THE GAA

A PEOPLE'S HISTORY

THE GAA

A PEOPLE'S HISTORY

Mike Cronin, Mark Duncan and Paul Rouse

The Collins Press

FIRST PUBLISHED IN 2009 BY
The Collins Press
West Link Park
Doughcloyne
Wilton
Cork

Reprinted 2010

British Library Cataloguing in Publication Data

Cronin, Mike.
    The Gaelic Athletic Association: a people's history.
    1. Gaelic Athletic Association—History. 2. Gaelic games—
Ireland—History. 3. Gaelic games—Social aspects—Ireland—
History.
    I. Title II. Duncan, Mark. III. Rouse, Paul.
    796'.06'0415-dc22

ISBN-13: 9781848890183

Design and typesetting by Anú Design, Tara
Typeset in Garamond
Printed in Singapore by Tien Wah Press Pte. Ltd.

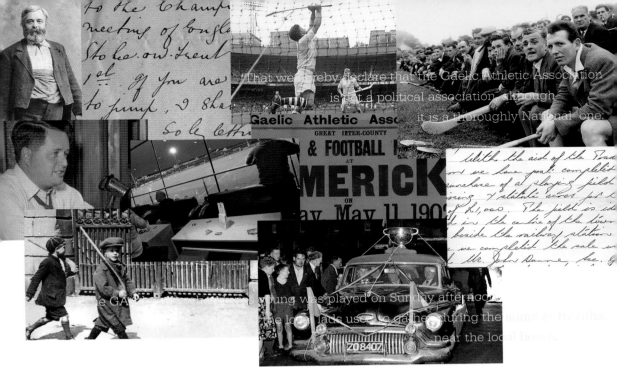

Contents

Acknowledgements

It has been a pleasure to write this book. More than anything, this book is the product of a huge collaborative effort and much thanks is due to the many people who have contributed. In writing this book we have had great assistance. The GAA Oral History Project, of which this book is part, has been funded by the Gaelic Athletic Association and we are grateful for the support given to us by President Christy Cooney, former President Nickey Brennan and Director General Paraic Duffy. As the project was suggested as part of the GAA's 125th anniversary celebrations, we owe a great debt of gratitude to Jarlath Burns and the 125 Committee, who warmly embraced the idea of a major history project as a means of marking the anniversary, and to Lisa Clancy for her ongoing input.

Boston College gave the project a home, and for all the assistance in making the project begin on time and for his good consul, we thank Eoghan Clear. Nothing at Boston College could happen without Thea Gilien. Colleagues in Boston have been invaluable, but most importantly we thank Rita Owens and Sarah Castricum for their technological know-how that continues to keep the material from the GAA Oral History Project associated with this book available on a day-to-day basis at www.gaahistory.com.

The preparation of this book took over not only our lives, but also those of the researchers working on the Oral History Project. Put simply, without their contribution, this book would not have been completed. Ann-Marie Smith kept the Oral History Project alive while other eyes were focused on this book and also found time to contribute to the book. Sean Kearns did a typically superb job sourcing historical quotes. Our greatest debt is to Arlene Crampsie and Regina Fitzpatrick. Their work – on the road, in the archives and in collating and organising the material which forms the visual and documentary bedrock of this book – was immense.

This book, like any other, has drawn inspiration and ideas from what has been said and written before. We acknowledge the many authors, especially at a local level, who have written about the GAA. Many of these previous volumes contain important historical information which would otherwise have been lost. They also demonstrate a real grasp of the place of the GAA in Irish life. We also pay a particular thanks to the various contributors to the 2009 Sports History Ireland conference, which was held at Croke Park in April 2009. Those contributors were drawn from the ranks of the best academics working in this field and their research has profoundly influenced this book.

For the images and documents in this book we thank the various repositories and individuals that made material available including:

Mark Reynolds and Selina O'Regan at the GAA Museum and Archive; Catriona Crowe, Aideen Ireland and the National Archives of Ireland; James McGuire and the Dictionary of Irish Biography; Jimmy Deenihan; Eoin Kinsella, Naomh Olaf and UCD; Kieran Hoare at the James Hardiman Library at NUIG; Pat Walsh at Deerpark; Kevin Corrigan of the *Tullamore Tribune*; Pat Nolan of the Irish *Mirror*; Deirdre McMahon; Rónán O'Brien; Tom Butler; Mick O'Keeffe; Mary E. Daly; Margaret Ó hÓgartaigh; Dave Billings; Pádraig Conway; Dara Ó Briain; Seán Crosson; Michael Laffan; Simon Byrne; Tadhg Ó hAnnracháin; Tom O'Donoghue; Fr Tom Scully; Clare Ní Cholmáin; Ray Spain; Tullamore GAA Club; the Rouse family in Durrow, Tullamore, Kilkenny and Dublin; the Egan family in Gledswood; Durrow National School; Tullamore CBS; Meadhbh and Eoin; the late Ken Duncan; Barbara Duncan and family; Andrew and Mikey Duncan; Harry Hughes; Seán Cleary; the Pozzey family in Brisbane, Australia; Kilmacud Crokes GAA Club; Diarmaid Ferriter; Stephen Cullinane; Martin Walsh; Pat Leahy of the *Sunday Business Post*; Brendan Minnock, Offaly GAA; Mike Lynch from Meelick; Ann Coughlan, former Offaly County Librarian; Micheál O'Connell; Colm Tóibín; Niamh Brennan and Ciara Joyce, Donegal County Archives Service; Dónal McAnallen and the staff of the Cardinal Tomás Ó Fiaich Memorial Library and Archive; David and Edwin Davison, the Irish Picture Library; Brendan Scott and the staff of Cavan County Museum; Ross Moore and the staff of the Linenhall Library; Natalie Milne, RTÉ Stills Library; John Rattigan, Clare Museum; Marie McFeeley and the staff of the National Gallery of Ireland; Catriona Mulcahy, UCC Archives; Brian McGee and the staff of Cork County and City Archives; Maura Craig, Central Library, Derry; Bernadette Walsh, Derry City Archivist; Niall McGuirk, Sports Department, Fingal County Council; Margaret Kane, Enniskillen Central Library; Catherine Quinn, Fermanagh County Museum; Patria McWalter, Galway County Council Archives; Michael Lynch, Kerry County Archives; Billy Doolin, Fitzgerald Stadium, Killarney; Martin Morris, Leitrim and Longford Archives Services; Lorraine McCann and Jayne Hutchinson, Louth County Archives Service; Alan Hand, Reference and Local

History Library, Dundalk; Eugene Kavanagh, Drogheda Library; Brian Walsh and Anita Barrett, County Museum, Dundalk; Frances Tallon, Meath County Library; Theresa Loftus and the staff of Monaghan County Museum; William Fraher, Michael Fitzgerald and the staff at Waterford County Museum; Gráinne Doran, Wexford County Archives Service; Robin Doolin, Rights and Reproductions, Oakland Museum of California; Lucy Francis, Getty Images; Martin Fagan, Pontifical Irish College Archives, Rome; Dermot Mulligan, Carlow County Museum; Clodagh Kinsella, Carlow County Library; Philip Kinane, Sportsfile; Sara Smyth, Jenny Doyle and the staff of the National Photographic Archive; Fran Carroll, Gerry Kavanagh, Mary Broderick and the staff of the National Library; Derek Cullen, Fáilte Ireland; Kelly Fitzgerald and Críostóir Mac Carthaigh, Delargy Centre for Irish Folklore; Sinéad O'Connor, Liz Howard and the staff of Cumann Camógaíochta na nGael; Martin Burke, Tipperary; Damian Brett, Kilkenny County Library; Alicia Dunphy and the staff of Graiguenamanagh Library; Seán Ó Súilleabháin, Mary Conefray and Caroline Martin, Leitrim County Library; Mike McGuire and the staff of Limerick City Public Library; Brian Hodkinson, Limerick City Museum; John O'Gorman and the staff of Tipperary County Library; John FitzSimons and the staff of the *Westmeath Examiner*; Adrian Butler, *Limerick Leader*; Michael Dundon and John Guiton, *Tipperary Star*; C. J. Destelle Roe; Micheál Maher; Rebecca Grant and the staff of the Irish Film Archive; ITV Global Entertainment; the Ó Síocháin family; Gerard O'Regan and Adrienne Carolan, *Irish Independent*; P. J. Maxwell; Liam O'Donoghue; Brian Ó Chonchubhair for all his help with Irish language quotes; Mary Moran; Magnum Photographic Agency; Norman McCloskey, Inpho; Máire Harris, Gael Linn; Walsh Printers; Eddie Guilmartin; Timmy Delaney; Tom O'Keefe and Willie Dempsey; Shay Murphy; Betty Rice; Brendan Rice; Edward Dullard; Declan Malone, *The Kerryman*; Anne Kearney, *Irish Examiner*; Kathleen Bell, *Irish News*; John Ferris, Belfast Media Group; John Kelly; Michael O'Donnell; Anita at P. J. Browne's, New Ross; Michael Kiely; Joe Martin; Toni Carragher; Richard Gerrard; Wexford Supporters Club; Denis Cadogan; Brendan Quigley; Edward Laverty; Micheál Ó Liodáin; Colm O'Hehir; William Treacy; Padraig Hamilton; Jim Cronin; Seamus King; Fr Seamus Gardiner; Kate Mullan; Sean McGettigan; Phil McGinn; Michael Madine; Jack Ryan; Muiris Prenderville; Paul Ferguson, TCD; Thomas Grennan; Fred Reilly. Special thanks to William Murphy and Tom Hunt for their extensive comments on the text.

The Collins Press embraced the idea of the book enthusiastically and dealt with short deadlines and a complex range of material with good grace and a highly professional manner. A huge debt is also owed to Karen Carty of Anú Design.

This book is ultimately for everyone in the GAA – especially those who have taken part in the GAA Oral History Project and have made material available to us – but at a personal level it is for Moynagh, Ellen and Samson; Sophie; Nuala, Cáit, Éilis and Joe.

Mike Cronin
Mark Duncan
Paul Rouse
Dublin, 2009

Reamhrá

Agus scrúdú ar bith á dhéanamh againn ar Éirinn agus ar chaitheamh aimsire a muintire, ní féidir dúinn gan a chur san áireamh an gaol speisialta agus an ceangal idir Cumann Lúthchleas Gael agus iad siúd, pé sa bhaile nó i gcéin dóibh, árbh í Éire tír a ndúchais.

Tá sé mar aidhm ag an leabhar seo é sin díreach a dhéanamh, agus ag an am céanna ómós cuí a thabhairt don bhliain fé leith seo ag Cumann Lúthchleas Gael agus í ag ceiliúradh 125 bliain ar an saol.

Tá go leor cuntais críochnúil déanta cheana féin ag go leor scríbhneoirí ar chúrsaí an chumainn maidir le cluichí de anuas tríd na blianta agus fós cur síos go leor ar ghníomhartha gaile agus gaisce ar pháirc na himeartha, ach mar sin féin bhí i bhfad níos mó riamh ag baint le ballraíocht sa Chumann Lúthchleas Gael ná imirt cluichí amháin.

Is cúis mórtais dúinn bheith páirteach sa Chumann iontach seo, cé go dtógann sé súil eachtrannach ar uairibh chun tuiscint a thabhairt dúinn ar an spioraid ar leith a thugann brí don eagraíocht uathúil seo, eagraíocht nach bhfuil a sárú le fáil in aon áit ar domhan ó thaobh cúrsaí spóirt agus uile.

Is beag eile is mó a thugann an fhéiniúlacht chéanna nó an grá don áit dúchais do dhuine ná geansaí a chlub áitiúil a chur air. Is maith mar a sheas na luachanna seo dúinn sna blianta atá thart agus ní baol ná go seasfaidh fós dúinn sna blianta atá romhainn.

Is bua, thar bhuanna, an t-amaitéarachas, obair dheonach agus athbheochan an chultúir Gaelach í scéal Chumann Lúthchleas Gael ó bhonn tionscanta lag in 1884 go dtí an borradh as cuimse síos tríd na blianta.

Diaidh ar ndiaidh ón mbonn aníos a tógadh stair Chumann Lúthchleas Gael, le scéalta pearsanta na nglúnta Gael sna mílte pobal éagsúil sa bhaile agus i gcéin.

Toradh is ea an leabhar seo ar Thionscadal Stair Bhéil an Chumann Lúthchleas Gael a ndearna Cumann Lúthchleas Gael a choimisiúnú, d'fhonn go ndéanfaí taifeadadh agus caomhnú ar scéalta na ndaoine seo. Tionscadal ab ea é a raibh géar-ghá leis; cuirfidh sé cartlann ollmhór ar fáil dúinn a thabharfaidh léargas nua dúinn ar shaol Chumann Lúthchleas Gael agus ar phobal na hÉireann araon do na glúnta atá romhainn.

Ba mhaith liom aitheantas a thabhairt go háirithe don dúthracht agus don ghairmiúlacht a chaith muintir Boston College leis an obair agus don chúram faoi leith a rinneadar den tionscadal seo atá chomh tábhachtach san don Chumann sa bhliain speisialta seo.

Mar is léir ón leabhar álainn seo tá go leor leor le feiceáil agus le hinsint. Tá mé ag tnúth go mór le tabhairt faoi.

Criostóir Ó Cuana
Uachtarán Chumann Lúthchleas Gael

Preface

Any cursory examination of Ireland and how its people engage in pastimes quite simply must include an in-depth analysis of the special relationship and bond that exists between the GAA and those who call Ireland home, whether they be here or abroad.

This publication aims to do exactly that and in the process fittingly marks what is a milestone year for the GAA, celebrating as it does 125 years in existence.

While the playing and on-field affairs of our Association have been diligently chronicled by so many down through the years in meticulous records and expansive reports and accounts of matches and heroics feats and deeds, there has always been so much more to membership of the GAA than the playing of the games.

We pride ourselves in our affiliation with what is a remarkable Association and one that sometimes requires the company of those less familiar with the GAA to really underline the special ethos that underpins a unique organisation, one without rival anywhere whether in sporting or general terms.

Few if any outlets offer a similar sense of identity or an attachment to home, through the vehicle that is pulling on a home club jersey. These are values that have served us so well to date and will continue to do so.

The story of the GAA from its humble if soon to be remarkable beginnings back in 1884, is one of the triumph of amateurism and volunteerism and the revitalisation of Irish culture.

The history of the GAA is one, ultimately, that has been built from the ground up, from the personal experiences of generations of Irish people across thousands of communities at home and abroad.

This book is a product of the GAA Oral History Project, which has been commissioned by the GAA, to ensure these experiences are recorded and preserved. It is a unique and necessary undertaking which will build a vast archive and open a new window on GAA life and Irish society for future generations.

I want to acknowledge the thorough work and professionalism of the team at Boston College and the attention to detail that they brought to a project that is of utmost importance to the Association in this special year.

As this beautiful book demonstrates, there is much to see and tell and I look forward to the challenge of attempting to take it all in.

Rath Dé ar an obair.

Criostóir Ó Cuana
Uachtarán Chumann Lúthchleas Gael

An Irish game with an international reach:
action from a hurling match between Kilkenny
and Offaly at Gaelic Park, New York in the early 1950s.
(*Picklow Collection, NUIG*)

Introduction

Since its establishment in November 1884, the Gaelic Athletic Association (GAA) has made a profound impact on Irish social, cultural, political and economic life. The story of the GAA is rooted in the appeal of its games and in the strength of the local allegiances fostered by the way the Association is organised. Its network of community-based clubs provides much more than a means of recreational distraction. The GAA is the focal point for the social life of entire communities, with clubs acting as a cohesive force, building relationships and a shared sense of place. It is a simple truth that generations of Irish people have spent the hours between work and sleep enthralled by Gaelic games and the Association that organises them.

Despite its importance – and despite the work of dedicated volunteers all over Ireland – the history of the GAA has received only piecemeal attention. Too much of what has been written about the GAA focuses on its politics, not least on its apparent contribution to the revolution which brought about the creation of the Irish Free State. Obviously, politics are an important part of the GAA's history, but only a particular part of that history. The story of the GAA over the last 125 years lies at the very heart of the Irish experience. Its development is rooted in wider social and economic forces: the spread of the railways, the cultural revival, the drift from the land, emigration and much else.

This book does not offer a straightforward chronological account of 125 years and is not an attempt to record fully everything important that has happened. Instead, it is intended as an overview of the broad sweep of the Association's history. It is divided into thematic chapters which document many aspects of the story of the GAA. The scope of the chapters – embracing areas as diverse as music and travel, exile and religion, as well as looking at the games, the grounds and the politics of the GAA – offers as full a view as possible of what it has been like to play, to watch and to organise Gaelic games over the first 125 years of the Association's history.

Throughout the book we have sought to introduce the words of players, officials, historians, commentators and many more. We have included a treasure of photographs, documents and miscellaneous memorabilia, many of which have never been reproduced before. All of this is by way of providing a history that documents what happens on the field of play, but also chronicles the glorious diversity of GAA life beyond the sidelines.

The great triumph of the GAA is that it means so much to so many people. It inspires a passion that is not always evident in many areas of life. Mostly that passion is manifested in positive ways, but the GAA has also made its fair share of mistakes. In acknowledging the obvious successes of the GAA, we must also document these mistakes and failures. Success and failure, alike, are part of the GAA's glorious ability to create controversy. As always with controversy, the dispute often lies not merely with what did or did not happen, but also with how and why that controversy occurred. Accordingly, there will be people who have entirely different memories of events from the ones recorded in these pages. There will also be people who will be disappointed at the failure to mention or give due regard to a whole range of activities undertaken or events organised by the Association. This is inevitable. Every individual will have their own understanding of what the GAA has been about and no book can possibly compete with the experience of a lived history. That is not to walk away from any of the views expressed in this book, merely to recognise that many GAA members and those who look at the Association from outside will dissent from some (or, maybe, more than some) of those views. If nothing else, we hope that this book will stir the embers of old controversies – or maybe even start a few new ones. If it succeeds in that ambition, it will reflect the diversity, the passion and the sheer fascination of 125 years of GAA history.

Players, people and place:
Galway footballers are chaired
from the field after winning
their third All-Ireland title
in a row, 1966. (*Fáilte Ireland*)

Maurice Davin, former champion athlete and first President of the GAA, throws the hammer on the sportsground at his home at Deerpark, Carrick-on-Suir. In his prime, Davin was considered the finest athlete in Ireland. This picture was taken when Davin was in his sixties. (*GAA Museum*)

Beginnings

'They had loosed an avalanche on its natural course and were helpless to recall it.' —

This was how the GAA journalist and historian
P. J. Devlin described the early development of the
GAA in *Our Native Games* (1935), p. 37.

'You are earnestly requested to attend a meeting which will be held
at Thurles on the 1st of November to take steps for the formation of
a Gaelic Association for the preservation and cultivation of
our National Pastime and for providing rational amusement for the Irish people
during their leisure hours.'

'That we hereby declare that the Gaelic Athletic Association is not a
political association, although it is a
thoroughly National one: that our objects are, as we have already stated,
the preservation and cultivation of national pastimes,
that our platform is sufficiently wide
for Irishmen of all creeds and classes

At 3 p.m. on Saturday 1 November 1884 a small group of men met in the billiards' room of Lizzie Hayes' Hotel in Thurles, County Tipperary. Michael Cusack and Maurice Davin had organised the meeting and immediately took centre stage. Cusack spoke first and stated that their purpose was the establishment of a new athletics association for Ireland. Davin then made a speech and outlined the reasons for establishing such an association, one which would run Irish sports for Irish people using Irish rules. It was not that there was anything wrong with British rules in themselves, he said, merely that they did not suit Irish sports.

As if to deflect from the poor turnout, Michael Cusack read aloud sixty letters of support from people across Ireland. Amongst the letters was one from the leader of the Land League, Michael Davitt, which promised his full support. By the end of the meeting it was proposed that Davitt, along with the nationalist leader, Charles Stewart Parnell, and Archbishop Thomas Croke of Cashel, would be patrons of the new Association. The choice of patrons was a reflection of the remarkable decade into which the GAA was born. The 1880s were a decade defined by the struggle for land and freedom. Debates on Irish affairs dominated the House of Commons in London and the establishment of a home rule parliament in Dublin had emerged as a genuine possibility. Wrapped up with political upheaval was a dramatic battle over land between landlords and their tenants. Month after month, whole swathes of the countryside were convulsed with evictions, boycotting and agrarian outrages.

To emphasise the political context of the establishment of the GAA, the men who attended the first meeting included several members of the Irish Republican

'You are earnestly requested to attend a meeting which will be held at Thurles on the 1st of November to take steps for the formation of a Gaelic Association for the preservation and cultivation of our National Pastimes and for providing rational amusement for the Irish people during their leisure hours.' – Circular invitation issued prior to the first meeting of the GAA, *United Ireland*, 11 October 1884.

Brotherhood (IRB), a secret revolutionary organisation dedicated to the overthrow of British rule in Ireland. Their presence lent credence to speculation by officials in Dublin Castle and amongst members of the police that the new Association – which became known as the Gaelic Athletic Association – was really the creation of the IRB. This speculation, however, was a triumph of conspiracy over reason. The reality was that the Thurles meeting was the product of the desire of Michael Cusack and Maurice Davin to change how sport was organised in Ireland.

The alliance of Cusack and Davin was an unlikely one. Cusack was a self-made man who had left the poverty of a small farming background in Clare to carve out a career as a teacher in some of the most prestigious secondary schools in Ireland. Davin, on the other hand, was born into middle-class comfort to a Tipperary family of large farmers who operated a river haulage business along the Suir. Differences in background were compounded by differences in temperament.

Cusack was a singular man whose self-confidence had exploded after he had established his own school in Dublin in 1877. Cusack's Academy thrived to the point where it was soon considered to be one of the most successful in Dublin in preparing students for the examinations which brought entry into the civil service of the British Empire. Buoyed by this success, Cusack spoke his mind on everything that he saw around him. There was a restlessness, an individuality, a bluntness to everything he did. His warmth and generosity allowed him to make friends wherever he travelled; his impetuous nature saw him create enemies with similar ease. For example, when his one-time friend John Dunbar wrote to Cusack proposing truce and compromise in the midst of a dispute, Cusack replied simply: 'Dear Sir, I received your letter this morning and burned it.'

Maurice Davin was an altogether more measured individual. The eldest boy in a large family, he inherited the running of the family farm and business before he had turned eighteen. As a student he had been given private tuition in the violin, becoming an accomplished player, and, in general, was considered a diligent and studious boy.

Crowds gather on the main square in Thurles, County Tipperary for a meeting of the National League in 1885. In November of the previous year, Hayes' Hotel on the square was the location for the founding meeting of the GAA. Over the following years some of the most dramatic scenes in the history of the GAA took place around this square. (William Corbett and William Nolan (eds.), *Thurles: The Cathedral Town. Essays in Honour of Archbishop Thomas Morris* (1989))

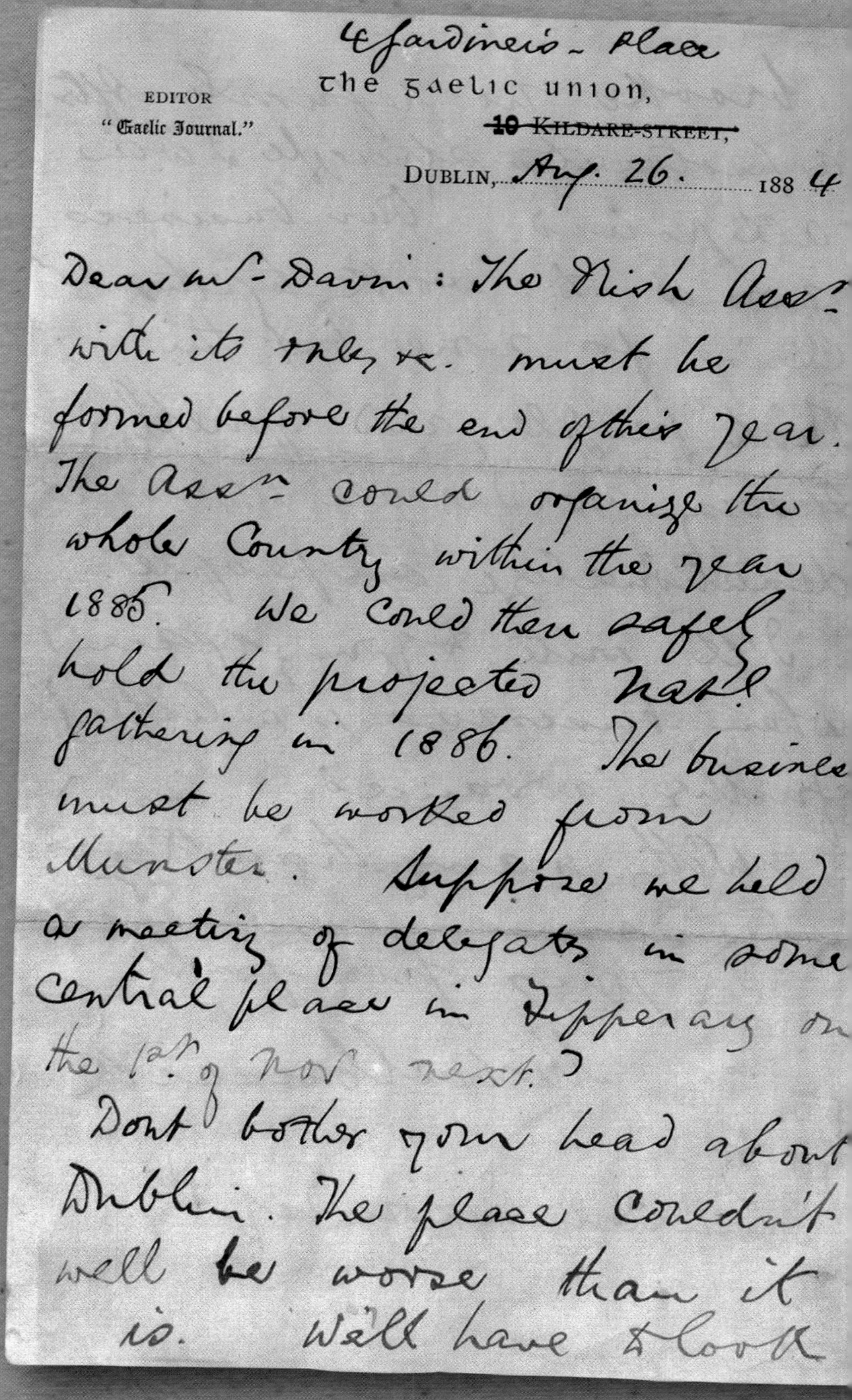

4 Gardiner's - Place

THE GAELIC UNION,

EDITOR
"Gaelic Journal."

~~10~~ KILDARE-STREET,

DUBLIN, Aug. 26. 188 4

Dear Mr Davin : The Irish Assn
with its rules &c. must be
formed before the end of this year.
The Assn could organize the
whole Country within the year
1885. We could then safely
hold the projected Natl
gathering in 1886. The business
must be worked from
Munster. Suppose we held
a meeting of delegates in some
central place in Tipperary on
the 1st of Nov next ?

Don't bother your head about
Dublin. The place couldn't
well be worse than it
is. We'll have to look

Letter from Michael Cusack to Maurice Davin discussing the setting up of the GAA and fixing a date for the first meeting. Cusack makes clear that the impetus in establishing a new sporting organisation would have to come from the provinces, not Dublin.
(GAA Museum)

to the provinces for men.

Dublin will have to fall
in, or keep up the connection
with England.

I have written to Cork this
day telling them that you have
responded most heartily. I am
sure Mr Stack of Listowel
will look after north
Kerry. Although I am not a
member of the Nat! League
I think I am not without
influence with several of its
leading members. The Nat!
press will give me room
for squibs when I am ready.
The Shamrock is also at my
disposal. I hope to see it

enlarged in about a month,
and then the education of the
people could start in earne[st]
the paragraphs, on athletics in United
Ireland are exploding like
shells in the enemy's ranks.

Of course they know it is
my doing and that therefore
the paper is not likely to hang fire
soon.

I have found it to be
utterly hopeless to revive
our nat'. pastimes without
the assistance of the leade[rs]
of the people; and I have no
hesitated to urge my clai[m]
on them with a persistency that

brooks no refusal. After
a protracted struggle I won
all round. Our business
now is to work together
caring for none but the
Irish people, and quietly
shoving aside all who would
denationalize these people.

I'll write to you again
when business is a little
further advanced.

With many thanks
I am
Yours faithfully

Michael Cusack

Maurice Davin Esq."

'Mother Erin, I think I understand what you want. Many of your children are having a hard struggle of it, striving to keep a grip of the land that bore them. You seem to think that I should make an effort to brighten their lives with the music of the Caman. I have been living in Ireland for upwards of three thousand years, and during all that time the hurling field was the great recreation ground of my brethren. Of late years, unfortunately, the spirit of the people has been drooping, and it will be difficult to straighten them up. I'll take hold of the first caman that comes in my way, call the boys together, make a beginning, and ask the people to join us.' – **Michael Cusack writing about the inspiration behind the setting up of the GAA in** *The Celtic Times,* **1887, quoted in P. J. Devlin,** *Our Native Games* **(1935), p. 18.**

Davin maintained this approach throughout his life, constantly striving to expand his store of knowledge by buying encyclopaedias and compendiums. He used this knowledge to design and build his own boats, most notably a 35-ft four-oared racing gig (named the *Cruiskeen Lawn*), which he raced at regattas around the south-east of Ireland.

What brought Michael Cusack and Maurice Davin together was the dramatic change during their lifetimes in how people played sport. Traditions of play were as old as history itself, but the nineteenth century brought a revolution in sport that had its roots in the profound social and economic change which was transforming life in England. The industrial revolution turned England from an agricultural society into an urban one. The masses now passed their days in factories and offices, not in fields. To meet the rapid expansion in the British economy the number and size of public schools was increased throughout the nineteenth century. In these schools traditional classical education was redesigned in an attempt to encourage values of manliness, strength, loyalty, discipline and leadership. Sport was seen as the perfect vehicle to do this. Between the schools

'He was reserved and even aloof at times and he considered controversy among members as useless and even counter-productive. It was a recurring theme with Davin that the association was founded to end dissension and not to perpetuate it.' – Séamus Ó Riain, *Maurice Davin (1841–1917): First President of the GAA* (1994), p. 96.

A portrait of Michael Cusack. (*NUIG*)

Throughout the second half of the nineteenth century attendance at sporting events became an increasingly important aspect of social life in Ireland. In this picture, taken in 1859, racegoers strain to get a better view of the action at the Punchestown races. At the time, this was one of Ireland's premier horse race meetings. (*Getty Images*)

and the industrial cities, patterns of play were remoulded. The informal, traditional recreations of previous generations were recast on an urban stage as modern, codified sports. Centralised organisations such as the Football Association and the Rugby Football Union now set rules for football in England, changing a game which had previously been played according to local rules in communities all across the country. Other sports such as athletics and rowing were also now organised by central associations. Sport became more commercialised as events involving amateur and professional competitors drew enormous crowds to purpose-built stadiums across English cities, while many more played games in the parks and pavilions of the growing suburbs.

Crucially, by the late nineteenth century, the British Empire had expanded to the point where it covered one-fifth of the land mass of the world. Everywhere the British went they brought their sports with them, making it inevitable that the sports revolution would spread to Ireland, which had seen a British colonial presence since the Middle Ages. A key factor in the spread of organised sport across Ireland was the education system. Irish students were sent to public school in England and brought organised games home with them. The most obvious example of this was the establishment of the Dublin University Football Club at Trinity College in 1854 by old boys of English public schools. From here, Trinity graduates took the games to the towns and schools of Ireland. In addition, over the following decades, just as had happened in England, sport – in particular rugby and cricket – came to find a central place in the growing number of elite schools in Ireland.

Michael Cusack's entry into Ireland's Anglocentric world of sport was through the education system. Cusack had trained to be a schoolteacher and subsequently taught during the 1870s at St Colman's College in Newry, County Down, at Kilkenny College, at the French College at Blackrock in Dublin, and at Clongowes Wood in Kildare. After he established his Cusack's Academy in 1877, he placed sport at

Boys play a game of cricket in east Galway *c*. 1880. Prior to the foundation of the GAA, the popularity of cricket was growing, its appeal transcending class divisions. In 1873, for example, the *Nenagh Guardian* reported that: 'The English game of cricket is very much in vogue in Ireland. It has completely displaced the old athletic exercise of hurling so prevalent some years ago. Hurling is almost unknown to the rising generation . . . every town and village, every hamlet and populous nook has either its [cricket] club or is in connection with some neighbouring one.' (*Clon 85, National Library of Ireland*)

the centre of the curriculum. Cusack wrote admiringly of how schools in England carefully provided physical recreation for their students and how this provided students with the stamina for working life. Cusack wrote that there was no better game for boys than cricket, and that every town and village in Ireland should have its own cricket field. For the 1879–80 season, he founded the Cusack's Academy Football Club and affiliated it to the Irish Rugby Football Union. The team played out of the Phoenix Park. Cusack was club secretary and trainer, as well as playing in the forwards, where he built a reputation as a powerful operator.

By then rugby was an established game in towns across Ireland, cricket was even more widely played, while soccer was just beginning to make inroads. The adoption of the sports of the Empire was not a straightforward process, however. The sporting revolution in England was not merely passed across the Irish Sea and adopted unchanged; local factors coloured the way in which the new sports were organised. In Dublin and Belfast, acceptance of English ways was most pronounced, but beyond the cities old traditions were not easily displaced.

Athletics were a case in point. The first modern athletics meeting to be held in Ireland took place in College Park, Trinity College, in 1857, when the Dublin University Football Club staged an event similar to the type of formal athletics meetings which had originated in England over the previous decade. The meeting in College Park drew a massive crowd, including the most important British official in Ireland, the Lord Lieutenant. The annual 'College Races' quickly became a phenomenon in the city – an extraordinary social event which was so popular that it was soon extended to two days and regularly drew crowds in excess of 20,000.

Through the 1860s the notion of holding athletics meetings spread across Ireland. In most areas of the country there was already a long tradition of athletics – running, jumping and, particularly, weight-throwing – where men gathered together to compete on Sunday afternoons or during the long nights of summer. Now, though, towns and villages of all sizes began to hold formal sports days. Weight-throwing was perceived to be a great form of exercise and was practised in many variations across the countryside. In Cavan, for instance, men would gather weights at the end of a rope and attempt to lift them with their teeth. Several of these old-style practices – including 'Throwing the Blacksmith's Sledge' and throwing a wheelstock, which had a rope inserted in the axle shaft – were included in the new sports days. In many places, despite the obvious influence of the English sports revolution, the Irish rural sports day was often considered 'more of a holiday than of a purely athletic gathering'. Mostly, it was only local men who competed and this was the target for occasional sneers from the Dublin press.

Having initially founded a rugby team in his own school, the Cusack's Academy, Michael Cusack then went to play for the Phoenix rugby club, with whom he is pictured here in 1881 (front row, second from left). Cusack seems to have acquired something of a reputation for the black arts in his play, leading one journalist to observe darkly: 'Everybody knows what Cusack is in a scrummage.' (*NUIG*)

While attending a sports meeting at Kilmallock, County Limerick, one reporter laughed at the attempt to stage a two-mile bicycle race, saying that he had had time to go and eat his dinner during the race and was still back in time for the finish. The reporter also recounted with relish that the meeting had ended up in a free fight.

Michael Cusack emerged from the rural tradition of weight-throwing and, when he arrived in Dublin, it was a natural progression for him to join in athletic activity in the city. In May 1875 he competed in the Dublin Amateur Athletic Club sports and won the 16 lb and 42 lb weight-throwing events. It was in that same year that he first met Maurice Davin, most probably in Lansdowne Road at the Irish athletics championships on a suitably wild and tempestuous day. Cusack came to regard Davin as the greatest authority he had ever met on the sport of athletics – both national and international. In the 1870s, Maurice Davin had revolutionised preparation for athletics events. A notebook which Davin used through the 1870s details the extent of his astonishing preparations. He constructed what might be considered a mini-gymnasium at his home in Deerpark, Carrick-on-Suir, County Tipperary, where he practiced weight-lifting, and used dumb-bells and assorted weighted clubs to increase the power in his muscles. He developed his throwing technique for the power events at which he became supreme. He was meticulous in his diet, neither drank nor smoked, believing that anyone who used cigarettes would never be any good at anything.

Davin became the dominant figure at the Irish athletics championships and went on to win ten gold medals for performances in weight-throwing events. In some years he was reckoned to be so untouchable that he was given a walk-over. Later, in 1881, Davin actually came out of retirement at the age of thirty-nine, having been goaded by suggestions in the English press that there were no good athletes left in Ireland. On the strength of two weeks' training, he travelled to compete in the British Amateur Athletic Championships, the most prestigious athletics event in the world at that time, and won the hammer and the shot putt. In common with Cusack, however, Davin disapproved of the manner in which Irish athletics had developed. The early promise of a vibrant, organised athletics scene had fallen away and what had emerged by the early 1880s was a shambles. No one club or federation had managed to elevate itself and establish proper control over Irish athletics. The sport was also dogged by petty internal squabbles, personal disputes and gambling. The annual athletics championship was on the verge of collapse on several occasions and the entire sport suffered for the want of a proper organisational structure.

'In the English parts of Ireland, the term "athletics" has very often of late been applied to that thing which a number of oldish young persons of doubtful gender do in fine weather after having undergone several weeks of careful nursing and when nobody outside their own class is allowed to compete.' – **This was how Michael Cusack lampooned the spread of 'English' athletics across Ireland in an article in** *The Shamrock* **in February 1883.**

In the early 1880s the British Amateur Athletic Association (AAA) began to fill this vacuum, its rules being accepted by increasing numbers of clubs along the east coast of Ireland. The expansion of the British AAA rules offended Cusack for several reasons. On a matter of sporting taste, the British AAA were concerned more with running than with the weight-throwing events, which Cusack believed were most suited to the Irish character. Cusack was also irked that officially recognised athletics meetings were held on Saturdays, yet the traditional day for sport in rural Ireland was Sunday, and that the rules of the British AAA narrowed the range of athletes who could compete. This was sport not for the 'amateur', but for the 'gentleman amateur'. In general, Cusack abhorred the increasing tendency of certain sporting organisations in Victorian Britain to move towards elitism and to seek to preserve their events for people from a certain class.

Through 1883 and 1884 more and more athletics meetings across Ireland were organised under AAA rules. Cusack and Davin resolved to act. An exchange of letters between the two in the summer of 1884 led to a general plan to hold a meeting in Tipperary on 1 November 1884 to establish an Irish athletics association. On 11 October 1884 the pair went public when Cusack published his famous epistle 'A word about Irish athletics' in *United Ireland,* the popular nationalist weekly newspaper. Cusack railed against the Britishness of everything now associated with Irish sport and called on the Irish people to take the management of their games into their own hands. In the following edition of the paper, Maurice Davin offered unequivocal support. To lend a sense of gathering momentum, Cusack and Davin combined to issue a circular calling for the meeting that took place in Hayes' Hotel on 1 November 1884.

The idea of reforming athletics dominated the meeting. Davin told those present that they needed to establish a proper code of rules for Irish athletics and to design those rules in such a way that they would provide recreation for the bulk of the people of the country, especially the working man, who, he said, seemed now to be born to no inheritance other than an everlasting round of labour. It

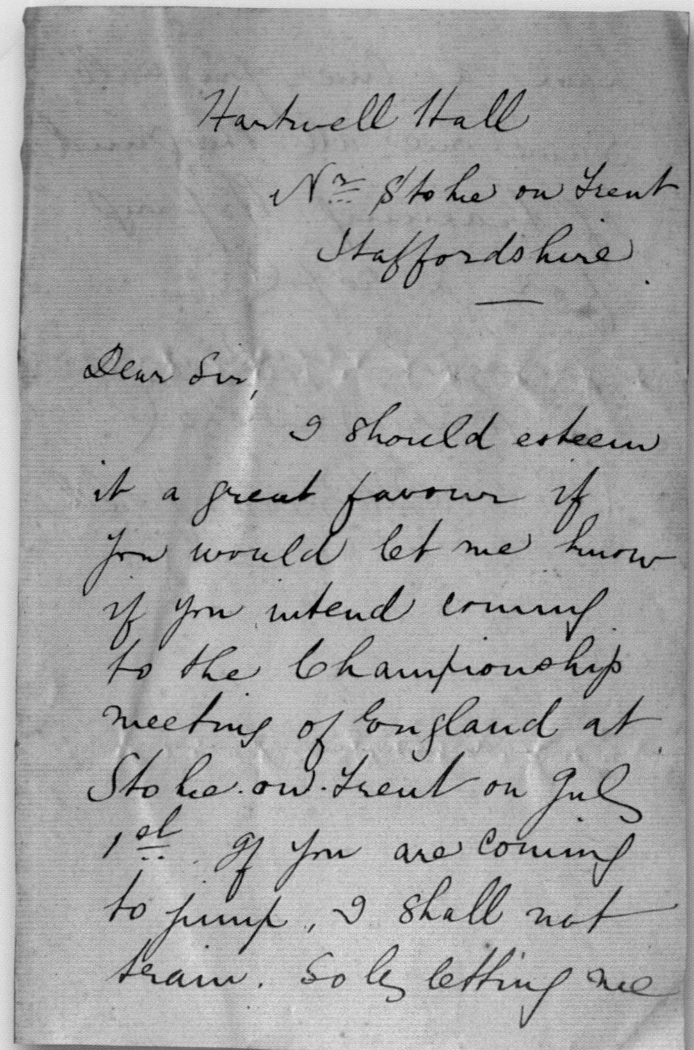

Hartwell Hall
Nr Stoke on Trent
Staffordshire.

Dear Sir,

I should esteem
it a great favour if
you would let me know
if you intend coming
to the Championship
meeting of England at
Stoke-on-Trent on July
1st. If you are coming
to jump, I shall not
train. So by letting me

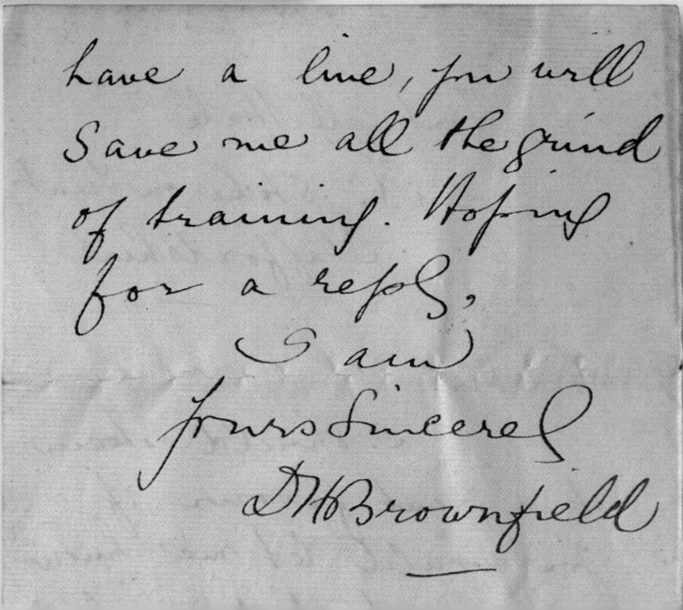

have a line, you will
save me all the grind
of training. Hoping
for a reply,
I am
Yours sincerely
DH Brownfield

A letter from D. H. Brownfield, an English athlete, inquires whether Maurice Davin's brother, Pat, intends competing at an upcoming championship meeting in England. Such was Pat Davin's pre-eminence in jumping events that Brownfield was not inclined to train should he have to face Davin. Brownfield was an accomplished cricketer who went on to play for an English XI against Australia. (*GAA Museum*)

was almost as an afterthought that the GAA set about drawing up what Davin called proper rules for hurling and football. In the case of football, that essentially meant inventing the game of Gaelic football. Various types of football had existed in Ireland – just as they had in Britain, across Europe and in other regions – for centuries. This folk football had evolved into soccer and rugby in England in the middle of the nineteenth century, and Cusack and Davin now set about developing their own football game.

Hurling was altogether another matter. This was a game which had resonated through the ages in Ireland, flitting between mythology and history. Hurling was a game, but more than just a game. The literature of ancient Ireland paints hurling as the sport of mythical figures such as Cúchulainn. In the old texts, hurling became a metaphor for the bravery and ability of the greatest figures of Ireland's lost past. This notion of the romance of hurling was repeated in classical poetry from the thirteenth century onwards, where hurling and hurlers appear on numerous occasions. By the late 1700s, matches were often played for wagers of money and porter, were advertised in the newspapers and drew huge crowds. Hurling declined in the nineteenth century, however. Across Ireland, as the century progressed, cricket pitches were laid down in manorial estates and grand hurling matches were replaced by similarly conceived cricket contests. The advent of famine in the 1840s placed it under even greater pressure. Even areas previously regarded as strongholds suffered a decline in hurling. There were several reasons for this. The

Pat Davin prepares for the high jump at Clonmel Sports, 1882. The spread of such sports days across Ireland, though hugely popular in rural areas, was frequently derided by the Dublin press. (*Pat Walsh*)

A pen and ink drawing of a hurling scene by Charles MacKenzie c. 1805. (*PD 4199 TX 1, National Library of Ireland*)

rise of the temperance movement and the increased power of the Catholic Church
left hurling less acceptable. More practically and more obviously, emigration
affected hurling. Interestingly, reports survive of hurling matches played in America,
Australia and Britain in the decades immediately after the Famine, but, in Ireland,
fewer people ensured fewer games. However, hurling did not simply disappear.
Between the end of the Famine and the founding of the GAA, hurling was still
played in the parts of Ireland where it had been practised for centuries in some form
or other – in north Tipperary, east Galway, around Cork city and elsewhere.

The Victorian games revolution, with its passion for uniformity and centralised
control, did not bring immediate change to the hurlers of Ireland – there was no
move to establish formal hurling clubs in rural Ireland. In those places where
hurling survived, it did so in much the same form as it always had. As with so
much else in modern Irish sport, Trinity College, Dublin was involved in changing
the way in which hurling was organised in Ireland. A game called 'hurley' had been
played by a club at the college at least since the 1860s. The rules included provisions
for off-side, hitting off one side of the stick only, and might be considered more a
forerunner to modern hockey, rather than to modern hurling. Amongst those
who played the game was Edward Carson, later a founding father of Northern
Ireland. Through the 1870s the game was spread out of the university and into the
city by Trinity graduates. The steady growth in the number of players led to the
establishment of the Irish Hurley Union at Trinity College on 24 January 1879. The
Hurley Union sought to draw its own rules closer to the game of hockey as played in
England. The impact of these changes was to make the game of hurley progressively
less physical and this seems to have led to a disaffection amongst certain players,
several of whom were instrumental in founding the Dublin Hurling Club.

The first meeting of the Dublin Hurling Club took place in the College
of Surgeons on York Street in December 1882 in the lecture room of Dr Hugh
Alexander Auchinleck. One of those who attended the meeting was Michael

Hurling on the Derrynane estate of Daniel O'Connell, as depicted by John Fogarty, 1831.
(*National Gallery of Ireland*)

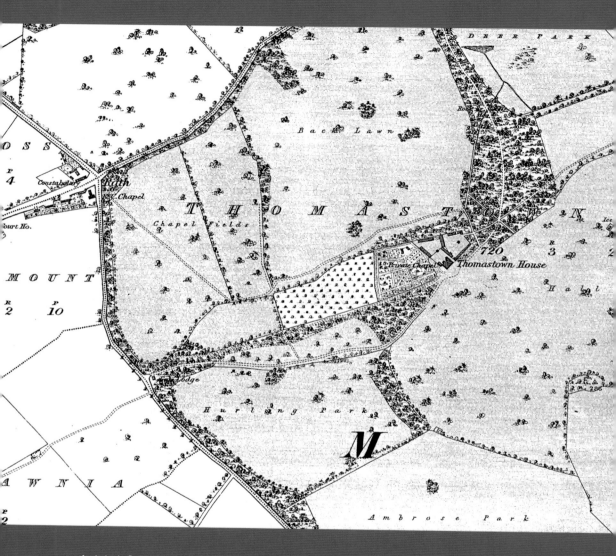

A six-inch Ordnance Survey map of Offaly, 1840, shows a dedicated hurling field in the foothills of the Slieve Bloom mountains. (*Reproduced from a map in Trinity College Library, Dublin, with the permission of the Board of Trinity College*)

Cusack, who became vice-president of the club. Four times in early 1883 the Dublin Hurling Club played matches amongst themselves in the Phoenix Park. Around twenty players turned up, many of whom were Dublin Protestants and part of the established hurley clubs of the city. Despite the apparent promise of the club, it disintegrated as suddenly as it had formed. The reason for the sudden demise of the Dublin Hurling Club in the spring of 1883 was clear cut. Following its establishment, hurley clubs had immediately sensed the threat of a rival organisation that would poach its players and they launched a counter-attack. Initially, several players had taken part in both hurling and hurley matches on the same weekend, hoping to combine the two games. Faced with confrontation between rival bodies, those players drifted back to hurley and the Dublin Hurling Club collapsed.

Cusack was undaunted. He began to gather hurling enthusiasts in the Phoenix Park on Saturday afternoons. At first there were just four of them, but their numbers grew until they were in a position to form the Metropolitan Hurling Club. This they did at a meeting in Cusack's Academy at 4 Gardiner Place on 5 December 1883. Michael Cusack was later in no doubt that this was the club out of which the GAA sprang. By the spring of 1884 there were sometimes fifty hurlers on the field on Saturday afternoons. It was enough to suggest to Cusack that it was time to expand his horizons. The opportunity for expansion came from County Galway. In the stretch of east Galway that bordered the River Shannon, hurling had never died. From Ballinasloe across to Loughrea and down to Portumna and Gort, hurling matches remained a regular feature of the social life of the people. Killimor were believed to be the finest team in the area and a match was fixed between them and Cusack's Metropolitans for the Fair Green in the middle of Ballinasloe on Easter Monday, 13 April 1884.

'Some of these foster fathers of the Gaelic Athletic renaissance were obstinate; some of them too adaptable. There can be no doubt that most of them were sincere. Those who earliest lent weight to the new movement must, for all time, share the credit for the success which attended it and for what it is today. Even had they ever so wished, they could not have recalled in pique what they had given whole-heartedly at the beginning. They had loosed an avalanche on its natural course and were helpless to recall it.' –
P. J. Devlin, *Our Native Games* (1935), p. 36.

Hurley, a game codified at Trinity College, Dublin, spread out from the college into some schools. This is a picture of the King's Hospital hurley players in 1879.
(*National Library of Ireland*)

'That we hereby declare that the Gaelic Athletic Association is not a political association, although it is a thoroughly National one: that our objects are, as we have already stated, the preservation and cultivation of national pastimes, that our platform is sufficiently wide for Irishmen of all creeds and classes: that whilst we welcome assistance from every quarter, we do not stand in need of any support from any organisation external to our own . . . – **Resolution adopted by the GAA, 18 July 1885, referred to in** T. F. O'Sullivan, *Story of the GAA* (1916), p. 13.

A huge crowd turned out. It was immediately apparent that the Killimor men were too strong and quickly scored a goal. Before they could score a second, Michael Cusack intervened. The play of the Galway men, he said, was too rough, not least because they slashed in a reckless and savage manner. As if to emphasise his point, Cusack then asked that the field be cleared so that the Metropolitans could play an exhibition match in order to demonstrate the proper rules of the game to the Killimor men. When this exhibition was complete, the Killimor men came back onto the field and played an exhibition of their own. After the exhibitions finished, Cusack refused to restart the match and Killimor were declared victorious. The Metropolitans returned to Dublin under something of a cloud, but the day was not without success for Michael Cusack. A letter to the *Western News* made a public plea for the nationwide revival of hurling, a relic of a time that was the golden age of Ireland.

Cusack and Davin integrated the idea of the revival of hurling and the organisation of football into their proposed athletics association. It proved a masterstroke. It gave the GAA a breadth of activities which immediately distinguished it from its rivals. It also allowed the GAA to stress the 'Irish' aspect of its endeavour. In the context of the social and political upheavals of the 1880s this was to prove a potent weapon. In time, of course, hurling and football overwhelmed athletics but, as the first members of the newly formed GAA left Hayes' Hotel, the challenge was first to survive and then to prosper. Michael Cusack and Maurice Davin were not to know it, but they had just turned Irish sport on its head.

A portrait of Maurice Davin. (*GAA Museum*)

The people's games: subs and
supporters follow the action at
a championship match in
Mullingar, 1962. (*Magnum*)

2

Games

'Like a city on fire, where the crackling of burning timber and the hissing of the flames swell into the roar of conflagration.' —

Michael Cusack describes hurling in the 1880s in his newspaper, *The Celtic Times*, 2 April 1887.

'. . . to see these young men of splendid physique contending like the Greeks of old in their Isthmikan games, and throwing every resource of strength and agility into the contest. As we watched on Sunday afternoon, and noticed their fine athletic forms . . . their sinews like whipchord and lungs . . . an ex-military father, a retired officer said they reminded him of the fighting tribes in the Himalayas, the warriors of the Ghourka'.

time play was . . .
the closing stages
. . . an scored a fur. . .
. . . sumption of play. . .
. . . tremely rough, + o. . .
. . . to retire owing . . .
. . . e was caused accidentally. . .
. . . gh this stage of the g. . .

The GAA wants, and will have, no one but men who will stand by its laws, and can well afford to do without the namby-pamby athletes who could 'go with the hare and run with the hounds'.

T he first matches played by the hurlers and footballers of the GAA were raw and often fierce. Style, skill and open play drew favourable comment, but what enthralled most was what Michael Cusack called 'men lovingly at war'. Teams drove at each other as they sought to drive the ball along the ground towards the opposition goal. A glue of players, arms and legs in every direction, rumbled around the field. Along the fringes, the weaker and quicker players waited for the ball to come close to them. Scores were a rarity, but this was not necessarily a cause of lament amidst the blood and thunder of battle.

The rules for hurling and football were framed by Maurice Davin, the GAA's first President, and were passed at a meeting in Thurles on 17 January 1885, less than three months after the GAA had been formed in that same town. The game of Gaelic football, which Davin invented, drew from the laws that had already been devised to regulate football in England. This meant, for example, that when a ball was kicked out over the sideline by one team, a throw-in was awarded to the opposition. In inventing Gaelic football, however, Davin also drew from the traditions of the Irish countryside and so the rules permitted that players from either team could break off from the play to wrestle with each other. For the most part, the rules were somewhat vague, and amounted to little more than guiding principles of play. This suited players who relished physical battle. It says much for the intense nature of the play that, when Callan played a team from Kilkenny city in the first ever game of Gaelic football in February 1885, the match ended in a scoreless draw.

Controversy surrounded the GAA's first rules for hurling. Turning age-old pastimes into modern sport involved distilling tradition and a certain element of compromise. When the men of Meelick, County Galway, saw the new rules of

'The play that followed was very fine; indeed I have seldom seen it equalled, never excelled. A quarter of an hour excelled without any score. The Kilmannon men now made a rush for their opponents' goal, and they narrowly missed obtaining a point. The ball was then kicked from goal, and hit a Ballymittyman, from whom it rebounded in the direction of the posts, with a Kilmannon man in pursuit. As the ball was coming straight for the goal, the goalkeeper advanced to meet it, and missed. Amid great cheering, the ball rolled in between the posts, thus giving a goal to Kilmannon.' – **A report of an early football match in Wexford**, *The Celtic Times*, 5 March 1887.

hurling, they were not impressed. One of their number – who signed his name as 'Old Hurler' – wrote to the *Western News* in Ballinasloe saying that this new game was only 'a slight improvement on those effeminate games, croquet and lawn tennis'. The 'Old Hurler' concluded by defending the traditional hurling rules of east Galway, saying that 'nothing vicious or unchristian is tolerated amongst them'. Nonetheless, it is remarkable how willingly most areas left centuries of local traditions to one side in favour of GAA rules. Even those areas – including Meelick – which were not immediately enthusiastic in their response to the GAA rules for hurling, quickly fell into line. The explanation for this was straightforward: the GAA was spreading rapidly across Ireland and those who did not accept the new organisation were left isolated. By the spring of 1886 reports suggest that all hurling played in Ireland was played under GAA rules.

The spread of the GAA was not rooted in its ability to organise rules for football and hurling, however. Instead, it was its involvement in athletics which was central to its early development. At its founding meeting the GAA had promised to draw up rules which suited those forms of athletics perceived as being particularly suited to the Irish. This meant introducing special provisions for weight-throwing and jumping competitions, while at the same time agreeing to follow accepted British AAA practices in the running events. What ensured the GAA's success in athletics, though, was not the rules it drew up, rather the reaction of existing athletic clubs in the Dublin area, which promptly came together to oppose the GAA.

'The GAA wants, and will have, no one but men who will stand by its laws, and can well afford to do without the namby-pamby athletes who could go with the hare and run with the hounds.' – *The Celtic Times*, 11 June 1887.

GAELIC ATHLETIC ASSOCIATION.

PROGRAMME

OF THE

FIRST GRAND

INTER-COUNTY CONTEST,

WICKLOW V. WEXFORD,

Under the Rules of the G.A.A.,

AT AVONDALE,

The Seat of the distinguished Leader of the Irish People,

C. S. PARNELL, Esq., M.P.,

ON SUNDAY, 31st OF OCTOBER, 1886,

To commence at 12 o'clock sharp.

GENERAL MANAGERS :

Messrs. E. WALSH, Wexford; and P. M'DONNELL, Bray.

REFEREES :

Messrs. E. J. KENNEDY, V.P., G.A.A., and JOHN CLANCY, T.C., Sub-Sheriff, Dublin.

UMPIRES :

WICKLOW—Mr. PETER ROBINSON, Bray, (Field) ; Messrs. A. M'DANIEL and COLCLOUGH BYRNE (Goals).

WEXFORD—Messrs. P. COUSINS and W. PETTIT (Field) ; N. KAVANAGH, and J. STAFFORD, Wexford ; W. KELLY, Rosslare ; JOHN SCALLAN, Piercestown ; JAMES MURPHY, Crossabeg ; EDMUND PIERCE, Lady's Island (Goal)

TIMEKEEPERS :

WICKLOW—DR. M. C. DWYER, Rathdrum ; and Mr. LEE CULLEN, Cronukerry.

WEXFORD—Messrs. J. F. WALSH, Wexford ; and M. DOYLE, Cottage.

HON. SECS.—Messrs. P. M'DONNELL and N. KEHOE.

MATCHES AND TEAMS :

The Programme of the Six Matches, commencing at 12 o'clock sharp. (Time for each Match 40 minutes).

12 o'clock—Wicklow Town v. Wexford Town.
12.45 p.m.—Tughor v. Rosslare.
1.30 p.m.—Avondale v. Crossabeg.
2.15 p.m.—Ashford v. Ballymore.
3 p.m.—Barndurrig v. Piercestown.
3.45 p.m.—Rathnure v. Castlebridge.

Trains—From Wexford, 9.15 a.m.; from Dublin, 5 p.m.; from Rathdrum (for Wexford), 6.20 p.m.; from Rathdrum (for Dublin), 6.20 p.m.

PUBLISHED BY JAMES DWYER, JOHN-ST., WEXFORD.

Printed at "The People" Office, Wexford.

The front page of a programme issued for a series of games played between clubs from Wexford and Wicklow on the estate of Charles Stewart Parnell at Avondale, County Wicklow, 31 October 1886. The organisation of inter-county fixtures such as these was facilitated by the availability of train services to and from venues. (*GAA Museum*)

Their opposition was driven by several forces, including an unwillingness to cede power to a new upstart organisation, as well as a dislike of Michael Cusack with whom several of the prominent members of these clubs had had personal disagreements. They established the Irish Amateur Athletic Association (IAAA), determined 'to quash the Gaelic Union'. The bitter row which ensued between the two sides was fought out in the pages of the popular press. The fact that the IAAA pledged its loyalty to the rules of the British AAA allowed the GAA to present a simple equation to the Irish people. As Michael Cusack put it, Irish sportsmen were faced with a stark choice 'between Irish and foreign laws'. Against the backdrop of political and social division in Ireland, most sportsmen, with the middle ground cut from beneath their feet, chose 'Irish laws'. Throughout 1885, more and more sports meetings were held under GAA rules, with traditional Irish weight-throwing and jumping events given greater prominence on the athletics programme. By the end of 1885 the GAA was in control of Irish athletics, its meetings drawing huge crowds in towns across Ireland.

In later decades, of course, athletics were lost in the long shadows cast by the appeal of hurling and football. In the beginning, though, it was athletics which did so much to promote hurling and football. When big Gaelic tournaments were staged, athletics events shared the programme with football and hurling matches. As spectacles of sport, colour and music, these tournaments offered wonderful entertainment. By eschewing any prohibition on Sunday play – a feature of most rival sports at the time – the GAA helped to bring organised games within the reach of those usually excluded from the experience. Those who came to see local athletes were captivated by hurling and football. This captivation was often the product of local loyalties. In 1887 the GAA ruled that the dividing lines between clubs were to be the boundaries of a parish. This rule was not slavishly adhered to – it was not applied, for example, to Dublin and in the countryside various clubs were also allowed (on request) to represent areas both smaller and larger than parishes, should a certain community make a compelling case. Nonetheless, the idea of one parish, one club became the hallmark of the GAA and, immediately, Gaelic games were defined by a passion for place.

The need to define the boundaries of clubs was largely due to the fact that, in 1887, the Association established an All-Ireland championship for football and hurling. The decision to establish the championships was influenced by several factors. Firstly, inter-club contests were wildly popular and began to draw huge crowds. Clubs started to travel across the country to play against each other and these matches generated intense interest as the newspapers began to speculate

Athletics at Jones' Road, later Croke Park, *c.* 1910. Athletics events were integral to the early success of the GAA. Eclipsed over time by the popularity of football and hurling, the GAA ceded responsibility for the organisation of athletics to a new body, the National Athletics and Cycling Association (NACA), in 1922.
(*GAA Museum*)

which teams might be considered the best in the country. Secondly, although the number of clubs was growing, many were slow to affiliate to the Association, leaving it short of money. Establishing a central championship held the prospect of enticing GAA clubs to process their affiliations, just as the establishment of the FA Cup had done so much in the 1870s to promote the development of the Football Association in England. The arrangements for the first All-Ireland championships were finalised in January 1887. The championships were open to all affiliated clubs who would first compete in county-based competitions, to be run by newly established county committees. The winners of each county championship would then proceed to represent that county in the All-Ireland championships.

These two basic ideas – county championships between local clubs and national competition between competing counties – provided the framework for the GAA's long-term development. They became the focal point of every team which aspired to success and, in the process, drove a refinement in the way the games were played. In Gaelic football the first team to move beyond the 'kick and rush' style to a new 'catch and kick' style was reputed to be the Young Irelands team in Dublin. Under the captaincy of John Kennedy, the players adopted a style which involved strict positional play and an avoidance of the usual congested midfield rushes. The tactics brought immediate dividends. Young Irelands won the Dublin championship in 1890 and then, in 1891, progressed to meet Cork side Clondrohid in the All-Ireland final. In the first half, the Cork side was bamboozled by the Young Ireland team's open play and trailed at the break by 2-1 to 0-2. Aware that in the scoring system in place at the time a goal outnumbered any number of points, Kennedy abandoned open play for the second half and instructed his entire team to retreat to their own goalmouth and to line up in front of the posts. Young Irelands did not score again, but their defensive effort brought them victory and a first All-Ireland championship. Immediately afterwards, the scoring rules were changed to make a goal worth five points. The change did nothing to deflect the progress of Young Irelands who adapted their game and went on to win two more All-Irelands.

By and large, early GAA players were young, Catholic men from the lower middle classes. They played for fun, for the thrill and excitement of competition and for the diversion it provided from the rigours of working life. And yet, when set against the backdrop of a nascent Irish-Ireland movement, the very act of playing football and hurling came freighted with added meaning. Players were held up as exemplars of Irish manhood, with GAA writers routinely extolling the physical and moral virtues of involvement in Gaelic football and hurling. In 1908, the journalist P. J. Devlin, writing under the pseudonym 'Celt', maintained that you could not 'walk the streets of our metropolis without meeting a specimen of what hurling has made, developed or maintained'.

Across those early years, a series of rule changes – in particular the reduction of team sizes from twenty-one to seventeen and then to fifteen players – helped to enhance the games by reducing the tendency of players to gather in a bunch. As it became easier to move the ball faster into open spaces, the quality of games improved. Gaelic sport retained its devotion to physical combat, but became more accommodating of the idea of skilful play. The public responded by attending matches in ever increasing numbers, with many travelling on trains laid on specially by business-savvy railway companies. Thousands came to support teams that, by the early twentieth century, increasingly stood for a county rather than a club identity.

From the very first All-Ireland championships in 1887, a trend developed where the champion clubs of each county selected a number of players from other clubs to assist them in inter-county matches. Over time, more and more players were brought in to supplement the county champions. Selection of county teams became the preserve of the county committee, rather than the champion club. And, as the club affiliations of the players who represented a county broadened, so the jerseys they wore were refined. For the first twenty-five years of the GAA, the representatives of a county usually wore the colours of their champion club. The extent to which teams representing counties became genuinely representative of the county as a whole can be gauged by the gradual adoption of distinctive county colours. Kilkenny won seven All-Ireland hurling titles between 1904 and 1913. Photographs show that the first four of these were won in the colours of the various champion clubs – Tullaroan or Mooncoin – in any given year. The last All-Ireland winning Kilkenny team to be photographed in a club strip was that of 1909.

Two teams gather in the middle of the pitch for the start of a hurling match at the Gaelic Field (now known as Fraher Field), Dungarvan, *c.* 1900. This photograph was taken at a time when Gaelic games were in the midst of a phase of rapid evolution. The character of the games was changing on the back of a series of alterations affecting the system of scoring and team sizes. By 1900 teams had been reduced from twenty-one to seventeen a side, forfeit points had been abolished and the value of a goal had been reduced from five points to three. It was not until 1910 that the present-day scoring area was arrived at, while the fifteen-a-side game was introduced in 1913. (*Waterford County Images*)

When the combined Mooncoin and Tullaroan clubs returned to win a further three All-Ireland titles in a row between 1911 and 1913 they did so as a united county team, with 'Kilkenny' sewn across each player's jersey. It was the most obvious way for players from different clubs to accept the idea of a unity of equals. All this underlined the idea of a county identity and, in turn, helped lend momentum to the creation of that identity.

This helped to widen the base of support for the All-Ireland championship. By 1913, indeed, the spectator appeal of Gaelic football was such that the gate receipts from two games – played out between Kerry and Louth for the Dr Croke Memorial Cup – were sufficient for the GAA to buy the ground at Jones' Road in Dublin which became Croke Park. One player who loomed large in both those games was Dick Fitzgerald, captain of the Kerry side. In 1914, Fitzgerald published a book called *How to Play Gaelic Football*. Its publication – the first book written on the GAA – signalled the emergence of Fitzgerald as a national sporting figure, a GAA player who had transcended the local. The book underlined the extent to which Gaelic football had evolved from its chaotic 'rough and tumble' origins into something that was 'scientific' and skills-based. As far as Fitzgerald was concerned, there was no football code to equal Gaelic – with no off-side or knock-on rules, the Irish game was, he insisted, mercifully free of the 'artificiality' of soccer or rugby. On top of that, the flexibility of its scoring system, by allowing goals and points, had served to minimise the element of luck in deciding games. But the real 'genius' of the game, Fitzgerald believed, was its ability to prize combination team play and still leave room for displays of individual brilliance. This book was more than simply a homage to Gaelic football, however. It offered practical advice to readers and used photographs to demonstrate how the core skills of catching and kicking might be better practised and perfected.

How to Play Gaelic Football opened a window on the changing world of Gaelic games and exposed the growing seriousness with which the top teams approached their sport. Training was mostly confined to the weeks in the run-up to major games, but it was still 'systematic' in nature. Trainers were engaged and special team training funds established. The money was raised by subscriptions and used, in part, to enable players to take time off from their work and dedicate themselves to the improvement of their game. Sometimes this was more of an aspiration than a reality as not all players were willing, or in a position, to meet this type of commitment. Still, what underpinned these new training regimes was an under-standing of the importance of physical fitness, skill-based drills and practice games. Without them, top teams could not expect to compete, let alone win – a

All-Ireland winning Kerry captain, Dick Fitzgerald. This photograph appeared in his landmark book *How to Play Gaelic Football* and was also used in newspaper advertisements to promote it. Although written primarily to benefit Gaelic footballers, Fitzgerald believed that his advice on positional play and tactics could be 'adopted almost in their entirety' by hurlers. (*GAA Oral History Project Archive*)

CATCHING.   **Three men required - A B C**
B and A stand about 30 yards apart. B pucks the ball with all his strength at A. A catches and strikes off as fast and hard as possible towards C who strikes back to B. This practice will tend to overcome a weakness in our men.

FREE PUCKS.   . Four or five men to be trained specially for these, each taking about 30 pucks each evening from different points on 70 line, and other parts of field. A record to be kept of pucks and surest scorer to take pucks in match. (See rule re Free Pucks).

SIDE PUCKS.   Four wing back men to be trained for these pucks.

FIGHTING FOR POSSESSION.   Two men required. Each man required to send ball in his own direction. Run a short distance for ball and fight for possession somewhat like two dogs for a hare. There is no practice better suited to give endurance and grip on a ball than this. When possession is gained possessor should strike as far as possible in his own direction.

DRIBBLING.   A fast dribble or run with ball, keeping control of it all the time and changing the course now and then to avoid an opponent, should be practised by all players. Ball might be passed to a comrade and passed back again immediatley.

The eight men in back division should endeavour to send ball as far forward as possible. Quickness and Vim at end of stroke tends far more to give distance to stroke than mere strength. The forward division should train as to direction and control of stroke rather than distance. The Centre right and left wing forwards should be well able to stop balls going for end line.

PRACTICE MATCHES.   In practise matches 9 forward players should be placed against 9 backs, play to take place over 100 yards in length of field. When ball passes over 100 yards line it is to be struck in from side line. A strict referee to be always in charge.

COMBINATION.   To be looked after in practice matches.

STRIKING.   Ground play must be practised. Clare men too fast and determined for fancy work. Men must practice striking ground balls when running at top speed. Centre men should practice to "let with" the ball on all occasions.

A note on training drills to be used by Laois hurlers prior to their 1914 All-Ireland final meeting with Clare. Although they lost, Laois claimed their first All-Ireland title the following year, defeating Cork in the final at Croke Park. (*GAA/Laois/73, GAA Museum*)

Borris - in - Ossory
7th Sept 1914.

My Dear Higgins,

I forgot to mention yesterday that we will have to pay a man to take Tim Hyland's place also. He is a coach-builder. He is working at home but they are a very large family and they could not very well afford to to have Tim away so long. Lalor is a game-keeper for Coursing Club & probably a man must be got to do his work, I don't know rightly what Kelly is at. Of course Jack works his farm & he has also a road but still if it could be afforded we should get a man to help him. Of course all this will involve a big sum of money and it will go near the £80 that I had in my head

A letter from Robert O'Keefe – player and later GAA President – to John J. Higgins, Honorary Secretary of the Laois hurling team training fund, stressing the need for substitute workers to be found so that players could, in the run-up to the All-Ireland final, take time from their work to prepare properly.
(*GAA/Laois/4, GAA Museum*)

all along. I would not like, if at all possible to have every man free of any loss whatever.
You can form that Committee you were talking about & put it down as being sanctioned.
Best wishes
Yours v. sincerely
R. O'Keeffe.

point trenchantly made in an anonymous letter to the secretary of the Laois County Committee in October 1914. With the county's hurlers preparing to face Clare in the All-Ireland final, the letter implored the players to 'leave off work and train. If ye do not', the writer added, 'ye will be not only beaten, but disgraced.'

In the decade following that final, the vagaries of war at home and abroad caused massive disruption to Gaelic games. It was not until the mid-1920s that fixtures fell back in step with the calendar year. The GAA had, by then, evolved into a markedly different organisation from the one envisaged by Michael Cusack and Maurice Davin. The place of athletics within the GAA was emblematic of the evolution of the Association. Where it had initially been envisaged that athletics would sit at the core of everything the GAA was attempting to achieve, over the decades athletics were, instead, pushed to the margins. Athletics retained a loyal and passionate following, but became increasingly peripheral to the progress of the GAA and their popularity paled beside that of hurling and football. This process was confirmed when, in 1922, the GAA ceded control of athletics to the newly formed National Athletics and Cycling Association (NACA).

Throughout the 1920s and early 1930s, the GAA steadily expanded. Record numbers of clubs (there were more than 1,600 by 1935) entered the county championships and the inter-county scene thrived. National Leagues at inter-county level for football and hurling were introduced in 1926, bringing with them an added media profile for the games and a growing celebrity for the players, whose faces now appeared on everything from the sports pages of newspapers to cigarette cards. The rise of stars such as Larry Stanley and Joe Keohane in football, and Lory Meagher and Mick Mackey in hurling, fuelled the popular imagination. Crowds attending championships increased year after year, with football drawing larger crowds than hurling. By the end of the 1920s more than 30,000 people were attending the All-Ireland football final and by the end of the 1930s, that number had passed beyond 50,000. Celebrated matches almost immediately passed into popular lore. The 1930s were bookended by the three matches it took to separate Cork and Kilkenny in the 1931 All-Ireland hurling final and by the remarkable 1939 'Thunder and Lightning' hurling final played out in a ferocious storm, again by Cork and Kilkenny, just after Adolf Hitler had sent his troops across the Polish border. Despite the weather in Dublin and the war in Europe, 40,000 people were in Croke Park to see Kilkenny win one of the most famous finals of all time.

The rise in the popular appeal of Gaelic games reflected improvements in the standards of play. The games became faster, more open, more thrilling and the

The growing celebrity of GAA players was reflected in the desire of commercial companies to associate them with their products. In the 1920s this series of hurling-themed cigarette cards was produced by the British manufacturer, Wills. The faces of the hurlers appeared on one side with profiles extolling their sporting qualities on the other. Introduced in the late nineteenth century, cigarette cards became popular collectors' items in many countries where they featured a range of sports, including cricket, baseball, boxing and Association football. It was not until the 1950s that health risks associated with cigarette smoking became a subject of widespread public debate and government action. (*National Library of Ireland*)

Gaelic footballers are put through their paces at a training session at Turners Cross, Cork, in August 1937. By this time there was a general acceptance that fitness and practice were essential to achieving success in football and hurling. Even so, most players at club and county level continued to train on their own, with teams only coming together in the weeks before important games. (*Irish Examiner*)

Involvement in Gaelic pastimes did not only increase among men in the 1920s and 1930s; women were also more inclined to participate. This photograph shows action from a camogie match in the Phoenix Park in the 1930s. The sport, founded in the early years of the century, was effectively relaunched in the 1930s, when an All-Ireland inter-county championship was introduced. The burgeoning appeal was perhaps best captured by one newspaper headline from 1934 which proclaimed: 'When work interferes with camogie - Stop Work!' (*Cumann Camógaíochta na nGael*)

'The training of a county team is an expensive item, costing our county £82 8s this year. Can it be said that collective training of teams has been a success in our county? It is my opinion that enthusiastic members of a team can train as well, if not much better, in their home grounds' – Report of County Board Secretary, D. Ó Duinn, to the Offaly GAA Annual Convention, *Irish Independent*, 27 January 1939.

number of scores registered grew steadily. Despite the rise in quality, a core of GAA officials worried that football and hurling were being coarsened by on-field indiscipline and a win-at-all-costs mentality. The matter was raised repeatedly at the GAA's Annual Congress where it was argued that a new ethos was being powered by the growing culture of whole-time collective training. This involved teams who reached All-Ireland finals retreating into camps for two weeks to prepare for the match. The practice even extended to junior and minor teams preparing for All-Ireland finals. Throughout the 1940s, some inter-county teams took to retreating into training camps for earlier rounds as well. The reason for this was the widespread belief that it achieved the 'best results'. That was certainly the view of Dr Eamonn O'Sullivan, the physician who trained Kerry to eight All-Ireland titles between the 1920s and the 1960s. Throughout this period, O'Sullivan's Kerry teams used their training camps to perfect his ideas of a rigid system of play, which confined players to their own sectors of the field and compelled them to win their individual battles. It was a style of football built on the principle of catch-and-kick and was designed to avoid bunching and 'disorganised effort', particularly in front of goal. The Kerry trainer was the most celebrated proponent of whole-time collective training. In his memorable 1958 book *The Art and Science of Gaelic Football*, he wrote of the value of subjecting players to a 'daily 24 hour schedule of alternating exercise, tuition, rest and play.' It was a routine aimed at both the collective and the individual. By bringing players together, it not only enabled teams to attain

'8.30 – Rise. 9.30 – Breakfast. 10.30 – Walk. 12.45 – Spongeing and towelling. 1.30 – Dinner. 3.30 – To St. Coman's Park for limbering, free exercises, hurdling, sprinting: place kicking and general practice: tactics. 5.30 – Baths and attention to injuries. 6.30 – Tea. 8p.m. – Short Walk. 9.45 – Supper. 10.30 – Retire.' – Collective training, the Roscommon way. This was the daily routine for Roscommon footballers prior to the 1946 All-Ireland final, *Irish Independent*, 19 September 1946.

Letterkenny (Pats) v Bundoran.   Daisy Hill,
                                  15 - 12 - 32

A chara,

I took charge of above teams at Ballybofey
on Sunday 11-12-32 in the semi-final of the
charity cup competition.   The match got going
prompt to time & before starting I warned
both teams against rough play, or using language
not in keeping with the spirit of the game.

Play from the outset was rather vigorous
as both sides were all out to win, & I had to
hold up for a good many fouls particularly
on the part of the Pats.   Bundoran had
the advantage of the breeze & forced the play
being rewarded with a point early on. Letterkenny
became more aggresive after this score & I had
to warn Mulhern (Pats) for dangerous play, the game
continued with a good deal of heat being
introduced, & also interference on the pitch by
Letterkenny supporters, this holding up the match
repeatedly. // About this stage of the game
Letterkenny scored a goal which was disallowed
by both Umpires owing to an infringement by
a Letterkenny player.

A referee's report of a football game between Letterkenny and Bundoran at Ballybofey, County Donegal, played on 11 December 1932. The report highlights the difficulties encountered by referees in controlling passions both on and off the field. Despite the increasing popularity of Gaelic games, concern with discipline was a constant. Officials and reporters frequently implored players to do nothing that might diminish the standing of the Association.
(Donegal County Archives Service)

This caused a good deal of resentment on the
part of the Letterkenny players, & supporters
& were it not for the fact that one of
the Umpires was a Guard in uniform certainly
it might have been an ugly scene.

For a time play was pretty well balanced
but during the closing stages of the first
half Bundoran scored a further point.

On the resumption of play after half time
play was extremely rough, & one of the Pats
players, had to retire owing to a leg injury
which I believe was caused accidently. A

All through this stage of the game play
was dangerous & in a tackle two of the players
came to blows I ordered both off, & immediately
they struck each other again.   I continued
the game as if it was held up, the spectators
rushed on the pitch, & delayed the play.

Towards the end of the game in a tussle
near the Bundoran goal a foul occoured,
(the free being for (Pats)) the Letterkenny player

'He was a great master of the cliché, but sometimes broke into originality, as when the time we were going for the county final he wouldn't let us touch a ball for a week previous as he wanted us to be "ball hungry".' – Patrick Kavanagh on his football trainer, in 'Diary', *Envoy*, No. 9 (1950), p. 80.

maximum fitness, it also allowed individuals to develop their skills by engaging in 'a long, continuous process of repetition'.

By the time of their publication in 1958, O'Sullivan's words were a lament for a lost era. Four years previously, in 1954, the GAA Congress had voted to abolish training camps on the grounds that full-time training ran counter to the amateur ideal. The special subcommittee that recommended their abolition made clear that it did not envisage an end to all training, but simply the sort that took players away from their normal employment and into camp, compensating them 'in cash or in kind'. The choice, therefore, was not between collective training and no training. As one Congress delegate pointed out, many counties – among them Tipperary and Cork – had enjoyed success by engaging in 'normal training', where players were brought together only in the evenings. That may have been so, but the debate surrounding the abolition of collective training revealed sharp divisions between counties in their approaches to training and gave voice to fears that standards would fall in the wake of its abolition.

They did not. If anything, approaches to games development became more innovative and inclusive. In the early 1960s, for instance, film was embraced as an instructional tool to demonstrate the skills of hurling and Gaelic football to a wider, more general audience. Gael Linn, the Irish language organisation, produced two colour films – *Peil* and *Christy Ring* – which were shown in cinemas throughout the country. The *Christy Ring* film was a remarkable piece of work. As well as offering a chronicle of the history and importance of hurling, it also captured the skills of the game as demonstrated by its greatest player. Ring had a status all to himself. The way he committed his life to hurling, to playing the game and to training for it, created an aura around him which grew into legend and song:

> *How oft I've watched him from the Hill move here and there in grace,*
> *In Cork, Killarney, Thurles town or by the Shannon's race,*
> *'Now Cork is bet; the hay is saved!' the thousands wildly sing.*
> *They speak too soon, my sweet garsun, for here comes Christy Ring.*

The beauty of the instructional part of the *Christy Ring* film is that the genius of his talent is preserved for future generations. Crucially, the film emerged not from

A group of men gather to watch a local hurling match in Clare in the early 1950s. On Sunday afternoons at GAA grounds across the country, similar gatherings were common. The games offered a diversion from everyday routines, an opportunity for social interaction and a chance to support the local team. (*Dorothea Lange Collection, the Oakland Museum of California, City of Oakland. Gift of Paul S. Taylor*)

A feature of the gathering momentum of the GAA was the increased number of competitions at various grades across club and county levels. This photograph shows a tussle for possession during a minor championship match between Armagh and Cavan in 1951. The All-Ireland minor championship had been introduced in 1928. (*Gaelic Games in Armagh CD, Cardinal Ó Fiaich Memorial Library*)

The making of *Christy Ring*. Cameraman Vincent Corcoran, film director Louis Marcus and Gael Linn's Pádraig Tyers observe as Christy Ring demonstrates the skills of hurling at the UCC Gaelic grounds in the Mardyke, Cork. When the film was launched at the Savoy Cinema in Cork in October 1964, the audience rose in a standing ovation for the county's most famous sporting son. And yet, for all the adulation he enjoyed, Ring said that hurling had always been simply 'a way of life' with him: 'It was never my ambition to play the game for the sake of winning All-Ireland medals or breaking records but to perfect the art as well as possible.' (*Gael Linn*)

a vacuum, but from a sporting culture that was increasingly conscious of the role that coaching played in improving standards of performance. Within the broad GAA fraternity, one of the most articulate advocates of coaching was Joe Lennon, a physical education teacher and author of two books on coaching and fitness for Gaelic football during the 1960s. Lennon had particular credibility in that he was part of the Down team that took the Sam Maguire Cup north of the border for the first time in 1960. In their meticulous approach to the game and the attention they paid to tactical matters, that Down team had redrawn the parameters of Gaelic football. For Joe Lennon, coaching was less about training than about education and, echoing an earlier call by Eamonn O'Sullivan, he stressed the need for a coaching system to be organised 'from school and club level to county and provincial level'. What Lennon was to football, Fr Tommy Maher and Tony Wall were to hurling. As a teacher at St. Kieran's College in Kilkenny, and outside the walls of that institution, Maher preached the importance of mastering the skills and shaped the thinking of many who would later take charge of teams. Wall, meanwhile,

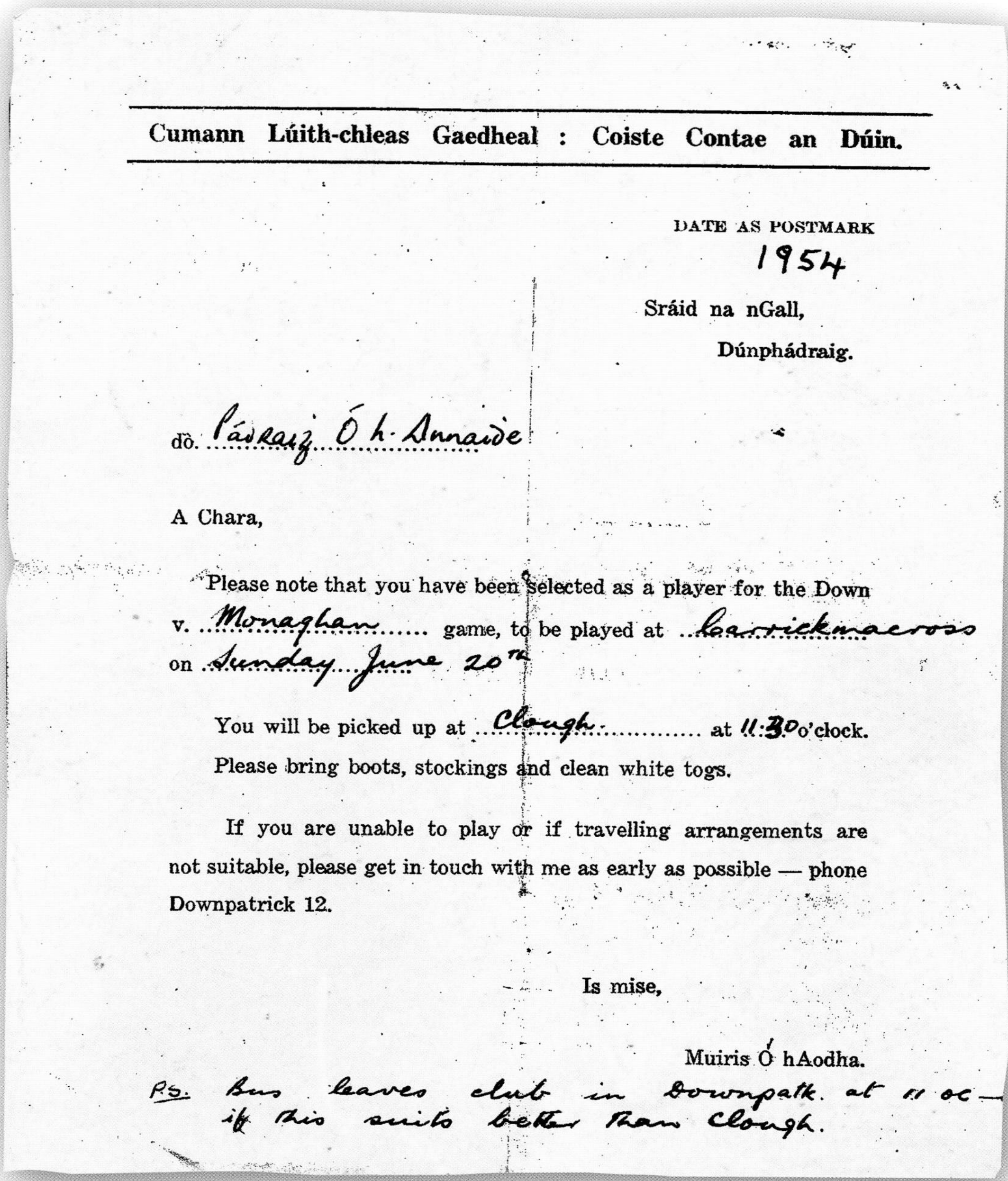

Cumann Lúith-chleas Gaedheal : Coiste Contae an Dúin.

DATE AS POSTMARK

1954

Sráid na nGall,

Dúnphádraig.

do. *Pádraig Ó h-Annaide*

A Chara,

Please note that you have been selected as a player for the Down

v. *Monaghan* game, to be played at *Carrickmacross*

on *Sunday June 20th*

You will be picked up at *Clough* at *11:30* o'clock.

Please bring boots, stockings and clean white togs.

If you are unable to play or if travelling arrangements are
not suitable, please get in touch with me as early as possible — phone
Downpatrick 12.

Is mise,

Muiris Ó hAodha.

P.S. *Bus leaves club in Downpatk. at 11 oc —
if this suits better than Clough.*

The formalities of the county call-up. Paddy Hanna receives notice from Maurice Hayes of the Down
County Board that he is required to represent the county in an upcoming fixture. Then, as now, selection
for the county team was regarded as a reward to the player and an honour for their club. (*Loughinisland GAC*)

Mick O'Connell in full flight for Kerry against Down in the 1968 All-Ireland final. Recognised as one of the most stylish players of all time, O'Connell's inter-county career spanned three decades, running from the 1950s to the 1970s. In 1975, he published an enthralling memoir in which he offered an insight into his singular devotion to training and sporting excellence. 'Training was somewhat of an obsession with me', he wrote. 'My everyday was geared to it, exercising, sleeping and even employment . . . Nothing was going to interfere with my regular pattern of life . . . Most of my training exercises, ninety per cent at least, were done at home on Valentia Island and alone.' (*Colman Doyle Collection, National Library of Ireland*)

Tom Moloughney, Jimmy Doyle and Kieran Carey relax in the Tipperary dressing room after defeating Dublin in the 1961 All-Ireland final. The team repeated the achievement the following year. Spreading the appeal of hurling beyond its traditional strongholds has been an ongoing challenge for GAA officials. In 1940 a special hurling commission was established. Its report recommended a push on the promotion of the game in primary schools and increased competitions for the Under-18 age groups. (*Jimmy Doyle*)

'I have always been fascinated by talk of the born hurler. He is reputed to be found somewhere in the South of Ireland yet I have searched and failed to find him. What I have found are boys and men who were reared where hurling is the chief form of recreation and the main topic of conversation. In this environment every boy has a hurley. He uses it for hunting home the cows, for "shooting Indians", for chasing the cat, but above all for hurling.' – Tony Wall, *Hurling* (1965), p. 11.

was an All-Ireland winning captain with Tipperary who, in 1965, published the first critical analysis on how hurling was and should be played.

For all that there were men like Lennon, Maher and Wall who advocated coaching, there was also a belief in certain quarters that it was not in keeping with the traditions of Gaelic games. It was not until 1971, when a special commission reported on the future of the GAA, that it was finally recognised that coaching could exercise a 'powerful influence for good'. The extent of the attitudinal change was extraordinary. Where, just a few years before, some leading officials decried the holding of coaching courses as tantamount to professionalism, now the Association promoted such courses as a means to advance their interests on many fronts. In addition to assisting in developing skills, improving standards of play, stimulating and sustaining player interest, and enhancing spectator experience, it was also hoped that coaching could add muscle to the GAA's ongoing mission to revive hurling.

Of all the games fostered by the GAA, hurling had always been the most cherished, yet the most difficult to promote. During its early years, the GAA had succeeded in its broad aim to revive hurling, but this had been only a qualified success. Although some newer areas took to the game, its heartlands remained confined to Munster, south Leinster, stretches of Galway, the Ards Peninsula and the Glens of Antrim. As if to emphasise the narrow base of the game, the All-Ireland senior hurling championship was dominated by just three counties – Cork, Kilkenny and Tipperary. The reasons for the failure to spread the game beyond these regions were many and complex. Competition from Gaelic football at local club and county level undoubtedly played a part, but the unique demands of the game presented their own challenge. For a start, hurling took more time and effort to master than football. It also required players to have access to hurling sticks and this added to the costs of participation for players and clubs. Securing a sufficient supply of ash and putting sticks in the hands of young players were therefore key to the revivalist cause and in the mid-1960s the GAA took to the bulk-ordering, subsidisation and distribution of hurleys throughout the country. This was originally part of a long-term plan to extend hurling to every parish in Ireland, but by the early 1970s the ambition had been lowered to focus on areas where hurling already existed or where there was a recognised potential for growth.

On their own, vision statements and grand schemes would never be enough to strengthen the roots or broaden the base of hurling. What was needed was support for the local effort of volunteers and practical assistance to build on the passion of those who played and taught the game. Occasional breakthroughs by counties long starved of success also helped to breathe life into the sport. In the 1950s, Wexford unexpectedly emerged from the hurling wilderness to win All-Ireland titles against the grain of history and tradition. In the early 1980s, Galway and Offaly did the same. For Galway, winning the 1980 All-Ireland title brought an end to a 57-year drought, while Offaly hurlers claimed their first ever senior title in 1981. Many hurling people rejoiced in these wins, not least because they understood that by challenging the hegemony of the traditional powers of the game, Galway and Offaly held open the possibility that other counties might follow in their path, that new hurling traditions might yet be forged.

It was just the timely injection of faith the game needed. During the 1970s hurling had paled beside Gaelic football, which was awash with new glamour. Dublin had emerged from the doldrums to win three All-Ireland titles in four years in the mid-1970s bringing with them a large urban youth support, a social catchment the GAA had traditionally struggled to reach. They did not do it alone: critical to the spectacular appeal of the Dublin footballers during this era was the rivalry they struck up with a young Kerry team whose achievements, in time, would surpass anything that went before. Rivalries between and within counties had always been at the core of Gaelic games culture and, over the course of a decade, Dublin and Kerry developed into a classic of the kind. Their encounters

'Movement would be Heffernan's *métier*. He went about his business with a winner's confidence. Heffernan ran the big man into the ground, smithereened his great heart under a merciless sun. It was pitiless, this exhibition of a new style of football built on motion and speed rather than long kicking and high catching.' – **An extract from Tom Humphries,** *Dublin v. Kerry: the Story of the Epic Rivalry that Changed Irish Sport* **(2006), p. 2.**

The birth of the Dubs, 1974. Supporters on Hill 16 celebrate as Kevin Heffernan's Dublin march to the first of three All-Ireland titles in four years. The success of the Dublin footballers in the 1970s galvanised the GAA in the city and its sprawling suburbs. Ever since, the crowd-pulling appeal of the Dublin footballers has been an Irish summer phenomenon, bringing colour and atmosphere to Croke Park and ensuring healthy gate receipts for the GAA. (*Fáilte Ireland*)

were popularly portrayed as meetings of opposites – urban versus rural – but, in truth, the teams had more in common than headline clichés permitted. Together, they effectively redefined Gaelic football with their approach to physical training, their use of the hand-pass and game-plans that were based around the quick transfer of possession, support play and fluid movement. The contrast with the games that had been played by the teams of the 1880s was stark. That it made for an attractive, fast-moving spectacle was undeniable. It was underpinned by a revolution in preparation with intense physical training prioritised over coaching. This was the lesson drawn by many ambitious counties and clubs who spent the following years trying to apply the formula to their own teams.

Dublin and Kerry changed football – so too did Australia. In 1984, during its centenary year, the GAA opened international links with Australians Rules football, the two indigenous sports combining to create a new hybrid code. It was a venture with a precedent in the late 1960s: struck by the similarities between the two games, Australian businessman Harry Beitzel had travelled to Ireland with an Australian Rules selection, which defeated then All-Ireland champions Meath in Croke Park. The following year, Meath exacted revenge, defeating the Australians on their own home ground. Nothing developed immediately from this exchange, but a trail had been laid. What distinguished attempts to revive contacts in the 1980s was the involvement of the governing bodies of the two sports, both of which were keen to establish a competitive international outlet for their games. In devising common rules, compromise was required: Gaelic footballers were given the advantage of playing with the round rather than the oval ball, but they had to contend with the more physical, rugby-style tackle of the Australian Rules game. The result of the experiment both fascinated and repelled. The game was open and fast, but marred by frequent violent outbursts. By trial and error, the rules evolved from the 1980s onwards, yet the game, for all its growing spectator appeal, never fully bridged the gulf between professional and amateur sporting cultures. International Rules did nevertheless feed into and improve the Gaelic game. The introduction of free kicks and sideline kicks from the hand, for instance, enhanced Gaelic football, making it faster and more free-flowing, if ultimately more demanding on players' fitness. Despite these changes, football remained more cynical than hurling, with the worst matches blighted by a plague of pulling-and-dragging. Defining legitimate tackles remained a problem and the inability to organise a streamlined, consistent, disciplinary process complicated the orderly running of games.

This was true for club teams, as well as for county ones. Across the country, year after year, clubs trained and played, won and lost, their fortunes rising and

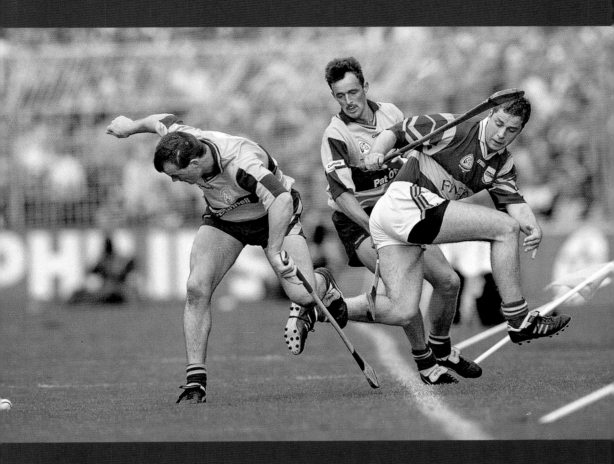

For hurling, the 1990s were what sportswriter Denis Walsh has called 'the revolution years'. A controversial 'back-door' championship system was introduced in 1997 and the All-Ireland final of that year threw up the novelty of an all-Munster pairing. In a classic match, one of many to adorn the decade, Clare defeated Tipperary by a single point. This photograph from that All-Ireland final shows Clare's Ollie Baker (left) and P. J. O'Connell tussling for possession with Tipperary's Liam McGrath. The back-door system added more games to the championship summer, but it did nothing to shift the power-base of the sport. As it was for much of the twentieth century, hurling in the first decade of the twenty-first century was dominated by Cork and Kilkenny. (*David Maher, Sportsfile*)

Brian Dooher (left) of Tyrone and Ronan Clarke of Armagh contest possession in the 2003 All-Ireland football final. Kerry apart, these two counties did more to define the way Gaelic football was played in the early twenty-first century. The great strength and appeal of Ulster football during these years was underscored by decisions to move three successive Ulster finals – 2004, 2005 and 2006 – out of the province to Croke Park. Although not universally popular, the move was considered necessary to meet spectator demand. (*Pat Murphy, Sportsfile*)

falling on the waves of their resources. Inter-county players playing with their clubs helped ensure that changes at inter-county level were quickly absorbed at club level and the very best club matches were considered at least on a par with most inter-county matches. County championships were fought out with a passion coloured by the intensity of local rivalry. The opening of an All-Ireland championship for clubs in the early 1970s was a great boon to the club game. Its winners are a roll-call of the greatest clubs in the history of the GAA. They also presented clubs from counties which were not to the fore at inter-county level with the opportunity to showcase their talent. Beyond playing for championships, there was much else on offer to club players. Regular challenge matches against clubs from other counties offered alternatives to local combat. So, too, did the informal calendar of carnival matches, seven-a-side competitions and gold-watch tournaments. Elite club players had much to challenge them, but there was also a large social element for those who wanted exercise and entertainment, without enduring undue hardship.

Throughout the 1990s, in the face of stiffening competition from rival sports, the GAA radically overhauled how its games were funded, promoted, presented and played. In the rush to modernise, old heresies became new orthodoxies. The controversial decision to allow sponsors' logos on team jerseys turned players into mobile billboards, enabling county boards to meet some of the escalating costs of preparing county teams. Sponsorship of the All-Ireland senior championships followed. This was accompanied by lavish, brilliantly executed advertisement campaigns which helped to revamp the popular image of the GAA, drawing on Irish mythology, ideas of localism and the unique qualities of the games and those who played them. The sponsors' timing was perfect. Their arrival coincided with an era in which Gaelic sports were undergoing a revolution.

In the early 1990s, the rise of Ulster football was marked by first-time All-Ireland wins for Donegal and Derry and two more for Down, a county whose Gaelic football tradition had been memorably forged in the 1960s. This democratisation of success had a galvanising effect on the sport, fuelling a belief in many counties that progress was possible if the right structures, the right management and a fully committed body of players could all come together. The story of hurling conveyed a similar message. All-Ireland wins for Clare in 1995 and Wexford in 1996 helped revitalise the game to a point where, for a number of years, it surfed a wave of unprecedented popularity. Underpinning both these unexpected break-throughs were charismatic management and an intensity of purpose born of years of underachievement. Under Ger Loughnane's management, Clare essentially did for hurling what Dublin and Kerry did for football in the 1970s. Training

The club and county scene has been transformed by the proliferation of floodlit grounds and all-weather facilities. Such improvements rendered GAA activity – training sessions and games – less dependent on congenial weather conditions and daylight hours, but it also impacted on the fixture programmes by facilitating the scheduling of games at night. This photograph shows a training match between a Cork selection and Glen Rovers at the Glen Rovers GAA Club grounds at Ballyvolane, County Cork on a Friday night in February 2008. (*Matt Browne, Sportsfile*)

became almost year-long and ferocious. At a field in Crusheen, a small village north of Ennis, players were subjected to a gruelling regime of hard winter training. As one player later recalled: 'At training you'd feel like getting sick, but you didn't quite because there was nothing there. You'd have nothing.' Crusheen became a byword for shared physical punishment and character formation. And because it worked for Clare, other teams went in search of a 'Crusheen' of their own.

As the physical demands of the games increased, so did their profile. Live television, radio, newspapers and sponsors played their part and, from the late 1990s, they were able to feed off a far larger diet of summer games. The All-Ireland football and hurling championships were revamped to allow a 'back-door' system whereby teams beaten in the early rounds were given a chance to re-enter the competition. This was a hugely significant move. It expanded the number of championship games, further elevating the status of the inter-county game. Against the back-drop of the booming Irish economy, the new championship format facilitated an increase in the level of commercial activity around the inter-county scene. As revenues rose, the GAA invested resources in games development, grounds and inter-county player welfare. A quiet revolution in Gaelic games was initiated through coaching programmes. The deployment of full-time coaches to deliver programmes to assist the voluntary effort in clubs and schools helped to transform the way hurling and football were taught and learned. The clear ambition was that coaching and games development would become vehicles to improve standards and level the playing fields across the country; that no one county or group of counties should have a monopoly on knowledge or expertise in such areas as sports science; and that the competitive base of the games would widen.

And yet, for all the investment of effort in grass-roots development, the GAA struggled to strike a proper balance between inter-county and club activity. Despite providing for the vast majority of the Association's playing membership, clubs in many counties found their seasons squeezed up against (or even into) the dark months of winter, when the weather and pitches were at their worst. Because of the expansion of the All-Ireland championships, summers were by and large sacrificed to the demands of county teams. In terms of the organisation of games, this presented the GAA with a major dilemma: how could it reconcile growing inter-county demands – critical for promotional and revenue purposes – with the need for a regular season of fixtures for clubs? Resolving this conundrum is one of the major challenges the Association has set for itself.

Modern Gaelic football and hurling may be unrecognisable from those games rapturously described in the early press reports of Michael Cusack, but they have never before been so popular. The games themselves are a product of evolution. Throughout their history, they have been shaped and re-shaped by rule changes, by the genius of generations of players and by a flow of new ideas on training, team preparation, tactics and skill development. Today, as if to underline the distance travelled from their early codified form, the emphasis of Gaelic games has shifted to a large extent from ball propulsion to ball retention. Winning and maintaining possession are now standard priorities. Whether the modern games are better or worse than those that went before is the stuff of bar-room debate and subjective analysis. It always has been.

Cyclists stop to watch a game of handball at Foxford, County Mayo, 1 August 1940. During the Second World War, with fuel rationed, many players, officials and supporters reverted to bicycles to ensure the continued conduct of GAA business. (*Irish Picture Library/Fr. F. M. Browne S.J. Collection*)

3

Travel

'We all came home from Thurles with the boots, togs and socks strung over our handlebars. Pat Stakelum tied the cup to the bicycle as well.' —

Tipperary hurler John Doyle recalls the aftermath of the 1949 Munster final, quoted in Seamus McRory, *The All-Ireland Dream* (2005), p. 119.

'Instead of forty train specials of 1938 we only had three last Sunday.
The petrol too was scarce but never before was there such a biking parade
to the Liffeyside. Cyclists lined the road in one continuous stream.
The trek which opened early in the week ended at 3pm on Sabbath day, though a few
stragglers with tyre troubles wheeled dusty cycles in,
sweating and very weary, round the half-time whistle.'

ON
Sunday, May 11, 1902
Killorglin v Shamrocks
(KERRY)   (TIPPERARY)
TWO O'CLOCK.
HURLING.
Kilmoyley v Two-Miles-Borris
(KERRY)   (TIPPERARY)
THREE O'CLOCK.

'In the 1950s very few of us would ever have got the opportunity of
travelling, particularly on a plane, were it not
for winning the National League. There were over 2,000 people
there to greet us [in New York] and they really gave us a rapturous welcome.
As emigration was rife at the time, the GAA was very strong in New York.

On the last Sunday in July 1898 several thousand Tipperary supporters squeezed onto a special train, which was heading to Cork for the Munster senior hurling and football semi-finals between teams from Cork and Tipperary. The huge crowd bore testimony to the rivalry that had already developed between the two counties. As the train attempted to climb the incline between Limerick Junction and Emly, its engine was unequal to the challenge and stalled. It proved impossible to pull the train full of Tipperary Gaels up the hill. The only answer was to split the train and haul the carriages, one after the next, over the incline. By the time the last carriages had made it across the brow of the hill, a second engine had arrived. The carriages of the train were once more united and, together, the two engines successfully pulled the train to Cork.

The semi-final matches to which the spectators were travelling were actually part of the 1897 Munster championship. Persistent difficulties in organising fixtures (not least in getting suitable grounds) routinely delayed local and national championships by at least a year, and sometimes even by two. By the time the matches were finally fixed for Cork on Sunday 31 July 1898, they attracted a crowd in excess of 15,000. That crowd eventually included the train-travellers, whose journey continued to be eventful even after their arrival in Cork. When they reached the pitch – Cork Park, a venue that the Cork GAA used from the very start of the GAA – they found just four turnstiles open. Newspaper reporters claimed such a crush developed outside the ground that the crowd 'clambered the high hoarding with the barbed wire on top, heedless of torn clothes and flesh'. In their haste to enter the ground the crowd seemed oblivious to the fact that the match was unlikely to start without them. After all, the spectators had been

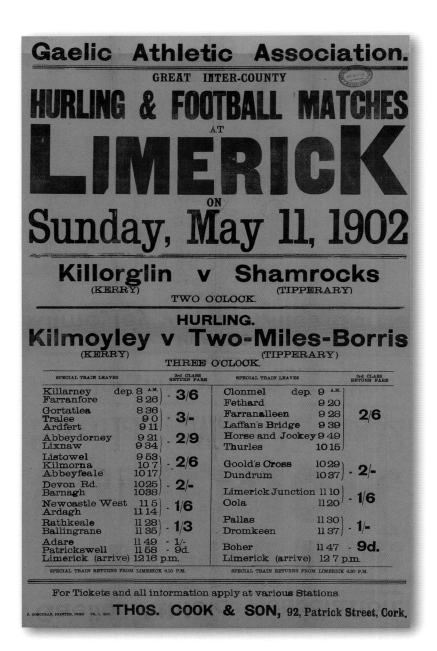

A poster used to advertise special train services to hurling and football matches at Limerick on Sunday 11 May 1902. The development of a national rail system in the nineteenth century made possible the organisation of inter-county, mass-spectator, sporting events. (*Limerick City Museum*)

'On last Sunday four of the leading clubs of the city of Limerick journeyed on the saloon steamer *Vandeleur* to Kilrush to meet two hurling and two football teams. The Commercials were the first to take the field, and though somewhat fatigued after the long river journey showed good form. When the Kilrush team entered the field many differed in opinion respecting the winner of the Cup presented by the ladies of Kilrush to the Gaelic boys of the parish. After a most warmly-contested match they were at last con-quered by the unbeaten Limerick Commercials . . . the No. 1 National Brass Band accompanied the excursion to Kilrush, where, much to the credit of the managing committee of the tournament, its members, as well as every one of the excursionists, were treated in a most hospitable fashion.' –
A report in *Sport* on 2 April 1887 of a tournament between clubs from Limerick and Clare.

accompanied on the train to Cork by the Tipperary teams. By the time the hurling match started, a full two-and-a-half hours after the appointed time, the Tipperary players were in no fit condition to play, 'having had no opportunity of getting lunch before they played', though even that cannot fully explain the fact that they lost by 4-16 to 0-2. The Tipperary footballers fared better, losing by just 4 points. Nonetheless, as they took the train home 'the Gaels of Tipperary, especially the hurling element, [were] to put it mildly, disappointed with the poor show'.

The place of rail transport on this and many other GAA Sundays is crucial to understanding the spread of the GAA. Without the railways, modern sport would have remained a much more localised affair and would have drawn far fewer spectators. For sporting organisations in America, in England, and elsewhere, the transport revolution of the nineteenth century was key to their growth. It facilitated the making of contests between teams who would not otherwise have been able to play each other. In addition, the mass movement of spectators increased atten-dances and drove commercial activity around sport. This, in turn, created a sense of excitement that would not otherwise have been possible.

Prior to the building of the railways, travel in Ireland was slow and haphazard, and was usually reliant on poor-quality roads and on various forms of horse-drawn travel. The building of the canals from the second half of the eighteenth century brought a measure of improvement, but it was the railway boom which meant that transport across Ireland became a less tortuous affair. The first Irish railway line, from Dublin to Kingstown (now Dún Laoghaire), was opened in 1834. It cost £300,000 to build the six miles of railway. Despite the success of the first line, only two others were built in Ireland before the onset of the Famine: in 1839 a seven-mile stretch was opened from Belfast to Lisburn, and this was followed in 1844 by a line from Dublin to Drogheda.

In the post-Famine years, a host of different companies won contracts from parliament to build and run railway services in Ireland. By the end of the nineteenth century there were eight major railway companies running national routes, and over thirty smaller businesses managing local routes, light railway systems and city-based tram services. Running between Listowel and Ballybunnion there was even the world's first commercial monorail, which ran from 1888 until 1924. At its height in the 1920s the Irish rail network ran for over 3,000 miles. When looking at the map of the national railway system at the turn of the century, it is striking how comprehensive that system was. In 1906, it was possible to travel from Dublin to the southwest, change trains and reach a series of towns and villages along the various peninsulas, including Kenmare, Schull and Baltimore. Later, with the rationalisation of the railways in the 1950s and 1960s, these lines, along with nearly 60 per cent of the whole network, were abandoned.

The founding of the GAA coincided with the height of the railway-building boom in Ireland and the impact of this was clear from the beginning. The very fact that Thurles was on a railway line was surely an influential factor in the choice of that town as the venue for the founding meeting of the GAA. On Saturday 1 November 1884, Michael Cusack was able to travel from Dublin to Thurles by train, and to return on the same day. John Wyse Power and John McKay most likely did the same in travelling from Kildare and Cork, respectively. The railways quickly became a central feature of life for those playing and competing in the GAA. When the first athletics meeting of the GAA was held on 11 November 1884, it was staged at Macroom, a town fully serviced by the railway. Indeed, all the important athletics meetings of the GAA, in its first year, were held in towns with major rail connections: Clonmel (February 1885), Tralee (June 1885) and New Ross (July 1885). The first national championships were held in Tramore (October 1885), a small fishing port that had been transformed by the arrival of the railway in 1853. Likewise, hurling and football, although promoted in the early months of the GAA by challenge matches between local clubs, were made national by the railways. In February 1886, when Cusack organised the first major hurling match to be played in Dublin under GAA rules, the teams from south Galway and north Tipperary travelled up to the city by train. This would have not been possible three

Railway stations became points of departure and return for sporting teams through the decades. In the early days of the Association, brass or pipe bands would often lead teams and their supporters from the stations to the fields of play. In the twentieth and twenty-first centuries, the railway station became the setting for scenes of mass public celebration or mourning when teams returned from big matches in either victory or defeat. This photograph, taken on 2 October 1938, shows members of the Dublin Camogie team at Amiens Street Station prior to boarding a train to Belfast for the camogie semi-final. The journey was a good one, the Dubliners returning with their place in the All-Ireland final secure. They went on to win the final. (*Cumann Camógaíochta na nGael*)

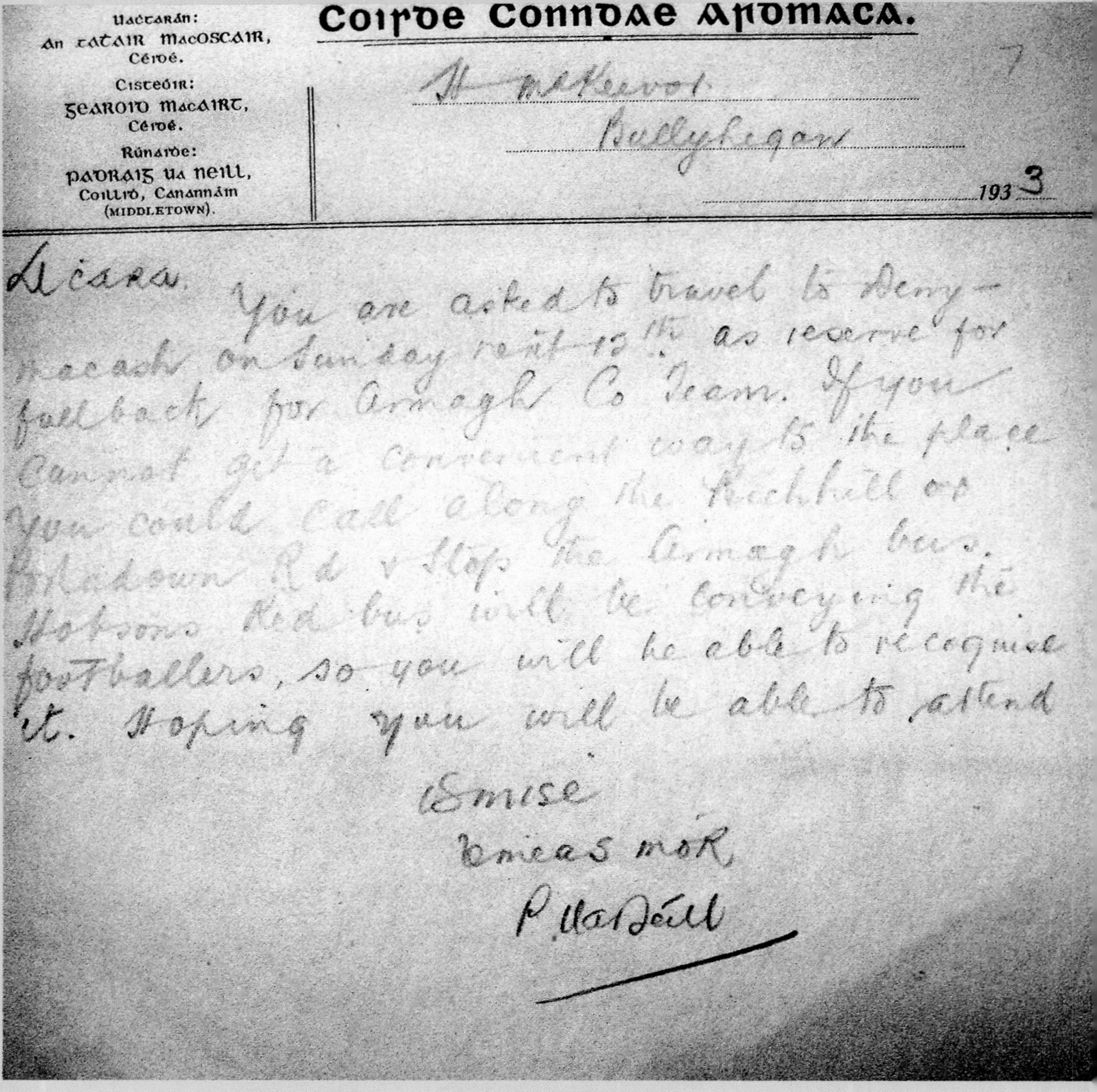

Uactarán:
An tATAIR MacOSCAIR,
Céide.

Cisteóir:
ᵹEAROID MacAIRT,
Céide.

Rúnaide:
PADRAIᵹ Ua NEILL,
Coillid, Canannám
(MIDDLETOWN).

Coirde Conndae Ardmaca.

St Patrickroe
Ballyhegan

7

193 **3**

A cara.

You are asked to travel to Derry-
nacash on Sunday next 13ᵗʰ as reserve for
full back for Armagh Co Team. If you
cannot get a convenient way to the place
you could call along the Hightull or
Tandown Rd & stop the Armagh bus.
Hotsons Red bus will be conveying the
footballers, so you will be able to recognise
it. Hoping you will be able to attend

Ismisé
Eneas mór,
P. Ua Néill

Notifying players and ensuring their transport to away games was part of the organisational responsibilities for many County Boards. This call-up to the Armagh County panel in 1933 came with advice to the player to intercept the team bus along the road. No guidance on time was given. (*Cardinal Ó Fiaich Memorial Library*)

decades earlier. Local lore around Gort suggests that several of the losing south Galway team were unwilling to take the train home for fear of recrimination.

The railways were not the only means of travel, of course. From the 1880s people walked, cycled and travelled by horse-and-car and pony-and-trap to local GAA tournaments. What made the railways so critical, however, was their ability to expand the boundaries of competitions to a national scale. There could have been no All-Ireland championships without the railways, and it is a simple fact that, Sunday after Sunday, trains were filled with GAA players and supporters moving to matches. This travel was an attraction in itself – a convivial world of card games, sing-songs, eating and drinking. It was a phenomenon which was a boon for railway companies who were delighted to be able to fill trains which would otherwise have stood empty on Sundays. Nonetheless, this was not a relationship without conflict. There were disputes between GAA officials and railway companies, which usually focused on the notion that those companies were making huge profits on the back of GAA members who were being herded about like cattle in overcrowded carriages. A dispute between Kerry and the Great Southern Railway actually ended with Kerry refusing to travel to the 1910 All-Ireland football final because of the manner in which their players and supporters were routinely treated. In Kerry's absence, Louth were awarded the match.

Ireland, along with many European countries of the time, had three classes of travel on most services. For GAA supporters, many of whom had restricted incomes, the availability of cheap third-class travel and match-day specials allowed them to traverse the country following their club or county. As many as 100 special trains could operate on certain Sundays. This travelling support was a boon to the GAA – the more people who could travel, the larger the crowd and the more profitable the gate receipts. The efficiency of the railway service, and its relatively low cost, is evidenced by the 1920 All-Ireland football final (played in June 1922) between Dublin and Tipperary, which drew a crowd of 17,000 people to Croke Park. GAA followers in the city could use the extensive city tram service to bring them into the city centre from Lucan, Blessington and Kingstown, as well as from all the major suburbs. For those travelling from the country to the match, four of the major railway companies ran match-day specials: the Great Southern and Western Railway had trains leaving from Carrick, Cahir, Cashel, Waterford Athlone and Tullow; the Midland and Great Western Railway special ran from Galway, Ballina, Westport and Sligo; the Dublin and South Eastern Railway ran a special from Wexford and Shillelagh; and the Great Northern Railway ran a train from Oldcastle, Navan and Drogheda. A return ticket from Galway cost four shillings.

Wexford, 1934. The St James, Ramsgrange, football team packs into Pat O'Brien's lorry to play a match in Clongeen. The previous year, in the course of a Dáil debate on a Road Traffic Bill, a number of deputies referred to the fact that, owing to the scarcity of public service vehicles, it was common for Gaelic clubs to use lorries for the conveyance of teams. Justifying the exclusion of GAA teams from stricter regulation of this practice, Martin Corry, a TD for Cork East, stated: 'The boys who engage in hurling and football are farmers' sons and farm labourers, and this is a very small concession to afford to those who have no other amusement than this game on Sunday, and who have no other means of travelling to the game than those afforded through the decency of a local tradesman who places his lorry at their disposal for the day.' (*Thomas Grennan*)

'Ah, I mind it all so clearly when the stars dance on the hills,
With their faces scrubbed and shiny and the powder in their hair,
And the tide across the sandbanks turning lazy in its sleep,
And a lonesome curlew bubbling here and there.
We all met at Keating's corner when 'twas midnight by the clock –
Casey's mouth organ made music like a lark,
And we gave the Kerry war-cry as we marched north two by two
To lep aboard the ghost train for Croke Park.' –
An extract from the ballad 'The Ghost Train to Croke Park' written by poet and songwriter Sigerson Clifford. The ballad recalls a journey taken by Clifford and friends from Cahersiveen, County Kerry to the 1926 All-Ireland football final.

For many, however, match-day journeys were much longer. Supporters from west Kerry who wished to make it to Dublin in time for an All-Ireland final had to make their way to Killarney for the 'ghost-train' which departed around midnight and arrived in Dublin in time for its passengers to go to Mass, get something to eat and make their way to Croke Park for the match. These tired and weary supporters eventually arrived back to Killarney a full twenty-four hours later, whereupon the people from outlying areas retrieved their bicycles and set out on the final leg of their journey home.

For many across Ireland, taking such trains to big matches marked their first excursion to Dublin, but these excursions were more often local than national. One observer remembered the excitement of the first diesel railcar excursion from Clonakilty for the local team's encounter with the St Nicholas team at the Cork Athletic Grounds in Cork city in October 1954:

I travelled with some friends on the empty train from Cork and on arrival at Clonakilty, we found the platform packed with men, women and children, all eagerly looking forward to this new mode of travel. Hundreds more were streaming up the steep MacCurtain Hill from the town. When the long train pulled out for Cork, it was packed tight with 640 on board. We picked up another 80 passengers at Ballinscarthy (possibly the whole population of the district!) and then sped non-stop to Cork with this grossly overloaded train. It was a remarkable sight to see 720 passengers alighting at the Albert Quay terminus at Cork. But that was not all. Shortly afterwards, another much shorter train pulled in from Bantry, Dunmanway and Bandon with as many passengers standing as sitting, a total of 461 more supporters. Altogether almost 1,200 people arrived at Albert Quay that morning, a record never surpassed afterwards. Three return trains left for the West that evening so the tired and disappointed fans (they lost the match) at least had a seat for the journey home.

For the brief, but remarkable, period of the Second World War known as the 'Emergency', trains were supplanted by bicycles as the most popular means of transport to matches. Cycling to matches was not, of course, a new phenomenon. Indeed, around the time the GAA was founded there was something of a cycling craze in Ireland. The invention of the modern bicycle had popularised cycling – an activity that had been introduced to Ireland in the 1850s, but had initially been a predominantly male pursuit as the first bikes, notably the penny-farthing, were unwieldy. In the 1890s both sexes took to the wheel, often to tour the countryside surrounding the areas in which they lived. Inevitably, this touring was tailored by some to include attendance at GAA events. Mostly, those who cycled to matches did so with the sole ambition of getting to the game, rather than marking it as just one stopping point on an itinerary. The bicycle aided not only spectators, but also players and officials. Sean O'Kennedy of Wexford was a star player (he was captain of the Wexford footballers for three of the four All-Irelands they won in a row between 1915 and 1918) who, like many of his contemporaries, cycled to training and matches. He subsequently served as county chairman and ran the county teams much as a modern manager might. In his pursuit of the best players for his panel, and driven by the need to cast his eye over all the players in various parishes, O'Kennedy was reported to have regularly cycled fifty miles in a day to watch a match.

Of course, travelling on a bicycle as a hurler presented its own unique set of problems. Not only did you have to find some way of carrying your kit and boots, you also had to balance your hurl. Paddy Wickham, another Wexford man, vividly described how he used to tie the laces of his boots together, throwing them over the handlebars. He put his knicks in one boot, his stockings in the other and his hurl would rest between the gear wheel of his bicycle and the handlebars.

During the Second World War, with other forms of transport constrained through the rationing of fuel, cycling to matches moved from being a local phenomenon to a national one. Streams of bikes rolled across the country to Croke Park, meeting on the North Circular Road like so many tributaries flowing into a broadening river. For a Leinster championship match between Wexford and Carlow at Croke Park in July 1941, the *Carlow Nationalist* wrote that 'with the shortage of fuel the bicycle

With the Sam Maguire trophy on the table opposite them, Kerry management, players and officials reflect on another triumphant trip to Croke Park, *c.* mid-1980s. Included in the photograph are (l–r): Kevin Griffin, Frank King (chairman of the Kerry County Board), Tony O'Keeffe and Mick O'Dwyer. Reflected in the window with the trophy is John McMahon, County Board treasurer. Kerry teams traditionally travelled by train to Dublin; however, a dispute with the Great Southern Railway Company in 1910 led to the county's withdrawal from the All-Ireland championship of that year. The Kerry action drew support from a range of public bodies within and without the county. The Ennis Branch of the Gaelic League, for instance, saluted the gesture for helping to 'bring to light the grave scandal which exists in the scant courtesy with which the chief Railway Company of Ireland treats the various national organisations in the matter of travelling facilities'. (*GAA/PH/KRY/005, GAA Museum*)

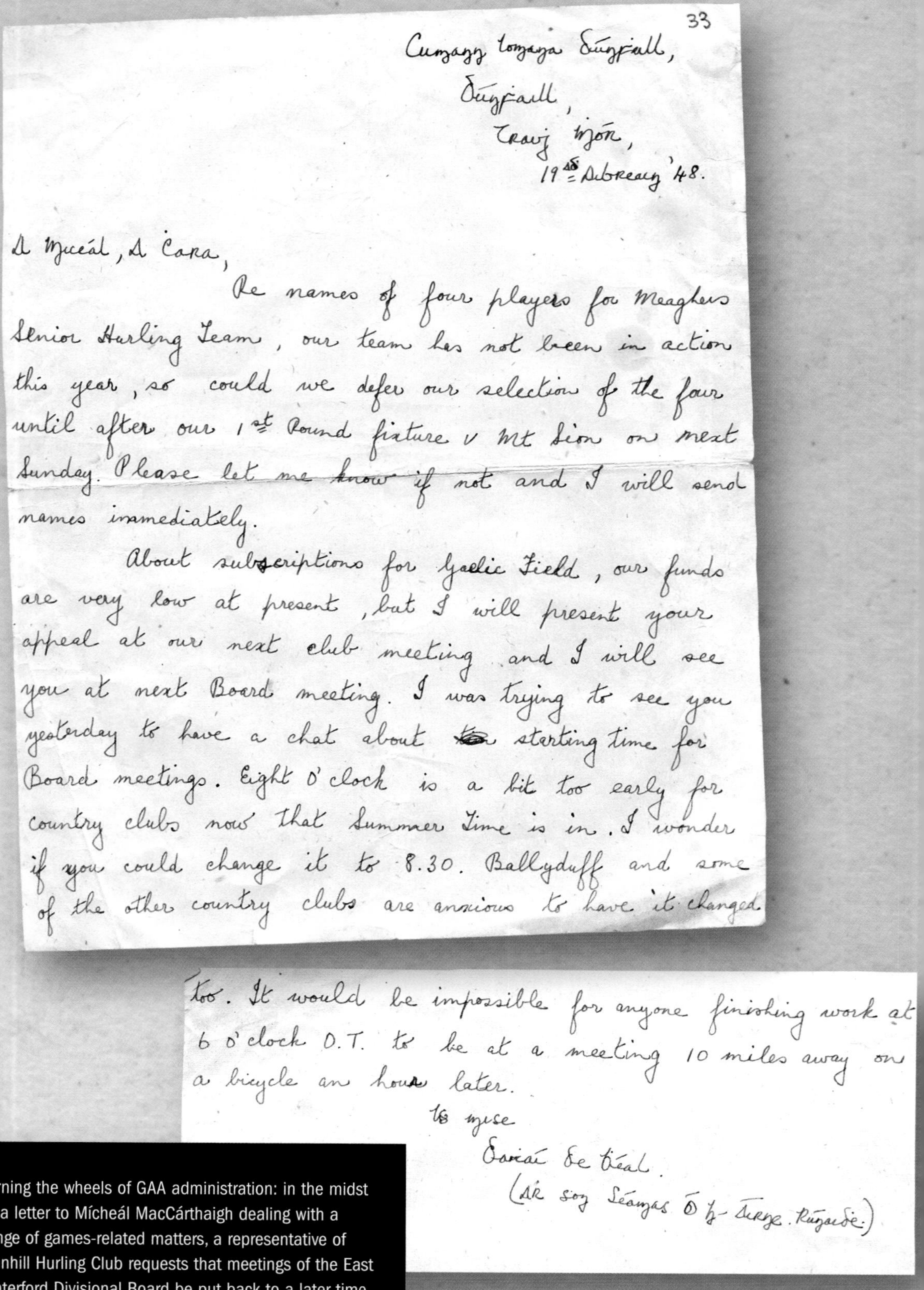

Cumann Iomána Dúnaill,
Dúnaill,
Tráig Mór,
19ᵃᵈ Aibreán '48.

A Míceál, A Cara,

Re names of four players for Meaghers
Senior Hurling Team, our team has not been in action
this year, so could we defer our selection of the four
until after our 1ˢᵗ Round fixture v Mt Sion on next
Sunday. Please let me know if not and I will send
names immediately.

About subscriptions for Gaelic Field, our funds
are very low at present, but I will present your
appeal at our next club meeting and I will see
you at next Board meeting. I was trying to see you
yesterday to have a chat about the starting time for
Board meetings. Eight o'clock is a bit too early for
country clubs now that Summer Time is in. I wonder
if you could change it to 8.30. Ballyduff and some
of the other country clubs are anxious to have it changed

too. It would be impossible for anyone finishing work at
6 o'clock O.T. to be at a meeting 10 miles away on
a bicycle an hour later.

Is mise
Dáiáí De Teál.
(Ar son Séamas Ó h-Áirge. Rúnaidhe.)

Turning the wheels of GAA administration: in the midst
of a letter to Mícheál MacCárthaigh dealing with a
range of games-related matters, a representative of
Dunhill Hurling Club requests that meetings of the East
Waterford Divisional Board be put back to a later time
to facilitate delegates who had to cycle long distances
to attend, 19 April 1948. (GAA/PL/PC1/33, GAA Museum)

Laurence J. Kettle,

M.Inst.C.E.I., M.I.Mech.E., M.I.E.E.

T.LEPHONE 92252 Dublin.

46 Cowper Road, Rathmines

XXXXXXXXXXXXXX XXXXXXXX

Dublin, Sept.20th. 19 51

Dear Taoiseach,

As you want the country to grow as much corn as possible does it not seem a strange and inappropriate thing to select the middle of the harvest season for the G.A.A. hurling and football championship finals? This means bringing perhaps 100,000 people away from the country to Dublin at a time when most of them would be doing good national work by staying at home. It is true that we don't usually do harvesting work on Sunday but you may take it that people who do the double journey from Kerry or Mayo are in no condition for work on Monday. Apart from this quite a number of these country visitors stay over Monday and even Tuesday in Dublin.

Church and State apparently identify themselves with these inappropriate arrangements. Surely these big sporting meetings could be arranged for a more suitable season of the year. All that would be necessary would be a word from you.

With kind regards

yours sincerely

Laurence J. Kettle

A letter from a Dublin resident, Dr Kettle, to Taoiseach Éamon de Valera expresses concerns that the exodus from rural Ireland on All-Ireland final Sundays was damaging agricultural efficiency. The correspondent made clear that those travelling long distances to attend the games were in no fit state to work the following day. In his response, de Valera explained that the dates for the final had now become 'traditional' and that he did not share Kettle's concerns. De Valera also recalled the occasion – in 1946 – when the GAA took the decision to postpone the All-Ireland football final in order to assist a national campaign to save the harvest. (D/Taoiseach, S 15147A, National Archives of Ireland)

'Instead of forty train specials of 1938 we only had three last Sunday. The petrol too was scarce but never before was there such a biking parade to the Liffeyside. Cyclists lined the road in one continuous stream. The trek which opened early in the week ended at 3pm on Sabbath day, though a few stragglers with tyre troubles wheeled dusty cycles in, sweating and very weary, round the half-time whistle.' – **The journalist 'Carbery' comments on the impact of the 'Emergency' on transport to the 1941 All-Ireland football final, quoted in P. D. Mehigan, *Vintage Carbery*, edited by Seán Kilfeather (1984), p. 181.**

was back to its own'. For those who had not been able to cycle up to the game, there was an alternative, as the newspaper noted, that 'during the hours of 4 p.m. to 6 p.m. on Sunday when the streets of the town and all roads in the neighbourhood were completely deserted by the male element and in every room where there was a wireless set, the air of expectation was at times so marked that you could hear the proverbial pin drop'. In the end it took Carlow four matches to beat Wexford and qualify for the Leinster final. They were due to play Dublin in that final, but because of the foot-and-mouth outbreak in the Carlow area, the Department of Agriculture refused to let the players travel and Dublin were selected to play Kerry.

What was remarkable was that attendances at GAA matches during this period reached new heights. The secretary of the Laois County Board, J. Drennan, noted at the annual convention in 1943 that the followers of the GAA in the county were

'The train, bedecked with the Roscommon colours, was greeted by supporters at every station that we passed through. At Athlone, where we crossed the river Shannon into our home province of Connacht, the platform and surrounding areas were packed with well-wishers and I got out and said a few words. All along the train route from Athlone to Roscommon town, a continuous line of bonfires blazed brightly on that lovely, mild and happy October evening. Along that route and six miles from Roscommon town lies Knockcroghery. There in my home village a massive bonfire blazed at the railway gate as children and adults in their hundreds marched in a torchlight procession.' – **Jimmy Murray of Roscommon on the journey home after winning the 1943 All-Ireland football final, quoted in Seamus McRory, *The All-Ireland Dream* (2005), p. 145.**

The last leg of the journey: a group of Waterford supporters from Aglish make their way up Dublin's O'Connell Street for the 1957 All-Ireland hurling final. Pictured here are Nicholas O'Donnell, Danny O'Neill, George Hennessy, Eddie Crotty and Roger Ryan. (*Waterford County Images*)

Crowds gather at Grattan Square and Bridge Street, Dungarvan, on the day of a Munster hurling championship match *c.* 1924. The changing pattern of travel to GAA games is apparent from the large number of cars in the photograph. Car ownership grew steadily during the following decades, but boomed from the 1960s onwards. (*Waterford County Images*)

to be commended for the many ways they were managing to travel to matches during the 'Emergency', noting that he had seen people travelling on bicycles, on foot, in cars, in carts and, on one occasion, on the back of a donkey. Most striking of all was the 1944 All-Ireland football final between Kerry and Roscommon. Almost 80,000 people turned up to watch that match. Breandán Ó hEithir later recalled meeting people who travelled to that match by the most extraordinary means, including a party from north Kerry who hired a traveller's horse-drawn caravan to bring them to Dublin.

People continued to travel by bicycle and by rail long after the Second World War, yet the irresistible shift in Irish life towards the private motor car brought inevitable change to GAA-related travel. This shift had been under way even during the heyday of the railway in Ireland. The first car in Ireland was owned by John Brown, Dunmurray, Belfast. In March 1896 he imported a Serpollet steamer, which he had purchased in France a few months earlier. The first petrol car seen in Ireland was owned by a Dubliner, Dr John Colohan, who imported a Benz Velo in November 1896. He was quickly followed by other prominent Dublin citizens such as H. M. Gillie, the editor of the *Freeman's Journal*, and Lord Iveagh.

Five friends, all from Roscrea, break for tea and sandwiches on the road to Fermoy for a Munster football championship match between Tipperary and Cork, 1943. Pictured are (l–r): L. T. Maher, Eddie Guilmartin, Tom Lawlor, Jack Fitzpatrick and Jack Maher. The car was owned by Tom Lawlor, a farmer who also ran a hackney service in Roscrea. Due to the fuel shortages and general expense, few cars were on Irish roads at the time. (*Eddie Guilmartin*)

The All-Ireland winning Tipperary hurlers pictured on board the SS *Bremen* in 1926. Tipperary were the first county team to tour the United States. Two days into their voyage, one of the travelling party wrote in his diary: 'We hurlers flock mostly together, so, being tired of walking the deck after lunch to-day, we induced Tim Crowe to bring out his violin, collect the few Irish girls on board, and danced lancers and quadrilles; while groups of Germans looked on, evidently amused at our kind of dance. Some step-dancing by Tim and Rody – quite a different day from yesterday. Not one of us to be seen yesterday – all dead sick.' (*GAA Oral History Project Archive*)

During the following decades, ownership of private cars spread from the moneyed elite to encompass every section of Irish society. This had profound implications for travel to GAA matches, bringing an entirely new dimension to the culture of match-day outings.

The number of private cars reached 170,000 in 1960 and rose dramatically to 796,000 in 1990. Roadside picnics, sandwiches from the boot of the car, new halfway houses, and the search for shortcuts to beat the traffic became the staple of big-match Sundays. The increase in car ownership also had an impact on playing and training. In time it changed the relationship between GAA players and their clubs by facilitating country players who had moved out of their home area to continue playing for their home club. This, in turn, had a negative impact on the number of players who transferred to Dublin clubs. Where once this was almost guaranteed, it became less certain with the growing use of the car. All of this also facilitated an increase in the number of training sessions held in the evenings and the tradition was spawned of lengthy road-trips to all parts of Ireland.

Travel by GAA teams extended far beyond Ireland from the early days of the GAA. The first ever GAA tour, the 'Invasion' of America, took place in 1888. For a fledgling organisation it was a bold step, and the travel involved was daunting. The touring athletes and hurlers came together in Dublin, before taking the train to Queenstown (now Cobh), with stops in Thurles and Cork. On 16 September 1888, fifty hurlers and athletes left on a nine-day voyage to America. GAA President Maurice Davin was the head of the party and his brother, Pat Davin, travelled to compete as an athlete and hurler. As they sailed away from the quay in Queenstown aboard the SS *Wisconsin* there were bands playing and massed crowds cheering on the quays.

The first night on the boat was idyllic. There was dancing on the deck until late in the evening with Germans, Russians and Swedes, but then came the storm. The hurlers, coming as most of them did from inland areas, were extremely badly affected, most of them vomiting continuously. At one o'clock in the morning the ship was almost lost when it was hit by a massive wave. Passengers were thrown about the place and, as Pat Davin later recalled, most of the hurlers 'remained up saying their prayers and expecting every minute to be their last'. Their state of mind was not improved by the sight of a small boat being driven around the sea with only the stump of its mast remaining. The hurlers survived and made it to America. During their month-long adventure, the players took some forty-five separate train journeys in order to complete the fixtures which were arranged. Seventeen of the original touring party of fifty remained permanently in America

'In the 1950s very few of us would ever have got the opportunity of travelling, particularly on a plane, were it not for winning the National League . . . There were over 2,000 people there to greet us [in New York] and they really gave us a rapturous welcome. As emigration was rife at the time, the GAA was very strong in New York. All the Irish people would meet for a social get-together every Sunday, in Gaelic Park. If you ever went to New York and you wanted to meet someone, Gaelic Park was the normal meeting venue.' – John Doyle of Tipperary on the benefits of winning the National League, quoted in Seamus McRory, *The All-Ireland Dream* (2005), p. 120.

and several more returned to Ireland only to tidy up their affairs before going back to live and work across the Atlantic. Maurice Davin was deeply upset on the afternoon of 31 October 1888 when their ship sailed out of New York, waved off by several hundred Irish emigrants and the remnant of his own Invaders. It was, wrote Pat Davin, a 'very affecting sight. Most of them never set eyes on their native shores again.'

Later, in the 1920s and 1930s, teams of All-Ireland winners travelled by sea to America and played teams of emigrants in exhibition matches in cities across the country. In time, sea travel was replaced by air travel. It was not a clean break, however. When the All-Ireland football final was staged in New York in 1947, the Cavan party mainly travelled by air, while their Kerry opponents travelled by sea. The victorious Cavan players were later to comment on the advantage of travelling by air as it gave them more time at home with their training and preparation for the final. Nonetheless, it did still take them twenty-seven hours to get to America by plane, with stops for refuelling in the Azores and Canada.

As the decades passed, the amount of travel undertaken by GAA teams, members and supporters continued to grow. The possibilities of air travel redrew the boundaries of where GAA teams might travel. The 1968 Meath All-Ireland winning team flew to Australia, for a groundbreaking tour which saw them play against an Australian Rules team. The tourists were sponsored by Aer Lingus, but the national carrier only flew as far east as Rome. The team transferred to three further flights, working their way through India and Southeast Asia before they made it to Australia. Trips to America became more and more frequent. And, yet, as air travel became cheaper and faster in the 1990s, overseas tours, club holidays and warm-weather training camps became a standard feature of the GAA year. This was true for clubs as well as for counties. People travelled in the opposite direction,

Hurling in the Polo Grounds, New York, 1954. The world shrank with developments in air travel and transatlantic tours, though still prized by county players, became less of the ordeal they were in the pre-Second World War era. By the late 1960s, indeed, GAA teams began looking even farther afield – to Australia. (*Getty Images*)

Car ownership facilitated more flexible travel arrangements to games, but it was not without its problems. This photograph was taken in August 1959 when a group of Kerry supporters suffered a puncture near Farranfore on their way to the Munster senior final. Help soon arrived: three cars of Kerry fans pulled up to change the wheel, which was quickly replaced with the spare while the flat tyre was put on the roof. The helpful Kerry fans were rewarded with tubs of ice-cream. The day, and the year, ended well for all: Kerry defeated Cork and went on to to win the All-Ireland title. (*Kennelly Archive*)

too, with Irish emigrants returning to see their clubs and counties play important championship matches.

In many respects the GAA world has become smaller. Teams travel more easily to play matches against each other and players travel longer distances to play and train. The possibilities of travel have impacted on other developments, not least the installation of floodlights to facilitate late-night midweek matches. Travel by road is almost unrecognisable from the journeys undertaken even twenty or thirty years ago. Before road safety legislation introduced the mandatory wearing of seat belts and maximum passenger numbers, whole teams (particularly school and underage teams) were ferried to and from training and matches in as few as two cars. Modern infrastructural developments have also altered journeys. The development and improvement of Ireland's network of motorways and national primary routes has resulted in greatly decreased journey times for supporters travelling to and from matches, as has the construction of bypasses around towns and villages along these routes. This has irrevocably altered match-day traditions, since favourite rest-stops and picnic locations are now off the beaten track, although so too are the traditional traffic jams and bottlenecks.

While some people prefer to travel by car to matches, many groups of friends and almost all supporters' clubs prefer the more atmospheric trip gained by travelling en masse aboard coaches and minibuses decked out in their county colours especially for the occasion. On All-Ireland final days the traditional bus-parking areas around the northern inner city, most notably Mountjoy Square, are filled with the sounds of supporters descending from buses and making their way to their favourite hostelries to soak up the pre-match atmosphere. Developments, such as the park-and-ride Luas facility at the Red Cow in Dublin, became new staging posts for GAA members. On a summer Sunday in Dublin, trams on the red line of the Luas often resemble game-day specials packed with supporters from outside the capital making the carriages their own. Ultimately, the same impulse which brought people on steam trains in the 1880s remains at work 125 years later.

Supporters stop at a cafe for refreshments when returning from a hurling match in Croke Park, 1964. In towns and cities across the country, the crowds drawn to GAA matches have boosted business in hotels, cafes and pubs. (*Magnum*)

The challenge to secure suitable playing grounds is one that, at some point, has confronted all GAA clubs, at home and abroad. This photograph shows members of the Garryowen Gaelic Football Club enjoying a kick about at the Greater London Council's playing field at Wormwood Scrubs on New Year's Day, 1967.
(*Getty Images*)

Places to Play

'The swelling hillside swarmed with people until it became a huge living pyramid of sightseers.' —

The *Freeman's Journal* reports on the huge crowd that stood behind the Railway End goals to watch Dublin play Kerry in the 1924 All-Ireland football final.

'A crowd estimated between 12,000 and 15,000 swarmed round the pitch. There were no stands, no embankments. The primitive arrangements had hitherto been sufficient for the spectators but nobody had visualised a crowd of those proportions. A rope served as a paling between spectators and the playing pitch.'

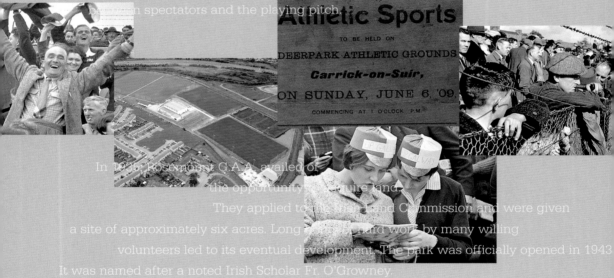

Athletic Sports
TO BE HELD ON
DEERPARK ATHLETIC GROUNDS
Carrick-on-Suir,
ON SUNDAY, JUNE 6, '09.
COMMENCING AT 1 O'CLOCK P.M.

In 1935, Rosemount G.A.A. availed of the opportunity to acquire land. They applied to the Irish Land Commission and were given a site of approximately six acres. Long hours of hard work by many willing volunteers led to its eventual development. The park was officially opened in 1943. It was named after a noted Irish Scholar Fr. O'Growney.

The early months of 1902 brought huge challenges for the Cork GAA clubs of Millstreet and Macroom. These challenges were laid bare in the pages of the *Southern Star* newspaper, which reported that both clubs had failed to secure pitches for the coming season. The Millstreet club had been leasing a field from the late 1890s but, by 1902, the lease had expired and had not been renewed. Negotiations were set in progress in an attempt to resolve the situation, but in the meantime the lack of a playing facility had interrupted the staging of the Millstreet football tournament. In Macroom, meanwhile, the club had been working unsuccessfully with the urban district council to secure lands. They had petitioned Lady Ardilaun to support them in securing a people's park for the town which would provide a space for the GAA. The writer glumly concluded that 'we have heard nothing of the Lady, the petition or the park since'.

There was nothing extraordinary about the experiences of Millstreet and Macroom. Finding a place to play was one of the great challenges facing GAA clubs as they sought to establish their presence in communities. The idea that sports clubs should have their own dedicated facilities was still an emerging one. Even after 1900 – almost two decades after the founding of the GAA – clubs relied on leasing or borrowing patches of land on which they could fashion a pitch. Too often, the work expended on preparing a pitch was later lost when use of the land was withdrawn. A lack of permanence undercut the potential for developing facilities. There was little point in investing in a facility which could be taken away within months. Landowners who leased land to GAA clubs were unwilling to sell the land – and even had they been willing, most clubs did not have the resources to complete the purchase. In cities, too, clubs moved from ground to ground, putting up posts on Sunday mornings and taking them down again in

Handballers play against the wall at Ferns Castle, County Wexford, 1 May 1930. This scene is evocative of the earliest depiction of handball in Irish art. In 1785 a painting by John Nixon showed the game being played against a castle ruin in Castleblayney, County Monaghan. (*Irish Picture Library/Fr. F. M. Browne S.J. Collection*)

'Civil servants, peelers, artillery-men, and garrison-folk, who always had
the happy knack of securing for themselves – whether by conquest,
confiscation, or whatever else you like – the fat tracks throughout all
unfortunate Erin, must have their pick of the open spaces, of which the
people at large are rightful proprietors . . . The plantation of Ulster is to be
superseded and eclipsed by the plantation of Dublin's grandest park –
Dublin's pride, and the world's admiration.' – *The Celtic Times* takes issue
with the restricted access to the cricket enclosures in the Phoenix Park,
4 June 1887.

the evenings. This was a story repeated in country parishes across Ireland, where
posts were fashioned from trees felled in local woods and erected and removed for
every match. The fields used were rarely level and pitches were marked either by
spreading lime along the edges or by placing the players' jumpers and coats along
the boundaries. Players changed in public houses, in ditches or behind trees. The
inability of GAA clubs to establish a place of their own signalled a hand-to-mouth
existence which had obvious implications for the progress of the Association.

The enclosure of grounds in the second half of the nineteenth century was a
central feature of the Victorian sports revolution. Across Britain and America, the
development of dedicated sports grounds was fuelled by the need to generate
income. Sports organisations – amateur and professional alike – sought to charge
spectators entrance fees. How this income was used depended on the organisation.
In some cases it was used to pay players; in others it was used to develop facilities;
in still more the money found its way into the pockets of entrepreneurs who saw
in the sports revolution a way of making considerable amounts of money. The
GAA did not need gate receipts to pay its players, but it did need income to cover
expenses and to develop structures. Finding suitable grounds was vital to building
the Association, but it was not a straightforward task.

From the beginning, the GAA struggled to get appropriate grounds. In Dublin
it played matches in the Phoenix Park where there was ample space. The problem
with the park was that it was impossible to collect admittance fees. Assorted
grounds were found across the city. The first Dublin championships – played in
1887 – were staged at grounds given by Lord Ffrench on the site of the current Elm
Park Golf Club to the south of the city. This was just a temporary home, however,
and clubs in the city scrambled year after year to secure a venue for their games.
Clubs across the country sometimes placed advertisements in the newspapers: a note

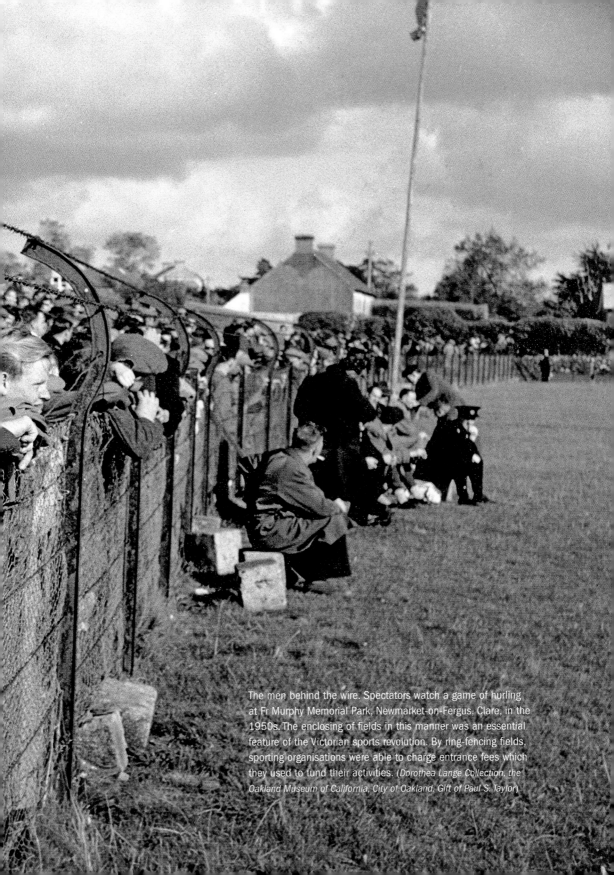

The men behind the wire. Spectators watch a game of hurling at Fr Murphy Memorial Park, Newmarket-on-Fergus, Clare, in the 1950s. The enclosing of fields in this manner was an essential feature of the Victorian sports revolution. By ring-fencing fields, sporting organisations were able to charge entrance fees which they used to fund their activities. (*Dorothea Lange Collection, the Oakland Museum of California, City of Oakland, Gift of Paul S. Taylor*)

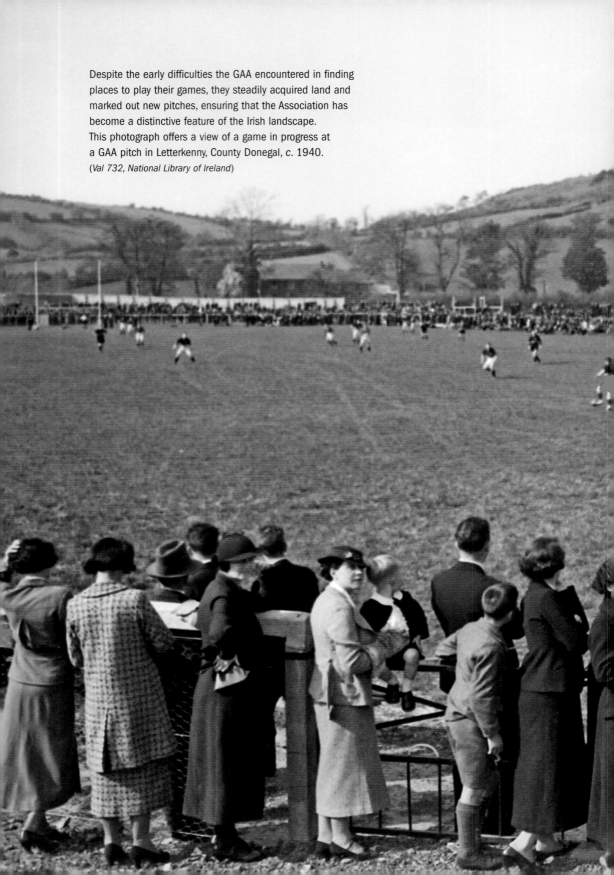

Despite the early difficulties the GAA encountered in finding places to play their games, they steadily acquired land and marked out new pitches, ensuring that the Association has become a distinctive feature of the Irish landscape. This photograph offers a view of a game in progress at a GAA pitch in Letterkenny, County Donegal, c. 1940. (*Val 732, National Library of Ireland*)

'A crowd estimated between 12,000 and 15,000 swarmed round the pitch. There were no stands, no embankments. The primitive arrangements had hitherto been sufficient for the spectators but nobody had visualised a crowd of those proportions. A rope served as a paling between spectators and the playing pitch. This often bulged inward from the pressure of the spectators, who, at intervals surged in over the field.' – **Description of the crowd at Tipperary for the 1903 All-Ireland football final between Kerry and Kildare, held on 23 July 1905, in P. F., *Kerry's Football Story* (1945), p. 31.**

in the *Midland Tribune* on 8 March 1888, read: 'Wanted: A field suitable for hurling, within a mile of Birr. For a suitable field £10 will be given for the season, ending December 1888. Apply to the secretary, St Brendan's club, GAA, Birr.' The first ever All-Ireland hurling final was played in that field three weeks later, but the St Brendan's club soon moved to a variety of different grounds around the town.

It is a measure of the problems faced by the GAA in securing grounds that it was difficult to put proper arrangements in place even for the playing of All-Ireland finals. These finals were fixed for places as disparate as the Great Southern and Western Railway Grounds in Inchicore and the Ashtown Trotting Grounds beside the Phoenix Park. The limitations of these arrangements were emphasised by the chaotic scenes which attended these finals. Pitch invasions, which interrupted the play, were a ritual, with no proper fencing to keep spectators off the field. Some of these invasions were inspired by excitement, others by boiling blood and an itch to contribute to proceedings. There were also ongoing problems with the suitability of the fields that were found. The 1893 All-Ireland finals were never actually played out at the Ashtown Trotting Grounds because, although 1,000 people paid in, the players refused to play because the grass was knee-high and there were no pitch markings. Undeterred, some players uprooted the goalposts and moved to a spot in the Phoenix Park where the games were duly completed.

More than half of the first twenty years of finals were played outside Dublin. Some matches were held on private grounds with the support of the owners, most notably the 1901 and 1904 All-Ireland hurling finals. Both of these finals were staged in a field at Maurice Davin's home, Deerpark, County Tipperary. The 1904 final – not played until 1906 – saw Kilkenny take their first ever All-Ireland championship when beating Cork. The case of Maurice Davin was, naturally, an exception. He was, after all, a central figure in the establishment of the GAA and, as a successful businessman, had the kind of property where games could be played.

Programme—4d. Each.

Athletic Sports

TO BE HELD ON

DEERPARK ATHLETIC GROUNDS

Carrick-on-Suir,

ON SUNDAY, JUNE 6, '09,

COMMENCING AT 1 O'CLOCK, P.M.

—RULES.—

In Foot Races the usual rules will apply.

In the Bagpipes' Competition each competitor will be required to play three pieces—First, a march or dance tune; second, slow air; third, a piece at option of competitor.

The decision of the Judges to be final.

The right is reserved of refusing any entry without assigning a reason, of postponing the meeting in case of very bad weather, and of making any alterations that may be deemed necessary.

Admission to Grounds, 6d.   Reserved Grounds, 6d. extra.

The programme cover for an athletics meeting held at Deerpark, Carrick-on-Suir, in June 1909. The grounds were owned by and home to Maurice Davin, the first President of the GAA. Three years before this meeting, the venue played host to the All-Ireland hurling final. It was ideally suited to the purpose: a level stretch of ground sandwiched between a main road and a railway line. (*GAA Museum*)

A summer day at the hurling, Thurles, 1953. When the showgrounds in Thurles were offered for sale in 1910, they were purchased by a group of local GAA people for £900. An issue of shares was subscribed to by the townspeople in order to meet the cost. Later renamed the Thurles Sportsfield, the grounds remained in the control of the shareholders until 1956 when they were transferred to the GAA. Since 1971 the venue has been known as Semple Stadium. (*Fáilte Ireland*)

'The showground had gone downhill, the show committee couldn't make it pay and they decided to sell and Fr M. K. then came to dad and said, will you do something about purchasing this field for the town and so they had a meeting then and they decided that they'd buy it and it went to £900 and the money had to be put up. So himself and Denis O'Keefe and Denis McCarthy put up the money but it was only for a very short space of time – £300 pounds each – but the place was bought and then the money was collected around the town. People became involved in it, and they bought it, and the men got their money back . . . for GAA purposes, that was the intention.' – **Micheál Maher on the purchase of the Thurles showgrounds, GAA Oral History Project Archive, 2008.**

Such figures were unusual in the Association, and it was not a way of hosting games on which the GAA could rely.

Although clubs were generally unable to acquire security of tenure, a measure of stability came when county boards began to secure longer-term leases on grounds. In Cork, for example, the GAA secured use of the Athletic Grounds in the city in the 1890s on a lease from the Munster Agricultural Company. The grounds were enclosed so that gate money could be taken and this was a definite step forward. It was not a step without complications, however. As the only such facility in the county, many championship and challenge matches, irrespective of who was playing, were staged there. At a meeting of the County Board in 1901, it was noted that this presented its own difficulties because 'the necessity of proceeding to the City from remote districts, to take part in the championship, is a great impediment'.

In the early years of the twentieth century the GAA began to acquire permanent grounds. Principal amongst these was what became Croke Park in Dublin. This patch of land at Jones' Road was owned, from the 1870s, by a city alderman, Maurice Butterly. It was used during his period of ownership as a sportsground, and was called the City and Suburban Sportsground, though it was usually simply referred to as Jones' Road. It was most frequently used as an athletics track, and was also home to Bohemians soccer club. As an available sporting space in the city, it was first used by the GAA for an athletics event in September 1892. Four years later, it was used as the venue for the Leinster football final played between O'Mahonys of Meath and Isles of the Sea from Dublin. Its emergence as a home for the GAA was further signalled in 1896 when the delayed 1895 All-Ireland hurling and football finals were played there. The GAA did not have a monopoly of use on the grounds, however, and it remained an occasional venue for the following decade.

Following the death of Butterly, the Jones' Road grounds were put up for sale in 1907. The GAA did not have the finances to make the purchase. Instead, the grounds were bought by journalist and GAA devotee Frank Dineen, who borrowed much of the £3,250 asking price to buy the fourteen-acre site in 1908. In his journalism Dineen had called for better facilities for Gaelic games and he immediately set about improving the stadium. He had the pitch rolled, the athletics track was redesigned and banks were constructed around the pitch to allow for better vantage points for spectators. Dineen was not a wealthy man, however, and struggled with the repayments on his outstanding loan. He received £10 from the GAA for every major match played at Jones' Road and he also sold four acres to the Jesuits of Belvedere College in 1910 for use as playing fields for their school.

The redevelopment of Jones' Road came precisely at the time that Gaelic games were reborn as mass-spectator sports. In 1913 the final of a special competition to honour the memory of Archbishop Croke – the Croke Cup – drew a crowd of more than 32,000 spectators to see Kerry play Louth. With the money earned from gate receipts, the GAA moved to purchase Jones' Road from Dineen. The sale was completed in December 1913 at a cost of £3,500 and the GAA's national

'Is í Páirc an Chrócaigh an amharclann náisiúnta', the writer Máirtín Ó Caidhin remarked in 1954. This photograph shows an aerial view of Croke Park on 5 September 1959. Since its acquisition by the GAA in 1913, the ground has been in a state of almost constant reinvention. Stands and terraces have been demolished and rebuilt over many decades. This photograph was taken following a major redevelopment of the Hogan Stand. (*Irish Independent Collection, National Library of Ireland*)

A view of a game of camogie at Croke Park in the 1930s. (*Cumann Camógaíochta na nGael*)

home was renamed 'Croke Memorial Park.' From then on Croke Park established itself as the focal point of the GAA at national level. Almost every subsequent All-Ireland final was played there. The stadium was redeveloped decade after decade. A succession of stands and terraces was added, one to the next. It became the biggest sports stadium in the country and the most modern. The stadium came to symbolise the capacity of the GAA for progress and innovation, while making it to Croke Park became the ambition of players and spectators alike.

Croke Park also became identified with a whole range of other events which tied it into the official life of independent Ireland. The murder of fourteen civilians by the British army at a match between Dublin and Tipperary in Croke Park on 21 November 1920 had already assured the stadium an iconic status in the history of the War of Independence. In the decade that followed, Croke Park was the venue for national and religious events. It staged the Tailteann Games in 1924, 1928 and 1932, a Mass in 1929 to celebrate the centenary of Catholic emancipation, a rally to honour the Golden Jubilee of the Pioneer and Total Abstinence Association in 1949 and a vast commemoration of the fiftieth anniversary of the 1916 Rising in 1966. Throughout this period the attendances at Croke Park for major championship matches increased dramatically: the replayed 1931 football final brought in £8,000 through the turn-stiles and, during the Second World War alone, nearly 600,000 people attended All-Ireland finals, paying gate receipts of more than £48,000. In this way, Croke Park became the engine that dragged the GAA's finances from deficit into surplus.

The story of Croke Park was repeated on a smaller scale across the country. The General Secretary of the GAA from 1929 to 1964 was Pádraig Ó Caoimh. A republican who had been imprisoned during the War of Independence, Ó Caoimh had masterminded the development of Croke Park and he was also a major figure

'Before me lies a green arena, its surface smooth as velvet.' This was how one reporter described the scene at the opening of Fitzgerald Stadium, Killarney, in 1936. Named in honour of the great Kerry footballer Dick Fitzgerald, crowds flocked to the town for the official ceremony and the accompanying entertainment. Visitors from places as distant as Belfast, Connemara, Wicklow and the Blasket Islands mingled with holidaymakers to create a carnival atmosphere around the town for the occasion. (*Irish Independent Collection, National Library of Ireland*)

NEW GAELIC GROUNDS
IN LIMERICK CITY

A Chairde,

The Limerick City Board of the G.A.A. have recently purchased extensive playing fields in the heart of the city for the use of the thousands of boys and young men playing Gaelic games and long handicapped by the absence of proper playing facilities.

The purchase and equipment of the new grounds will cost a considerable sum. The resources of the City Board are very limited, catering as they are in the most part for youths, and lacking any of the big gates associated with the more important games of the Gaelic year.

In confidence, we appeal to the many associated with Limerick City through business or other ties for assistance in this great work for the youth. Those subscribing will be registered as founder-members of what we hope will in time become a very active centre of Gaelic activity. The names of all helping in this manner will be included in the Souvenir Booklet we intend publishing on the occasion of the official opening, and subsequently kept on permanent record at our headquarters.

An appeal will be made to the many thousands of our members working in shops, factories and offices in Limerick City and district to give their enthusiastic and wholehearted support to all those who came to our assistance when we needed help urgently.

Appreciating the kindness of your consideration.

Please reply to : —

SEAMUS O CEALLAIGH, Chairman, City Board G.A.A.,
    " San Mairead," Ballinacurra, Limerick; or to:

VERY REV. E. CANON PUNCH, P.P., President, Co. Board
    G.A.A., Raheen, Co. Limerick;

DENIS MORAN, Chairman, Inter-Firm G.A.A. League,
    " Alcantara," Ballinacurra, Limerick;

TADGH O CEALLAIGH, O.S., Chairman, G.A.A. Schools'
    Board, 13 Belfield Park, Limerick.

Limerick Leader Ltd

Providing a place to play. The Limerick City Board of the GAA appeals to local traders to help meet the cost of purchasing and equipping new grounds in the city c. 1934. (*Limerick City Museum*)

in supporting the development of grounds around Ireland. A string of new county stadiums were opened during his years in office. McHale Park in Castlebar opened in 1931, the Gaelic Grounds in Limerick in 1934 (although they had been in use since 1926), Cusack Park in Ennis in 1936, the Fitzgerald Memorial Park in Killarney in 1935, Celtic Park in Derry in 1943, Casement Park in Belfast in 1953, and Pearse Stadium in Galway in 1957. The great bulk of the money for these grounds was raised locally by county committees, but some money was made available in grants by the central council of the GAA.

Clubs, too, were encouraged to acquire their own facilities. Cordial relations with the Land Commission, which was charged with the division of large landed estates, allowed various GAA clubs to acquire pitches. This was just one means, however, and grounds were acquired in any number of ways. The grounds used by Fethard GAA Club in Tipperary lay on what was once part of the Drill Ground used by the British Cavalry when stationed in the area. With the establishment of the Irish Free State, the Fethard barracks, in line with other former British army barracks, became part of state property. Throughout the 1920s the lands were let for grazing. Fethard GAA Club saw the grazing lands as an ideal space on which to play their games and frequently sought permission to use the fields during the season. The arrival in Fethard of Br Leo Slattery in 1931 transformed the situation. A GAA supporter, Slattery put in place a plan to acquire the former Drill Ground. Rather than relying on asking for permission to use the fields, which could be denied at any time, Slattery put together a plan, which was accepted, for Fethard GAA Club to lease the grounds on a permanent basis. Slattery's successor in Fethard, Br Albert Small, took the scheme one step further and arranged for the ground to be purchased by the club. A fund-raising drive was organised, and

'It is hard to realise to-day, when land is so valuable that in those days we hopped in over any "ditch" and hurled in Attridges big field at the Lios Cross, we played in Joe Coughlan's field opposite the Lodge, in Jim Bowen's field opposite the village, in Tom Hosford's field, in Kennefick's field opposite the school and in the Feis field, (now MacCarthy Park) which we finally made our playing pitch by paying a very small rent – I think £1.0.0 thanks to the generosity of Michael Kennefick, who later played on the team.' – Eamonn O'Carroll, 'Ballygarvan Hurling Club (1919–1930)', posted on Ballygarvan GAA website.

The official openings of club and county grounds were typically occasions of ceremony and entertainment. The festivities around the opening of Gaelic Park, Carlow, in August 1936 were a day-long affair. Beginning with a religious blessing and encompassing a series of exhibition matches, events were brought to a close with a late-night céilí in a local hostelry. (*Carlow County Museum*)

although it took over a decade to complete, the purchase went through in 1957, giving the Fethard club a permanent home of its own.

The expansion of GAA property in the middle decades of the twentieth century saw the number of grounds owned by the GAA increase from 16 in 1929 to 204 in 1950. The commitment to expanding ownership and to improving existing grounds was relentless. A grounds committee, set up by Central Council in 1963, augmented work being carried out by provincial councils in giving development grants. Clubs and counties which themselves established grounds committees and had a sustainable plan for developing grounds became eligible for grants. Then, in the 1970s, a grant-and-loan scheme was established to fund further the development of club grounds.

Overall, the dramatic transformation of the Irish economy in the 1990s and early 2000s had great implications for GAA grounds. By then, the ambition that every parish should have its own dedicated GAA pitch – an ambition stressed throughout the centenary year of the GAA in 1984 – had largely been achieved. More money in the economy meant greater possibilities for fund-raising. Club

'The Gaelic Athletic Association had no presence on the island where I grew up . . . Nature had seen to it that the level grass-covered land, necessary for the playing of hurling and football, was scarce and far too valuable to be trampled on and torn by the boots of vigorous young men . . . In the whole island there were about five or six fields suitable for a game of football but their owners guarded them fiercely. One of them had a shotgun and a reputation for ferocity that was deterrent enough without any additional armament.' – **Breandán Ó hEithir** on his early life on Inis Mór in the 1930s, quoted in Breandán Ó hEithir, *Over the Bar – A Personal Relationship with the GAA* (1984), p. 1.

'Mr. Seán Hayes asked the Minister for Lands and Fisheries whether it is the policy of his Department to give sympathetic consideration in the division of ranch lands to influential local representations for the provision of playing fields for national games.

Mr. Roddy: The Land Commission are prepared, where local conditions permit, to give favourable consideration to applications from branches of the Gaelic Athletic Association to purchase a field for use as a sports field.' – **An exchange in Dáil Éireann**, *Dáil Debates,* 26 March 1931, p. 2170.

On the outside looking in. Latecomers strain to get a view at the Cork Athletic Grounds, 1936. Officially opened in September 1904, the grounds were initially intended to cater for a range of sports. But for occasional games of hockey and Association football in the immediate wake of its acquisition, the new grounds were used exclusively for GAA games. (*Irish Examiner*)

Sráid na tEascair,
Tuaim.
13·5·'46.

A Cara,
With the aid of the Traders of Tuam we have just completed the purchase of a playing field comprising 7 statute acres for the sum of £1,000. The field is ideally situated in the centre of the town & just beside the railway station. Before we completed the sale we invited Mr. John Dunne, Sec. Galway Football Board (member of Central Council) & Mr. J. J. Nestor, a member of the Central Council, to inspect the site & they expressed complete satisfaction with our choice. That, of course, is only the first step.

We must now set about the

Once purchased, grounds still needed to be developed. In 1946, after acquiring a suitable field at the centre of Tuam town, the local GAA club stated it would require financial support from Central Council to bring the ground up to a modern standard. The purchase of the field had been made possible with the assistance of local traders, likely beneficiaries in the event of major games being held at the venue. This letter makes clear that the field would be used exclusively for Gaelic games. (*GAA Museum*)

task of developing this pitch along modern lines so that it will be capable of accomodating the many thousands who are sure to patronise the games as soon as things return to normal.

In this respect we feel that we are entitled to ask the Central Council for financial aid to meet part of the cost of this huge project. The field will, of course, be used solely for G. A. A. purposes.

We have already given an earnest of our enthusiasm & sincerity by raising over £1,000 for the purchase of the park & we feel confident that the Central Council will treat us as generously as they possibly can by way of a grant to enable us to equip the pitch in the shortest possible time to make it one

of the best in the country.

I would be greatly obliged if you will bring this matter before the next meeting of your Council & if you would communicate their decision to me at your earliest convenience.

Is mise, le meas mór ort,

Séamas Ó Maonaig.

Cathaoirleach Cumann Tuama C.L.G.

Galway supporters check the team list prior to the All-Ireland football final at Croke Park in 1966. For thousands of GAA people, attendance at Croke Park remains a summer ritual. (*Fáilte Ireland*)

and county committees showed their innovative, entrepreneurial skills in the range of fund-raisers they designed in order to purchase or improve their pitches and facilities. Perhaps the most successful have been the local lottos and annual development draws. In addition to these almost staple income generators, many clubs also run events such as race nights (for camels, horses and dogs), mock weddings, elections and fashion shows. Increased National Lottery funding was provided by the government to supplement locally raised money. Pitches were improved, stands were erected, floodlights were added and general facilities were extended. Clubhouses were built where none had previously existed, while existing ones were renovated. Some clubs used the boom to relocate. Soaring values of land meant that some GAA clubs were made offers by developers for their grounds. In towns across the country, clubs relocated to reap the benefit of new and larger purpose-built facilities, even if they lost something of their past by leaving their old grounds.

As if to underline the rejuvenation of the GAA's physical infrastructure in this period, Croke Park was completely rebuilt. The day after Derry won the 1993 All-Ireland football final, work on the demolition of the old Cusack Stand began. Over the following decade, redevelopment was continued in phases, funded by GAA money, bank loans and government grants. By 2004 the new stadium was completed. Its capacity pushed beyond 82,000, but the glory of the stadium lies not in its scale or in its architecture, rather in the atmosphere it generates. A full Croke Park, especially on All-Ireland Sunday, is like no other sporting venue on earth: the mix of supporters, the roar as the parade moves around the ground, the pride which GAA members feel in the fact that the stadium is one of the finest in the world – and that it is theirs.

'In 1935, Rosemount G.A.A. availed of the opportunity to acquire land. They applied to the Irish Land Commission and were given a site of approximately six acres. Long hours of hard work by many willing volunteers led to its eventual development. The park was officially opened in 1943. It was named after a noted Irish Scholar Fr. O'Growney. Over the years with the aid of loans and grants the pitch was greatly improved by drainage and levelling. In 1979, a new community centre was built in the parish on the grounds of the football pitch and for the first time the footballers had their own dressing rooms.' – The story of Fr O'Growney Park, home to Rosemount GAA Club, Westmeath, as told on the club's website. Many GAA clubs acquired and developed their grounds in a similar way.

Build it and they will come. Supporters enjoy the day out at the recently opened stadium at Tuam, September 1950. The official opening of Páirc Naomh Iarflaith had taken place earlier that summer when it was blessed by the Archbishop of Tuam, Rev Dr Walsh. The venue came to be regarded as the 'home of Galway football'. (*Getty Images*)

An aerial view of the Nemo Rangers GAA Club grounds in Cork. The club, which was once based at what are now the Turners Cross soccer grounds, has undergone a major transformation in the early twenty-first century. Against the backdrop of an unprecedented, and soon to end, property boom, the club sold for housing development grounds that it had acquired in the 1970s on the South Douglas Road. In a deal which involved both a land swap and a cash payment, Nemo Rangers moved half a mile down the same road into bigger grounds with vastly improved facilities. In 2006 these new club grounds opened with four outdoor pitches, one astroturf pitch and an indoor hurling arena. Included also were several meeting rooms, dressing rooms, a gym and a hall, which has become a meeting place for both GAA and non-GAA members of the community. (*The Fleming Group/Nemo Rangers GAA Club*)

Revolutionary hurlers: Michael Collins and Harry Boland enjoy a puck around in Croke Park prior to the Leinster hurling final, September 1921. Remarking upon the sight of Collins with a hurling stick in hand, the *Irish Independent* reported: 'For five minutes, the fifteen thousand spectators saw no longer a hunted fugitive or a Minister for Finance, but a schoolboy at play.' (*Collins 22 Society*)

Politics

'Playground of, more often than a player in, the revolution.' —

Historian Dr William Murphy, speaking on the role of the GAA in the War of Independence at a Michael Hogan commemorative lecture in Grangemockler, County Tipperary, May 2009.

'Moreover, the Gaelic Athletic Association
          holds that within the arena it provides, there is scope and
opportunity enough for the physical enjoyment of any Irishman,
               and that loyalty to any one distinctive possession implies acceptance
of every tenet of the national faith—political, cultural and creative.

'Where was the Rugby Union, the Soccer Association
or the Hockey Association then?
               It was not at Dalymount Park or Shelbourne Park or Lansdowne Road
          The Black and Tans looked for rebels and it was at Croke Park
they tried to perform deeds which shocked the civilized world.

On Easter Monday morning 1916, a group of GAA men were kicking a ball around the Nine Acres in the Phoenix Park in Dublin. Football practice on the Nine Acres was a commonplace sight, but this was no ordinary morning and these were no ordinary footballers. According to William Nolan's history of the GAA in Dublin, the practice was infiltrated by a group of Fianna Éireann (a republican youth movement) members who had joined with a specific objective, one unrelated to sporting development. When one of their number received the ball, he kicked it over the wall of the adjacent Magazine Fort, a British army munitions store. When the sentry turned to retrieve the ball he was attacked and the 'footballers' managed to secure a range of weapons and ammunition that were used during the 1916 Rising. They did not succeed in their primary objective, however, which was the detonation of the explosives store.

Throughout Easter Week, members of the GAA were amongst the rebels who fought to overthrow British rule in Ireland. There was no surprise in this. From the beginning, the GAA was identified with nationalism. Everyone – opponents of the GAA, as well as its supporters – accepted that the GAA was more than simply a sporting organisation. This, of course, is partly a function of the context in which the GAA was founded. The 1880s brought profound social and political upheaval in Ireland. The constitutional push for Home Rule for Ireland, led by Charles Stewart Parnell, was just one aspect of a sulphurous decade. Land agitation left whole areas of the country in uproar and, all the while, in the background the IRB were conspiring to foment a republican revolution. Wrapped around all this was the relationship between Catholicism and nationalism, and the undeniable reality that the Catholic Church was a formidable institution across the island.

Against this backdrop, it was inconceivable that the GAA should eschew politics. After all, existing sporting bodies, with their identification with the pillars of British rule in Ireland, also operated within definite political parameters. Accepting the patronage of the key figures of British rule in Ireland to their sports, flying the Union flag, inviting bands of the British army to play the music of the empire, all suggested their own particular allegiances.

The GAA was a clear reaction against this. From the first meeting of the Association there was an unambiguous identification with nationalism. This was most clearly illustrated through the choice of patrons for the GAA – Parnell, the leader of the Irish Parliamentary Party, Archbishop Thomas Croke, the leading Catholic cleric in the country and Michael Davitt, the leader of the Land League. The GAA did have a number of Protestants involved in its early affairs and it repeatedly stressed its non-sectarian nature. However, the reality of its politics – reflecting the reality of the politics of Ireland – saw it identified from the beginning with nationalism and Catholicism.

Maintaining a broad nationalist alliance in its first years was critical to the success of the GAA. It posited itself as the sporting organisation for Irishmen and characterised its opponents as allied to Britain. This was a powerful weapon in a decade as tumultuous as the 1880s. The rhetoric of nationalism was one element – though only one – in driving remarkable expansion. By the end of 1887 there were more than 600 affiliated clubs. The very success of the GAA almost proved to be its undoing. The IRB saw in that success the opportunity to further its particular agenda and to use the GAA to recruit men, earn money and advance the idea of republican revolution. IRB men had been present in the GAA from its very first meeting. By the beginning of 1887 they had moved to take complete control of the Association.

The opportunity to take control was related to a vacuum in the leadership of the GAA. Michael Cusack had been dismissed as secretary of the Association in the summer of 1886. The GAA was thriving beyond all expectation by that point, but Cusack had succeeded in alienating huge swathes of the Association, thanks to what one Cork GAA club noted was 'the unfortunate knack possessed by Mr. Cusack in a superlative degree of offending and insulting those with whom he comes in contact'. On top of that, his administrative and organisational shortcomings were on a biblical scale. With Cusack gone, the path was open for the IRB to seize control. By the beginning of 1887, only one member of the central committee of the GAA – Maurice Davin – was not a member of the IRB. The symbolic announcement of the ascent of the IRB was the invitation to its President, John O'Leary, to become the fourth patron of the GAA.

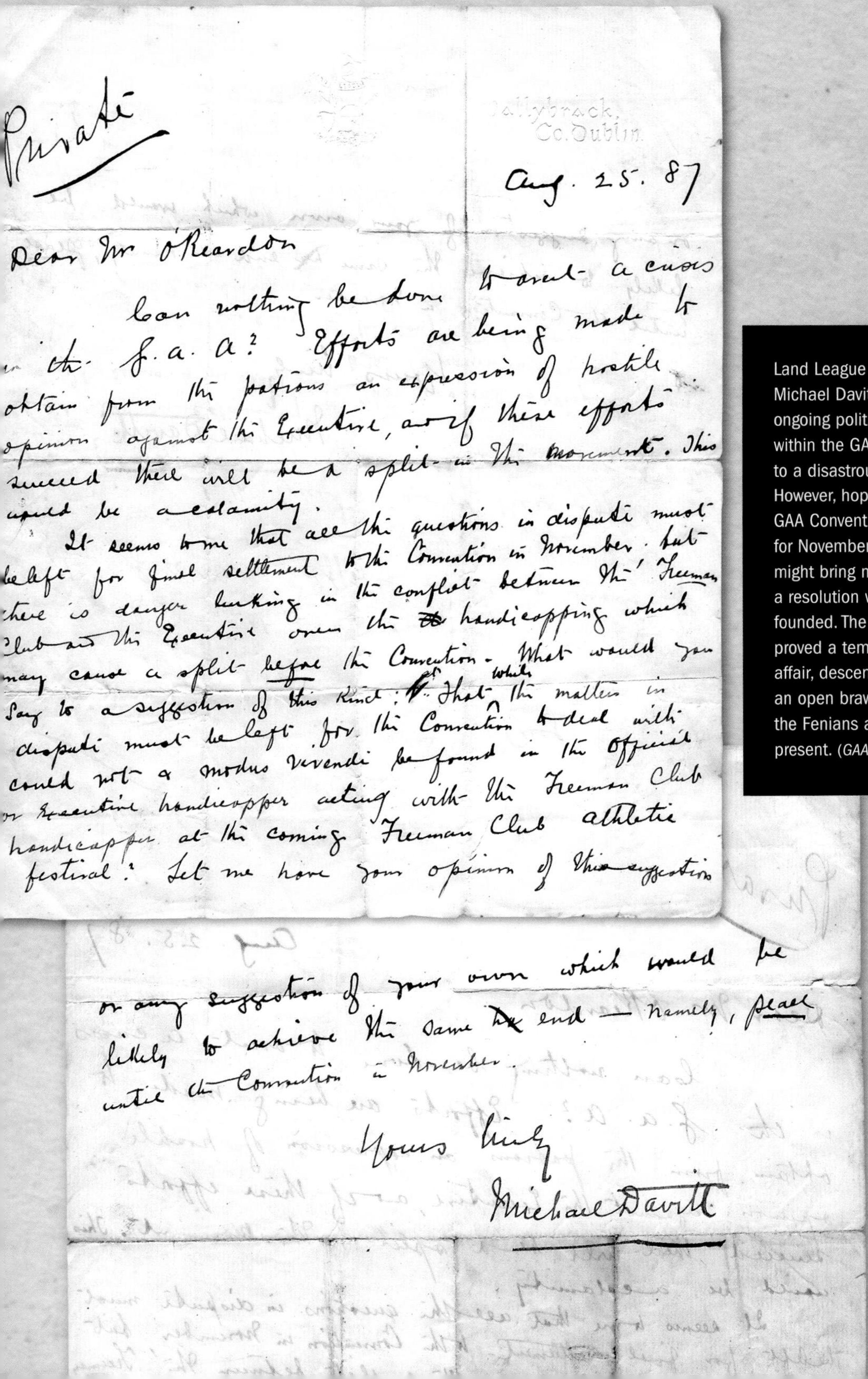

Private

Ballybrack,
Co. Dublin

Aug. 25. 87

Dear Mr O'Reardon

Can nothing be done to avert a crisis in the G.A.A.? Efforts are being made to obtain from the patrons an expression of hostile opinion against the Executive, & if these efforts succeed there will be a split in the movement. This would be a calamity.

It seems to me that all the questions in dispute must be left for final settlement to the Convention in November, but there is danger lurking in the conflict between the Freeman Club & the Executive over the handicapping which may cause a split before the Convention. What would you say to a suggestion of this kind: That while the matters in dispute must be left for the Convention to deal with could not a modus vivendi be found in the Official or Executive handicapper acting with the Freeman Club handicapper at the coming Freeman Club athletic festival? Let me have your opinion of this suggestion or any suggestion of your own which would be likely to achieve the same end — namely, peace until the Convention in November.

Yours truly

Michael Davitt

Land League leader Michael Davitt warns that ongoing political divisions within the GAA could lead to a disastrous split. However, hopes that the GAA Convention, planned for November 1887, might bring matters to a resolution were ill-founded. The Convention proved a tempestuous affair, descending into an open brawl between the Fenians and priests present. (*GAA Museum*)

'I think I have given our reverend friend sufficient latitude. I am very sorry that a gentleman of his profession should be the first to throw in the apple of discord. I know that I am watched by the authorities (loud cheers). But I consider it no crime to be watched by the authorities (loud and prolonged cheers). And though I take part in your proceedings here today, it's purely from a non-political point of view. I rule the gentleman out of order, and the business of the meeting is open (cheers and noise and interruptions).' – This was how the IRB's P. N. Fitzgerald dismissed attempts by the Nenagh curate, Fr John Scanlan, to stop the IRB gaining complete control of the GAA at the Association's Annual Convention in November 1887. The meeting was reported in *Sport*, 12 November 1887.

A year later the IRB's control took the form of a stranglehold: the organisation appointed all members of the executive as *ex officio* members of every county committee across the country, with full voting rights, and decreed that no GAA event could take place without the permission of the county committee. This meant, in effect, that no GAA event could take place without the say-so of the IRB. To compound the sense that the GAA was now allied to a certain political vision, all members of the police were banned from membership of the Association, and from competing in its sports. For the police, in the form of the Royal Irish Constabulary (RIC), such a move was unsurprising. In 1887, aware of the influence of the IRB in the Association, the RIC had begun infiltrating GAA clubs around the country and had sent men to attend the annual conventions.

In the same year Dublin Castle commissioned a special report on the political activities of the GAA (something that was done for the next thirty-five years), and

'Mr T. W. Russell: Everyone knew that the Gaelic Athletic Clubs in Ireland were political associations in everything but in name; and in a month they could be armed and would become an effective force.

An hon. Member: Bosh!

Another hon. Member: They are football clubs.

Mr T. W. Russell: said, nominally football clubs, these associations were the successors of the Fenians.' – An exchange between members of the House of Commons on 2 June 1893, from *Hansard*, vol. 13, cc 74-5.

concluded that, in the noises emanating from the Annual Convention, there was enough evidence to prove 'the dangerous political character of the Association'. Another observer, Maurice O'Halloran, from Clare, commenting on the success of the GAA in staging matches and athletics contests in front of large paying crowds, noted that, 'as the cool moderate people say, "'Tis only a swindle for Fenian organisers to make money out of"'.

In the wake of the IRB takeover, leading clerics, most noticeably Archbishop Logue of Armagh, were quick to condemn what they saw as the demoralising effect of the IRB on GAA members. Throughout the country, the Catholic Church was opposed to the activities of the IRB and even avowedly nationalist clerics fought to prevent that movement gaining traction. Eventually, and particularly after Maurice Davin resigned his presidency in 1889 having tired of fighting for control of the GAA, the Catholic Church set about destroying the GAA, rather than leaving it in the hands of the IRB. Condemned from the pulpit and in the press, there was a spectacular collapse in the number of GAA clubs. Having numbered more than 1,000 in 1888, by 1890 the number of clubs had dropped to 557. Later that year, things got even worse with the explosion of controversy around Charles Stewart Parnell's adulterous relationship with Katharine O'Shea. The majority of the Irish Parliamentary Party, the Catholic Church and many nationalists opposed Parnell, after news of his affair with the wife of one of the MPs in his party became public. Against that, the GAA's central committee (dominated by IRB men) decided in April 1891 to support Parnell. This support was most

'The establishment of the Gaelic Athletic Association by my old friend Michael Cusack – I was one of the first members – was an enormous step in the direction of Irish nationhood . . . Well-developed bodies with well-developed Irish brains ought to be the ideal of the GAA. I am sure it is, too, only it does not unfortunately show itself in action as one should expect that it would do. Thousands of Irishmen will go to see a hurling match because it is the national game who would never go to look at a cricket match. Yet very often the players never think of any other aspect of the Association than that of the match alone. The idea that they are really and powerfully contributing to the revival of Irish nationality has, I believe, never occurred to thousands of them.' – **Douglas Hyde, quoted in** *The Gaelic Athletic Annual and County Directory, 1908–9*.

P. J. Hoctor

Though Hoctor now resides at 19 Upper Mallow St. Limerick & is N.º 7 on our Divisional C B List he is more properly a suspect of the S.E. Division. He is the son of a publican at Newport, County Tipperary N.R. His father died about fifteen years ago, & after his death the business declined, & the subject of this history was then apprenticed to Mr. George Cullen a publican & draper in Newport, where he served seven years & at the age of 22 left Mr. Cullen's establishment. He was an advanced Nationalist on leaving Newport: in fact he never adopted the political creed of Mr. Parnell: but like M. Davitt, P. N. Fitzgerald, & C. Doran, is an ardent believer in the power of the physical force party to "free Ireland & establish a Republic." He was, after leaving Newport, a traveller in the double capacity of I.R.B. organizer, & seeking orders in the tea & spirit trade. He was one of the first to see the opportunity afforded by the starting of the G.A.A. to capture it for Fenian purposes. When the "Gael" newspaper was established he got on its Staff in Dublin, & worked hard with P. N. Fitzgerald & others in opposition to the clerical influence to establish the Gaelic Association on a Fenian foundation. He was, together with P. N. Fitzgerald & I. C. Forde of Cork, amongst the foremost speakers at the Thurles Convention in 1887, when the first open collision took place between the I.R.B. & Clerical parties in connexion with the Organization. However during the thick of the struggle Hoctor suddenly disappeared from the country — some say to France, others to America. He

evocatively demonstrated following Parnell's untimely death in the autumn of 1891. At his funeral, 2,000 GAA men followed the cortège to Glasnevin cemetery, each shouldering a hurley draped in black. The GAA had found itself as the only important national movement supporting the Parnellite cause. It was a disastrous decision: the GAA imploded as members left in their droves. Only fourteen men attended the 1893 convention and as few as three teams entered the hurling championship played in that same year. Political involvement had all but destroyed the GAA.

That the GAA survived the 1890s was due in no small part to the secretary-ship of Meath man Dick Blake. Elected secretary at the GAA's annual convention in April 1895, he moved to make the Association avowedly non-political, and banned all political discussions at convention. He made improvements to the game of football (standardising the size of the ball, allowing substitutes and introducing linesmen) and moved to bridge the gap that had emerged between the GAA and the Irish Amateur Athletics Association over the control of Irish athletics. Blake's period in office moved the GAA beyond the Parnell split. Club numbers increased again, and hurling and football matches developed a popular momentum that was never again lost.

The revival of the GAA continued in the first decade of the twentieth century. This decade brought a marked increase in the nationalist sentiment of the GAA, even if it continued to profess itself as a non-political organisation. Renewed nationalist sentiment (which reflected a broader trend in Irish life) manifested itself in several ways. During the Second Boer War – fought in what later became South Africa between the British and the Boers (descendants of European settlers seeking to defend their independent republics) from 1899 to 1902 – many Irish nationalists found common cause with the Boers. In a public display of support for the idea of fighting against British colonialism, many GAA clubs renamed themselves in honour of Boer leaders, and the annual conventions passed a series of resolutions supporting the embattled in South Africa. For example, what is now the Kilruane MacDonaghs Club of Tipperary was renamed in late 1900 as the Lahorna De Wets in honour of a famous Boer general of the time. The club also had a song, again not uncommon at the time, praising the general: 'Unconquered yet, are you De Wet, O may you never vary, The magic name that gained such fame, For gallant Tipperary'.

The idea that the GAA could be used to draw a distinction between 'Irish Ireland' and those portrayed as 'West British' brought the establishment of a set of rules which redefined membership of the GAA in the early years of the twentieth century. These rules – which were not supported by large sections of the GAA – banned from its membership anyone who played rugby, soccer, cricket or hockey. They also banned anyone who attended these 'foreign games', and all members of the police, the army, the navy and the prison service. Later, this suite of rules was extended to place a membership ban on anyone who attended dances run by the British armed forces or by 'foreign games' clubs.

The introduction of these rules presaged a decade of momentous political change. It began with the successful passage through the House of Commons of the Irish Home Rule Bill in 1912. The upshot of the bill was the renewed militarisation of Irish politics, this time with mass involvement and the threat of civil war. Rather than accept a home rule parliament in Dublin, unionists formed the Ulster Volunteer Force in January 1913. The nationalist response was the establishment of the Irish Volunteers. The GAA was involved in this force from the beginning. Although formally brought together at its first public meeting in November 1913 (a meeting addressed by the GAA Secretary, Luke O'Toole), activity had actually begun in Dublin during the summer of that year when James Strich, an old IRB figure, had started drilling men behind the Wolfe Tone's Club in Parnell Square. Key amongst their number were members of the GAA, led by Harry Boland, chairman of the Dublin County Board. There was a huge overlap between membership of the GAA and the Volunteers. Evidence of the close ties was readily apparent: the annual convention of 1914 was addressed by a member of the Volunteer Executive; the newspaper of the Volunteers, *The National Volunteer*, carried a weekly GAA column; GAA President James Nowlan urged Association members to join the Volunteers and 'learn to shoot straight'; and, in October 1914, the Kerry Board put forward a motion (which, ultimately, was not put before the annual convention) that rifle training be included in GAA activities at club level.

As a movement, the Irish Volunteers were closely tied to John Redmond and his Irish Parliamentary Party and, with the outbreak of the Great War in 1914, the Volunteers were urged by Redmond to join the British army and to fight in Europe. Thousands of GAA members followed this call and fought at the Western Front, in Italy and in the Dardanelles. Their story has largely been forgotten in the history of the GAA, but so great was their number that GAA clubs were left struggling in their absence. Killaloe GAA Club in Clare, for example, reported being 'badly hit as many of its members enlisted'. Various counties even considered lifting the ban on membership of the GAA for British soldiers, at least for the course of the war. This proposal never gathered momentum.

Members of the Irish National Volunteers use hurling sticks for drill practice in Strabane, County Tyrone, 1914. With Volunteer and GAA membership frequently overlapping, many GAA men inevitably followed the lead of John Redmond and the Irish Parliamentary Party, fighting for the British side in the Great War. Others stayed at home, some to play a part in the Easter Rising of 1916. (*Joseph Martin*)

GAELIC ATHLETIC ASSOCIATION, LIMITED.

NOTICE is hereby given, that an Extraordinary General Meeting of the Gaelic Athletic Association, Limited, will be held at Wynn's Hotel, Lower Abbey Street, Dublin, on Saturday, the 19th day of December, 1914, at 8 o'clock p.m., when the subjoined resolutions will be proposed as extraordinary resolutions :—

RESOLUTIONS.

1. That, in pursuance of the objects stated in the Memorandum of Association, the property, assets, debts, liabililities, and undertaking of the Gaelic Athletic Association and the Trustees thereof be acquired and taken over by the Gaelic Athletic Association, Limited, and that the said Gaelic Athletic Association, Limited, shall indemnify and keep indemnified the said Gaelic Athletic Association and the Trustees or any of them against said debts and liabilities.

2. That the Central Council of the Association are hereby instructed to execute and do all deeds and things necessary to carry the foregoing resolution into effect.

3. That the existing Rules of the Gaelic Athletic Association shall continue to apply, as far as applicable, to the Gaelic Athletic Association, Limited, until the Annual General Meeting, to be held in the year 1915.

" That, as the Gaelic Athletic Association is the largest and best organised body of its kind in the world, and as its constitution is National in the truest sense, and as we consider the present situation to be of the greatest concern to the Irish Nation, we, the Kerry County Committee, request the Central Council to summon immediately a Convention of the Association for the purpose (1) of amending the conditions of the Association so as to allow of the affiliation of Rifle Clubs in the same manner as Hurling and Football Clubs as now affiliated and (2) of promoting Inter-Club, Inter-County, Inter-Provincial and All-Ireland Championships in Rifle Shooting. And that copies of this Resolution be forwarded to the Secretary of the Association and the Secretaries of each Provincial Council and County Committee."

Proposed by Michael Griffin. Seconded by J. M. Collins.

JAMES McDONNELL, Hon. Secretary, Kerry County Committee.

AND NOTICE is hereby given that at said Meeting the subjoined Resolution will be proposed as an extraordinary Resolution.

AND NOTICE is hereby also given that a further Extraordinary General Meeting of the Company will be held on the 16th day of January, 1915, at the same time and place, for the purpose of receiving a Report of the proceedings at the above-mentioned Meeting, and of confirming (if thought fit) as a Special Resolution the subjoined resolution.

RESOLUTION.

That the Articles of Association be altered in manner following :—

1. The following words shall be added to Article 5 at the end thereof :—" The members of the Central Council and the Athletic Council for the time being and one delegate from each Province, as determined by the Association, to be elected by the registered Athletes and Cyclists of said Province, shall also be members of the Association." The following words shall be inserted in Article 7 after the end of the first sentence :—" The delegates from Provinces as provided in Article 5 shall also be elected before the Annual General Meeting, and remain members for a period of twelve months, unless re-elected. The members of the Central Council and Athletic Council shall be members of the Association from the termination of an Annual General Meeting to the termination of the next Annual General Meeting."

By Order,

LUKE J. O'TOOLE,
Secretary.

Croke Park, Jones' Road,
December, 1914.

19 December 1914: In view of the circumstances prevailing in the country, the Kerry County Committee proposes that rifle clubs be allowed to affiliate to the GAA. The motion was never put to the GAA convention.
(GAA/Laois/121, GAA Museum)

A small minority of volunteers split from the Redmondites and founded their own volunteer movement. They united with James Connolly's Irish Citizen Army and staged a rebellion against British rule at Easter 1916. Although not a national rising as first envisaged, the rebels held out for a week before their leader, Patrick Pearse, surrendered to British forces. Estimates of the numbers of GAA members involved in the fighting run to around 350. This is about one-fifth of the total number of rebels out on Easter Week. Five of the fifteen men executed after the Rising had a GAA connection, notably Patrick Pearse, who had been a strong advocate of the value of Gaelic games at his school, St Enda's in Dublin. At the Official Commission of Inquiry into the events of Easter Week, leading British civil servants and policemen implicated the GAA as an instigating factor in the rebellion. Immediately, the GAA issued a statement denying involvement and took particular issue with statements that the GAA had been used in furtherance of the objectives of the Irish Volunteers.

Nonetheless, when the British authorities took the decision to intern those it considered responsible for the Easter Rising, many GAA men found themselves jailed. Amongst the leading GAA men who were sent to prison were James Nowlan, J. J. Walsh, Pádraig Ó Caoimh and Harry Boland. Indeed, there were enough players in Frongoch to organise a series of games which kept prisoners busy during their periods of free association from 12.30 p.m. until 8 p.m. A board was established to run competitions. In Frongoch, the 1916 final of the Wolfe Tone tournament, between Kerry and Louth, saw Kerry, led by Dick Fitzgerald, win by one point. While the prisoners also wanted to play hurling, the camp commander, Colonel Haygate-Lambert, would not permit them to have hurleys in case they were used as weapons.

Most prisoners were released from internment camps by the end of 1916. In the months that followed, the rise and fall of the political temperature was reflected in the GAA's activities. Matches continued to be played, though not in the same numbers as previously. Particular GAA members became heavily identified with the emergence of Sinn Féin as a potent political force, one that in time destroyed the moderate Irish Parliamentary Party. The identification of the GAA with the politics of Sinn Féin took various forms. Tournaments were staged to raise money for republican prisoners and, when Clare reached the 1917 All-Ireland football final, the team paraded onto the pitch before every championship match behind the banner 'Up de Valera'.

Attempts by the British government to introduce military conscription to Ireland in 1918 saw a fresh wave of political unrest. Politicians, trade unionists, church leaders and GAA officials shared platforms of opposition. Increased unrest led to the British government, in July 1918, prohibiting the holding of any public meetings in Ireland except under official permit. The GAA chose to defy the prohibition and organised a mass protest for Sunday 4 August. County boards across the country were instructed to stage matches without permits at 3 p.m. In Dublin alone, twenty-four matches were played at different venues. When entry into Croke Park was barred by police and army, camogie players staged a match on the road outside. The success of their protest was the springboard for the resumption of widespread activity by GAA clubs across the country.

It was a major act of defiance, and one which linked the GAA to the gathering momentum of radical nationalism which led to the election victory of Sinn Féin in 1918. The electoral success of Sinn Féin led, in turn, to the establishment of the First Dáil and the initiation of the War of Independence in 1919. The GAA was involved in the emergence of the Irish Republican Army (IRA), and particular IRA leaders, including Eoin O'Duffy in Monaghan, most likely made use of their GAA connections to recruit. Throughout this period, the GAA continued to

NOTICE TO PERSONS WITH RESPECT TO WHOM
AN ORDER IS MADE UNDER REGULATION 14B.

Name of Prisoner	**Richard Fitzgerald.**
Address	**College Street, Killarney.**
W.O. Number	**955 B.**
H.O. Number	**313894.**

Notice is hereby given to the above-named that an Order has been made by the Secretary of State under Regulation 14 B of the Defence of the Realm Regulations directing that he shall be interned at the Place of Internment at Frongoch.

The Order is made on the ground that he is of hostile associations and a member of an organisation called the Irish Volunteers or of an organisation called the Citizen Army, which have promoted armed insurrection against His Majesty, and is reasonably suspected of having favoured, promoted or assisted in armed insurrection against His Majesty.

If within seven days from the date of his receiving this notice the above named prisoner submits to the Secretary of State any representations against the provisions of the said Order, such representations will be referred to the Advisory Committee appointed for the purpose of advising the Secretary of State with respect to the internment and deportation of aliens and presided over by a Judge of the High Court, and will be duly considered by the Committee. If the Secretary of State is satisfied by the report of the said Committee that the Order may, so far as it affects the above named prisoner, be revoked or varied without injury to the public safety or the defence of the realm, he will revoke or vary the Order accordingly by a further Order in writing under his hand. Failing such revocation or variation the Order will remain in force.

An order for the internment of Richard – more usually known as Dick – Fitzgerald at Frongoch prison camp, Wales. Better known as Kerry captain and one of the first true superstars of Gaelic football, Fitzgerald was by 1916 among a number of Kerry footballers and mentors imprisoned in Frongoch and other British prisons. Within the Frongoch camp, the only form of football tolerated by the Irish internees' leadership was Gaelic football. (*Fitzgerald Stadium Collection*)

organise matches for the Republican Prisoners' Dependants Fund. The spiral of violence inevitably intervened with the calendar of matches, though competitions at club and inter-county level were continued in many areas. There were also regular challenge matches which drew impressive crowds. Dublin and Kildare played before 5,000 spectators in October 1920. Then, on 21 November 1920, Dublin and Tipperary met at Croke Park in another inter-county football match. This match was eagerly awaited, but is now remembered as the most infamous in the history of the Association. On the morning of the match, IRA men directed by Michael Collins killed fourteen British intelligence officers in their flats, boarding houses and hotel rooms around the centre of Dublin. In reprisal, members of the British forces entered Croke Park as the Dublin and Tipperary match was in progress. Indiscriminate firing at players and spectators left fourteen people dead, amongst them the Tipperary player Michael Hogan. Of all the bloody days of the War of Independence, this was the bloodiest of them all – at least in terms of its impact on the public psyche. For the GAA, it lent an entirely new aspect to the place of Croke Park in the story of the Association. This was now more than merely a playing field: it was martyred ground, the place where people had been shot because they had attended a Gaelic football match.

The War of Independence ended in truce and then treaty in 1921. The divide over the relative merits of the deal struck with the British descended into bitter Civil War. During 1922 and 1923 the activities of the Association were severely hampered. Even after the Civil War ended in the summer of 1923, the GAA was affected by the inevitable fall-out. The continued imprisonment of members of anti-treaty forces was problematic for the GAA. In 1923 Kerry refused to play their All-Ireland final against Dublin in protest against the continued imprisonment of Austin Stack (an All-Ireland medal winner with Kerry and, by then, the president of the Kerry County Board). Cork, too, refused to play Offaly until their chairman Seán McCarthy was freed. It would be wrong to simplify or to overstate the role that the GAA played in healing the bitterness of the Civil War (or at least taking the edge off that bitterness). Nonetheless, it seems clear that by offering a neutral space for its members to play the games that they loved, irrespective of their political loyalties, the GAA played some part in fostering national reconciliation.

The central place of the GAA in the official life of the Irish Free State was made clear from the beginning. In 1924, the Free State government staged the Tailteann Games in Dublin. This was the biggest sporting event in the world that year – bigger even than the Paris Olympics. The games were organised by the Free State to celebrate national independence and to herald the dawn of a new era in Irish history.

Michael Collins meets the players before the Leinster hurling final, September 1921. 'You're not only upholding the great game, you are also upholding one of the most ancient and cherished traditions of Ireland', Collins reportedly remarked. Collins and other political leaders were conspicuous presences at Croke Park during this period. Their attendance and ceremonial roles in meeting players and throwing in the ball to start games helped cement the identification of Gaelic games with the Irish nationalist cause. Less than a year after this photograph was taken, Collins was killed in an ambush at Béal na mBláth in County Cork. (*GAA Museum*)

Growing up in a time of war: children in Dublin play soldiers
using hurley sticks as mock guns, 15 April 1922. In December
of that year, with the Civil War then in full stride, the GAA's
Central Council agreed to use its influence to bring the two
sides together and assist a cessation of hostilities. Their efforts
failed. (*Fitzellle Collection: Album 135, National Library of Ireland*)

The ancient Tailteann Games were supposed to have last been held in 1168 AD, the year before the Norman Invasion. Their restaging was designed to show the world that the Irish nation had survived colonisation, and to bring together Irish emigrant populations scattered across the world in a celebration of a global Irish culture and identity.

Croke Park was the focal point of the entire event. The GAA was given money by the government to rebuild part of the stadium for use during the Games, not least for the opening and closing ceremonies. More than 5,000 competitors took part – most were Irish or from Irish emigrant communities – but some, like Johnny Weissmuller (American swimmer and winner of five Olympic gold medals), were foreign stars included to add glamour and prestige. They competed in a remarkable range of sporting events. There was a full programme of athletic events, clay-pigeon shooting and chess, archery and golf, and much more across the two-week programme. Enormous crowds attended. Amongst the highlights was the success of Weissmuller – who soon went on to star as Tarzan in several Hollywood films – in the swimming competitions which were held in the pond in Dublin Zoo. Even more dramatic were the motorbike, sidecar and aeroplane races held around the Phoenix Park. Crowds of more than 50,000 came to the Park to be thrilled by the exploits of the top racers. Against the novelty of those sports, the Gaelic football and hurling matches were overshadowed, though the GAA was commended for the skill and commitment it displayed in ensuring the Games were a success.

The relationship of the GAA with successive governments in independent Ireland was not always smooth. The GAA demanded that it receive special treatment from government – treatment which would reflect the broader social and cultural mission of the Association. For example, when the Cumann na nGaedheal government of the 1920s sought to impose a tax on income generated by sports bodies, the GAA lobbied successfully for exclusion from that tax. More than that, though, the GAA argued that, because of its national service, it alone amongst sporting bodies should be excluded from paying the tax and this argument was accepted.

'Dr. Hyde's gesture in attending the Polish match became his position in the State. What do the Poles know of Gaelic football or hurling? Are we to have no manners, and no tolerance, where others are concerned in this new Ireland? Is a narrowminded and ignorant intolerance to represent Gaelicism in the eyes of the world?' – Patrick K. O'Horan, Rector of Achill, writing to the editor of the *Irish Independent*, 17 January 1939.

State-building: the revival of the ancient Tailteann Games begins with an Olympics-style opening ceremony at Croke Park, 1924, which included a march-past of all competing nations, who were accompanied by mythical figures from the court of Queen Tailte. This two-week event was planned by Postmaster General J. J. Walsh, a leading figure in the Cork GAA. (*INDH 523, National Library of Ireland*)

An......................Garda ....Siochana

> Division of Mayo
> Superintendents Office
> Claremorris
> 30th May 1934.

Ard Fheadh.
Caislean a Bharraigh.

RE/ Assault at Ballyglass dance hall on Sunday night the
27th May 1934.

> Submitted please.
> > On Sunday night the 27th inst. a
dance was held in Ballyglass dance hall (Ballindine sub-
district)under the auspices of the G.A.A.
> > The dance was conducted almost entirely
by the local Fianna Fail club,but the attendance included
all shades of political thought.

> > Just as the dance was about to conclude
at 12 m.n.Patrick Murphy Ballyglass,(Blue Shirt) struck
William Varley of the same address,and immediately he did
so a crowd -some wearing blue shirts.-rushed into the hall
with the object of defending Murphy should he be interfere
with.This crowd were apparently lying in wait outside the
hall.They did not attempt to assault Varley.

> > This occurrence was a sequel to a row a
fortnight previously between Murphy and Varley and in which
it appears Murphy (The Blue Shirt) got the worst of matter

> > It would appear Murphy organised this
crowd to help him avenge his defeat by Varly,but his plans
did not seem to carry as he and Varley had been separated
when the crowd entered the hall.
> > There were no blows struck except
between Murphy and Varley,but one of the Blue Shirts
called out in a loud voice in the hall,if there was any
man who would strike Murphy.This ended the incident and
the Blue Shirts left.
> > Varley,is not,the Garda are informed
a member of the local Fianna Fail club,but he has Republi
an sympathies.
> > The door was closed on the latch when the
Blue Shirts rushed in,and as the dance was about to
finish nobody in particular was at the door at the time.
> > The parties concerned are taking
action in the case,and the Garda although they investigated the incident and not interfering.

> *J.Kelly*

J.Kelly Superintendent.

A Garda Síochána report on a political fracas at a GAA dance at Ballindine, County Mayo, 27 May 1934. Civil War divisions defined the political culture of the Irish Free State and, following the emergence of the Blueshirt movement in the early 1930s, clashes with republicans were both frequent and violent. Although GAA members were to be found on either side of these clashes, many more stood apart, playing no role at all. (*Jus 8/119, National Archives of Ireland*)

UACHTARÁN NA hEIREANN

SGEUL.......... G. A. A.

FO-SGEUL.......... President as Patron.

SUGGESTED REMOVAL FROM OFFICE AS PATRON.

1.   On the 13th November the President attended the International Soccer Football Match between Poland and Ireland at Dalymount Park, Dublin (file P.794).

2.   It was anticipated that this action on the part of the President would not be acceptable to the G.A.A., a rule of which Association forbids its members to play or be present at what were termed foreign games - Association Football, Rugby, Criket, etc.

3.   A certain amount of dicussion and correspondence in the papers took place on this matter.

4.   In one case at least the proposal was made that the President's name should be removed from the list of patrons of the G.A.A. The Body concern-ed was the Patrick Pearse G.A.A.Club, Derry. The resolution to this effect took place on Sunday 4th Dec. A full report appears in the press of today's date.

5.   The report as published in the "Irish Press" is attached.

6.   I understand that a somewhat similar resolution was proposed by a branch of the G.A.A. in Cavan in the week preceding the Match, but I have been unable to locate it.

Foible—WI. 3277—Gp. 50—500—11/'37—P 4918.
WI. 1742—Gp. 50—3,000—7/'39—Q 3448.

5.12.38

A memorandum from the Office of the President gives the background to the decision to remove Douglas Hyde as Patron of the GAA. For Hyde to have snubbed the international soccer match would, a later memorandum made clear, have been to 'ally himself with the narrow parochial outlook of those who regard it as an offence against nationality to play or even look at any healthy game of which they do not approve'. Hyde had been appointed a Patron of the GAA in November 1902 due to his position as President of the Gaelic League. His removal in 1938 gave rise to a frenzy of newspaper coverage, much of it critical of the GAA. (*Pres 1/P 1131, National Archives of Ireland*)

'Moreover, the Gaelic Athletic Association holds that within the arena it provides, there is scope and opportunity enough for the physical enjoyment of any Irishman, and that loyalty to any one distinctive possession implies acceptance of every tenet of the national faith – political, cultural and creative. For this reason, restrictions and prohibitions had to be enforced . . . there is a moral obligation on every man who subscribes to a doctrine to honour it at all times or renounce it openly. He cannot be orthodox today and unfaithful tomorrow: Non-Gaelic on Saturday and Ultra-Gaelic on Sunday.' – P. J. Devlin, *Our Native Games* (1935), p. 48.

On other occasions, however, the GAA made decisions which undermined its relationship with government and which exposed the Association to popular ridicule. In 1938 the first President of Ireland, Douglas Hyde, attended an inter-national soccer match in Dublin in the course of the duties of his office. Hyde had been for many years a patron of the GAA, a titular role which recognised his contribution as a founding father of modern Ireland, a distinguished Gaelic scholar and the creator of the Gaelic League. When the matter was raised by a Connacht delegate at a Central Council meeting of the GAA, the President of the Association, Pádraig MacNamee, ruled that because of Hyde's actions, he had 'ceased to be a patron of the Association'. To deploy the ban rules against a man who had helped to invent the very ideal of an 'Irish Ireland', which the rules were supposed to help establish, was a perversion of common sense.

The decision reflected the challenge which faced the GAA as it sought to stake out its meaning in independent Ireland. How could the GAA help create the 'Irish Ireland' which was supposed to flow from political independence? For some within the Association, the promotion of Gaelic games and the other cultural activities were insufficient. Instead, they hardened the ban rules (to which Hyde fell victim) and forbade any GAA club from holding social functions at which 'foreign dances' were engaged in. On top of that, Vigilance Committees were established to attend 'foreign games' matches and to report if any GAA members attended. The irony of this was that in the years between 1922 and 1926 there had been a series of motions – led by the very men who had actually sponsored pro-ban motions in the early 1900s – to delete the ban rules on the grounds that it was outdated following the establishment of the Irish Free State. GAA stalwart and political activist Eoin O'Duffy led the campaign against removal of the ban rules, saying that the very idea of it was 'an outrage on the living and the dead'.

For four decades until the 1960s, periodic efforts to remove the ban rules were met with similarly emotive language. In 1953, the then President of the GAA, M. V. O'Donoghue, stated that the ban rules were there 'to remind members of the dishonour of associating with British imperialism', that they were crucial in opposing the subtle plan for proselytising Irish youths, who were being lured 'by various inducements to become happy little English children and heirs to the joy of a soccer paradise.' For all the posturing – and for all that there was a hard core of GAA activists who sincerely believed in the integrity of the ban rule and of its intrinsic value in the pursuit of the ideal of an 'Irish Ireland' – it had become clear by the 1960s that large numbers of GAA members were simply ignoring them. Change in Ireland discredited the use of the ban rules, even for those who believed in their value. After all, a GAA member could be banned for attending a soccer match, yet those members who watched that same match on television in their own homes were free from censure. A groundswell of opposition to the rules eventually led to the removal of many of their aspects in 1971 – though only after a decade of furious debate. The unfolding situation in Northern Ireland ensured that the ban on members of the British armed forces joining the GAA was retained. Equally, it was decided that the ban on rival sporting organisations using GAA grounds would also be retained.

By the time the ban rule on foreign games was amended in 1971, one of the most successful GAA players of all time – Jack Lynch – had been elected as Taoiseach. Lynch's career was stellar. He won six All-Ireland senior medals in a row between 1941 and 1946. Five were for hurling and one for football. He also won Cork senior championship medals in hurling and football and, as a schoolboy at North Monastery CBS, he won three Harty Cup medals. He is acknowledged as one of the finest hurlers of all time and was selected at midfield on the Team of the Century and the Team of the Millennium. With his career as a hurler drawing to a close, Lynch stood for Fianna Fáil in the 1948 general election. His party lost the election, but Lynch was elected. He was promoted through the ranks and served in various ministerial positions after Fianna Fáil regained power, before being elected Taoiseach in 1966.

'Personally, I found any rule or law that set one group of Irishmen to spy on another set of Irishmen, in the name of a spurious national purity, distasteful in the extreme. The Irish word *spiadóir* may have more of spit in it than the English word spy but the spit is there also.' – Breandán Ó hEithir, *Over the Bar: A Personal Relationship with the GAA* (1984), p. 213.

A Chara,

I will be pleased to act on the Vigilance Committee to the best of my ability. Shall it be necessary to attend foreign games myself or will it be sufficient to report on the reliable word of an informant?

For instance, I can very definitely state that F. Mulhern, J. Callaghan, J. Blake and McKinley (ex-Pats) have attended and played at soccer matches for Kilmacrenan. I believe they are already suspended. The suspension should be extended. D. Crampsie, I believe, has played rugby. As I am not certain about this, I will wait for another offence before reporting him for suspension.

On Monday at Donegal Mental Hospital cttee mtg. we had a discussion on question of granting the grounds for a rugby match. You will see it reported. Mr. M. D. O'Boyle adopted a most disappointing attitude. "One game is as good as another" he declared publicly. This is our ex-member of Handball committee. Little wonder it failed.

The application was very vague. Father McCauley said he understood that Father McMenamin (of St. Eunan's College) intended to apply for use of grounds for a rugby match, but he had received no such

Jack Lynch (left) in action for his club, Glen Rovers, against Imokilly in 1941. By the time he first stood for election in 1948, Lynch was recognised as one of the country's most celebrated sportsmen, the winner of six All-Ireland medals. Roscommon footballer Jack McQuillan – holder of two All-Ireland medals – was also elected to Dáil Éireann in 1948. (*Irish Examiner*)

Lynch stands as the ultimate example of one who enjoyed success in the GAA and in politics, but he was far from alone. Having a profile as a leading member of the GAA was a useful head start for aspiring politicians, particularly where constituency boundaries were contiguous with the counties whose jerseys had been sported. It was by no means a guarantee of success, however, for there were many GAA members who did not enjoy electoral success. Nevertheless, enough made it to ensure that the GAA had a sympathetic ear close to the centre of political power in the years after the founding of the Irish Free State.

While Jack Lynch was the ultimate example of the presence of the GAA in the south of Ireland, the story of the GAA in the north was much more difficult. This was a consequence of the wider political, social and cultural divide of the island in the aftermath of the partition of Ireland and the establishment of the Irish Free State in 1922. For all that people repeated the mantra that sport should remain above politics, the reality was that this statement resided in the realm of the fantastic. Irish sport sundered in ways that reflected the complexities of identity across the island. New accommodations were made – usually involving compromise or ambiguity. For example, many Catholics loved soccer and supported soccer teams that identified with their community (Derry City and Belfast Celtic, for example). Those teams, however, still played within a framework which *de facto* recognised partition – or, in the case of Glasgow Celtic, recast local enmities in a Scottish setting. The GAA offered an expression of identity which was unambiguous. Northern clubs offered the nationalist community a space in which to gather, to play Gaelic games and to stress an identity that was at odds with the state in which they lived. For nationalists, the GAA was a clear statement of allegiance to Irishness. This was a critical function in the decades after partition, with the forces of unionism controlling the symbols of official life in the north.

The rise of the civil rights movement in the 1960s, the subsequent outbreak of the Troubles and the eventual slide into a prolonged period of violence exerted a new set of pressures on the GAA. The ostentatious presence of the symbols of nationalism and of Catholicism at GAA events left unionists in no doubt as to which side of the cultural divide the GAA sat. The activities of loyalist paramilitaries had a profound impact. The decades after 1970 saw the murder of GAA members and the destruction of GAA property. The Ulster Freedom Fighters placed the GAA on its lists of 'legitimate' targets because of its 'continual sectarianism and support for the republican movement'. Amidst the repeated intimidation of members, men such as Sean Brown and Gerry Devlin were murdered by loyalist paramilitaries precisely because of their involvement in the GAA. The hostility of the

NORTHERN IRELAND CIVIL RIGHTS ASSOCIATION

Climax of Week of Protest against Repression
and for Democracy

ANTI-INTERNMENT
RALLY
AT CASEMENT PARK
SUNDAY, 12th SEPT. at 5 p.m.

Speakers:

Bernadette Devlin, M.P.   Joe Deighan

Kevin Boyle   Edwina Stewart, Hon. Sec. N.I.C.R.A.

Pat Fanning, President G.A.A.   Paddy Devlin, M.P.

Michael Keogh M.P.   Association for Legal Justice

British Labour M.P.   Chairman: Rory McShane

A Massive turn-out from all over Six Counties expected
● If we remain united and strong we shall overcome ●

"IRISH NEWS" LTD.

The introduction of internment by the Stormont administration in 1971 united all shades of northern nationalist opinion in opposition. This demonstration rally, held at the home of the GAA in Belfast that same year, brought together a number of prominent public figures, including GAA President Pat Fanning. Some months earlier, also in Belfast, Fanning had presided over the abolition of the controversial ban on foreign games. (*Museum of Free Derry*)

HOUSE OF COMMONS
LONDON SWIA OAA

7 May 1973

Mr T Walsh
Gaelic Athletic Association
Failte
69 Milton Avenue
Liverpool 14

Dear Mr Walsh

I have now had a letter from the Secretary of State concerning the occupation of Casement Park in Belfast. He states that it remainsnecessary for the Army to occupy Casement Park for the security reasons outline in my letter of 1 January.

He continues that he cannot propose that the Army should withdraw from Casement Park until he is certain that the security situation permits it. He goes on, "As to the last paragraph of the letter from the Association, I understand that the Army received information that ammunition had been hidden in the struts of the goalposts at the Shaws Road Playing Fields. They investigated this report, but found nothing. Unfortunately, while the goalposts were being dismantled one was damaged. The Army arranged to replace it and by about the middle of February the goalposts were again intact. Headquarters Northern Ireland have written to the Gaelic Athletic Association inviting them to discuss the provision of playing, spectator and bar facilities and the future use of the ground. You may wish to know that the facility already exists at the ground for playing and spectators but it would seem that they are more interested in bar facilities."

Do you know if discussions are taking place with the Army on this matter?

Yours sincerely

Merlyn Rees.

British Labour Party MP Merlyn Rees, a future Northern Ireland and British Home Secretary, explains why British soldiers would not be withdrawing from the GAA grounds at Casement Park, Belfast. The occupation of the ground and social facilities by British troops in 1972 led to a storm of protest by various GAA units and added a further strain to British–Irish government relations. Setting out the GAA's position in September 1972, Pat Fanning, the Association's President, declared that the 'British Army occupation of Casement Park has been effected by force and that the GAA does not and never will concede to the British Army the right to enter or hold this or any other GAA park or property.' (*GAA Museum*)

Surveying the wreckage: the aftermath of an arson attack by loyalist paramilitaries on St Joseph's GAA Club, Ballycran, County Down in May 1993. This was the seventh such attack on the Ballycran club over a period of twenty years. At the time club officials estimated that the cost of damage to the club was £750,000 sterling. Each time, the club picked itself up from the rubble and started again. Across the six counties many GAA clubs were subject to similar attacks. (*Irish News*)

British army, too, was a serious problem. This involved the requisition of GAA grounds, most famously the use of the Crossmaglen Rangers' ground in south Armagh as a helicopter base, and repeated stop-and-search harassment of members. Many GAA matches had their start times delayed as groups of players and supporters were subjected to prolonged searches en route to games. While GAA supporters in the south left home and travelled in cars decked out in club and county colours, in the north GAA flags and buntings would be removed or hidden while travelling through particularly hostile towns and villages. Attacks on supporters' buses and trains were commonplace. For those players and supporters who ventured into Northern Ireland from the south during the Troubles, border checkpoints were part and parcel of match-day rituals. Most notorious of all was the murder in 1988 of Aidan McAnespie from Aughnacloy. In February 1988 McAnespie was walking to a junior match at Aghaloo Club in Tyrone when he was killed by a soldier at a checkpoint who fired three shots into his back.

The risks people in the north took to maintain involvement in the Association were not always recognised by GAA members in the south. Answering the question of what precisely the GAA's nationalism meant was not an easy task. For many in the south, reflecting a wider response to the conflict in the north, the tendency was simply to disengage. This brought inevitable irritation amongst northern GAA members. But even in the north itself, there were divides on how to react during the Troubles. Individual members and various clubs were much more nationalist in their allegiances than others. During the hunger strikes of 1981, for instance, amongst the men who died was Kevin Lynch from Dungiven in Derry. Lynch had played for the St Patrick's Club and had captained Derry to the All-Ireland Under-16 final in 1972. He was also a member of the Irish National

'The House will be aware that a considerable amount of ratepayers' and taxpayers' money is provided to fund that organisation. It has been a sad and sorry spectacle on our television screens during the past few weeks to see the banners and flags of the GAA in the forefront of the protest being carried out on behalf of the murderers and gunmen in the Maze prison in Belfast. It is obvious to everyone who reads the *Irish News* that advertisements are placed almost every day by that same so-called sporting organisation in support of what some term as the brave men in the Maze prison.' – **Peter Robinson of the Democratic Unionist Party, speaking in the House of Commons, 10 December 1980, from** *Hansard*, **vol. 995, cc 984.**

To All GAA Fans

• Kevin Lynch, who died after 71 days on hunger-strike, captained the County Derry side to win the 1972 All-Ireland under-16 hurling final at Croke Park.

Once again it is time to enjoy the All-Ireland Football Final, between Kerry and Offaly, and rightly so. But as you do, remember that in the past year ten men, some of whom were keen Gaelic players in their youth and one of whom, Kevin Lynch, won honours at junior county level for Derry, have died an agonising death on hunger-strike in the H-Blocks of Long Kesh for seeking 5 simple demands which would recognise their special position as political prisoners.

Thatcher and the British authorities have pursued a vicious death policy in the H-Blocks and have got away with it because successive Dublin governments, as well as the Catholic hierarchy and SDLP, have refused to take serious action to force Britain to back down, by isolating her at every level, national and international.

Its sad to have to say that some weeks ago they got some unexpected support from the Executive Council of the GAA, when they issued a directive barring county boards, clubs, etc. from becoming actively involved in what they called a 'party political' campaign, i.e. the H-Block campaign, and invoked Rule 7. It is of course no such thing, being a broad front of individuals who support the prisoners' demands and nothing else.

Fortunately, but not surprisingly, the South Antrim Executive of the GAA quickly disowned the directive and was supported by other sections in the six-counties who have direct experience of British army harassment including occupation of their pitches over the past ten years.

We call on the ranks of the GAA, as a whole, to force the Executive to withdraw the directive. Now, more than ever, with seven more hunger-strikers engaged on a fast to death to secure their demands, thirty-two county nationalist unity against the British is vital. Those who play Britain's divide and rule game will be remembered with ignominy

JOIN THE CAMPAIGN IN YOUR LOCAL AREAS, AND INVOLVE YOUR COLLEAGUES AND CLUBS WHERE YOU ARE A MEMBER.

support the hunger-strikers

Crowds attending the 1981 All-Ireland football final were met with requests to support the demands of the Maze Prison hunger strikers. This poster, which appeared on routes leading to Croke Park, displayed the image of Kevin Lynch, a former hurler and footballer from Dungiven, County Derry. Aged twenty-five years, Lynch had died on hunger strike the month before. In total, ten men would die as part of the 1981 hunger strikes. As the criticism contained in the poster makes clear, the heightened political tensions caused by the strike created difficulties for the GAA hierarchy, which maintained that the Association was non-political. Others within the GAA saw matters differently – in Dungiven, Kevin Lynch's club was renamed in his honour.

Children wear hurling helmets as protective headgear at an anti-H-Block/Armagh Prison parade on Springfield Road, Belfast, June 1981. The *Andersonstown News* reported that the demonstration had been organised in response to the killing and injury of children in non-riot situations by the British army. (*Andersonstown News*)

Demonstrations accompany the opening of Croke Park to rugby and soccer in February 2007. While a sizeable number of GAA members remained uneasy about the move, on-street protests – like this outside Croke Park – were small-scale and attracted a mostly non-GAA crowd. (*Shay Murphy*)

'This is the first opportunity I have had in the House to congratulate the Gaelic Athletic Association which took a decision on a 32 county basis, as it has always done, to accept the Police Service of Northern Ireland. That 32 county decision is in keeping with a real united Ireland approach and the way in which we should do our business in regard to these issues. It was a clear affirmation by a sports organisation with deep embedded links with the Nationalist community on both sides of the Border – that regrettable land frontier – that it was happy to accept the Police Service of Northern Ireland. There is a message in this on which we must act.' –
Brian Lenihan, speaking during a Dáil Éireann debate on paramilitary organisations, *Dáil Debates,* 7 April 2004, p. 948.

Liberation Army (INLA). After he died on hunger strike, the St Patrick's Club was renamed 'Kevin Lynchs'. The support for the hunger strikers and for other nationalist causes created tensions within the GAA. The hierarchy of the Association struggled to resist the demands of clubs for a greater politicisation. The leaders of the GAA clung to the idea that the Association – though avowedly nationalist – was non-political. This was not an option for those whose daily lives were coloured by conflict and whose very involvement in the GAA was perceived as a political act.

The peace process of the 1990s eventually allowed for a new departure in northern politics. The end of large-scale violence, the signing of the Good Friday Agreement in 1998 and the establishment of the Northern Assembly redrew the parameters of life in the north. This change was reflected in the GAA. The momentum towards reconciliation in the north placed the GAA under increasing pressure to remove Rule 21, which banned members of the British security forces from joining the GAA. The history of the Association, both recent and long-term, ensured that debate was emotive and divisive. Ultimately, the rule was deleted at a special congress in Dublin in November 2001. Equally emotive was the debate over Rule 42 – the prohibition on the playing of 'foreign games' in GAA grounds. With Lansdowne Road being redeveloped, the GAA was asked to open Croke Park to permit the playing of rugby and soccer internationals during the period of reconstruction. Despite considerable opposition from many members, it was eventually decided to open the ground. February and March 2007 saw the first rugby and soccer matches at Croke Park. Most notable was the visit of the English rugby team to the site of Bloody Sunday and the playing there of the British national anthem; it was not a moment that could have been envisaged during the Troubles. Overall, the opening of Croke Park was a move which drew considerable praise for the Association and increased the international profile of the stadium. The general prohibition on the playing of 'foreign games' on GAA grounds was retained, however, even if it is clear that the opening of Croke Park means that things will never be quite the same again.

As if to emphasise the change in the political life of the island since the reordering of northern politics, the GAA has engaged in a series of initiatives to draw members of the unionist community into Gaelic games. These include the 'Game of 3 Halves', which is a summer scheme run in partnership with the Presbyterian Church in east Belfast incorporating the three main sports of Gaelic football, rugby and soccer. The Ulster Council of the GAA has recently launched a six-year strategy entitled 'Ulster GAA Strategic Vision and Action Plan: Lifelong Promotion of Gaelic Games, Culture, Community and Family'. Within that strategy, the Ulster Council has committed to developing outreach initiatives focused on forming links and promoting understanding with the unionist community. The history of the Association and the manner in which clubs are rooted in local communities ensures that this will not be an easy process. It is a measure of the evolving politics of Ireland that the endeavour is under way at all.

August 1961: months before the
launch of Telefís Éireann, men gather
at a local shop in north Louth to
listen to a GAA match commentary.
(*Edward Laverty*)

Media

'Once Michael O'Hehir's voice crackled from the Cossor, the tension was unbearable.' —

John McGahern, *Memoir* (2005), p. 164.

'Life goes on and the grip of the games seems never to loosen.
This community within a community seems to endure forever.
I see men and boys buried in their graves with their jerseys draped over their coffins.
I see families marry into each other and becoming Gaelic town dynasties.
I see entire communities consumed by the passion of a season, generations
welded together by the love of the game.

'The GAA locally when I was young was played on Sunday afternoon.
All the local lads used to gather, during the summer months,
near the local beach. One of the group used to have a portable radio,
which was a rarity, and we used to listen to Michael O'Hehir
commentating on the matches Sunday after Sunday.

One Sunday in the summer of 1926, P. D. Mehigan, a well-known GAA journalist, sat behind a table in the press stand in Croke Park. On the table was a large mahogany box with wires and screws and numerous mysterious gadgets. Attached to the mahogany box was a wire which led to a leather headset. The headset was placed on Mehigan and a yellow brass tube was positioned in front of his mouth. A signal came from an office beneath the Hogan Stand that they were 'on air'. With just the two teams on a slip of paper in front of him, P. D. Mehigan began the first radio broadcast of a GAA match – the 1926 All-Ireland hurling semi-final between Galway and Kilkenny.

Mehigan began with a preview of the game, then commentated on the first half, filled half-time with summary and resumed commentary for the second half. By the time he was finished, he remembered being extremely tired, but was boosted by the elation of the radio engineers who had pioneered the broadcast. It was one of the first live sports broadcasts in Europe, such was the scale of the achievement. Indeed, the very notion of the live broadcast of sport had only recently been experimented with in the United States and there were many who doubted that it was technically possible to achieve what was done in Croke Park on that day.

Preparation for the commentary had been organised by the then secretary of the Department of Posts and Telegraphs, P. S. O'Hegarty. That department had control over the new national radio service, 2RN (which later became Radio Éireann and then RTÉ Radio), which had been established in January 1926. O'Hegarty and J. J. Walsh, the minister in charge of that department, were Cork GAA members and devotees of hurling. They quickly identified the possibilities of using the new

'The crowd around me got out of hand. I could see nothing. Stewards were helpless. I stood on a chair and tried to keep the commentary going. I was hit on the poll, in the ear and on the shoulders with clods and grass sods, some of them hard enough. The crowd swarmed around me and swept the phones away; the match was abandoned and the broadcast broke down.' – quoted in P. D. Mehigan, *Vintage Carbery*, edited by Seán Kilfeather (1984), p. 32.

radio service to identify the Irish Free State with its national games, as well as with the Irish language and Irish music.

Not everyone was enthusiastic about the achievement. Mehigan described his first commentary as 'constant shouting' and it greatly upset his colleagues in the press box trying to take notes. At Mehigan's suggestion, subsequent commentaries were shifted to the sidelines of the field. This, in turn, brought its own problems. Mehigan recalled broadcasting a hurling match in Cork, when the crowd got out of hand and swarmed around the commentary position to the point where he could see nothing of the game. He stood on a chair to try to keep the commentary going, but still the crowds came. Eventually, his equipment was swept away and the broadcast broke down. One of Mehigan's successors, Éamonn de Barra, the editor of the GAA-related *An Gaedheal* magazine, was also reported to have had one of his broadcasts interrupted: while commentating on the 1933 All-Ireland football final between Cavan and Galway, de Barra was said to have been told at the point of a gun to stop speaking. An unknown voice told listeners to support the republican prisoners then on hunger strike in Mountjoy Jail. When the protestors left the box, according to legend, de Barra continued his commentary.

'Could some improvement be made in the running commentaries on Gaelic Games? Many of us here in the north are very interested in Gaelic Games and can only hope with the aid of a good commentary to visualise the play. Can't we have announced to us the flight of the ball in its principal movements – movements that count in the game? Can't we be told who plays the ball, to what side frees are given, who takes them and the result?' – Letter from 'Enthusiast' to the *Irish Independent*, 14 August 1933, quoted in Seán Óg Ó Ceallacháin, *Seán Óg Ó Ceallacháin – His Own Story* (1988).

A group of young Galway supporters on the terraces tune into radio coverage of the 1966 All-Ireland football final. Despite competition from television, the popular appeal of radio has endured. Sunday after Sunday, many supporters still bend their ears to radio commentaries of games being played in front of them or at other grounds around the country. (*Fáilte Ireland*)

Michael O'Hehir at the microphone on 29 September 1953.
In his autobiography, published in 1986, O'Hehir recalled that in his early years as a broadcaster, he would picture in his mind's eye a man called Patrick Garry, from Ballycorrig in Clare. 'For some years before I started broadcasting, he had been bedridden', O'Hehir wrote. 'So I'd imagine myself talking directly to him . . . In those formative years it was not the people of Ireland or anywhere I was speaking to, but to Patrick Garry, doing my best to tell him what was happening.' (*Irish Independent Collection, National Library of Ireland*)

'As a child I remember what seemed like many but were probably just a few All-Ireland Sunday afternoons, when we would have the entire town to ourselves as Michael's voice boomed from every window. Even then I thought it was surreal. We could walk the length of the town and back twice without meeting another soul, and all the while to be accompanied by this voice.' – **Writer and commentator John Waters, describing his childhood memory of growing up in Roscommon, quoted in John Waters, *An Intelligent Person's Guide to Modern Ireland* (1997), p. 59.**

Through the 1930s a range of different commentators broadcast Gaelic games, including the Clare priest, Fr Michael Hamilton, before the debut in 1938 of Michael O'Hehir. O'Hehir was a Dublin schoolboy whose father was a GAA official, and for the next five decades he dominated the broadcasting of Gaelic games. If the GAA are credited with bringing colour and character to the lives of so many, O'Hehir is rightly acknowledged as their accomplice. The image of the extended family and community gathered around the wet-battery radio hanging on the words of O'Hehir is central to any understanding of social life in mid-twentieth-century Ireland. His status as a commentator is linked as much to the fact that his was the central voice during the golden age of radio through the 1940s and 1950s, as it is to his remarkable ability to turn a phrase or capture a moment.

O'Hehir commentated on ninety-nine All-Ireland finals between 1938 and 1985, but his most significant GAA broadcast was the 1947 All-Ireland football final, which was played in the Polo Grounds in New York between Cavan and Kerry. It was believed to have had the largest listenership of the time for Radio Éireann. Across Dublin city, it was reported that groups of people congregated around parked cars whose radios transmitted O'Hehir's commentary. In Cavan, the end of the broadcast saw bonfires lit and a long night of singing.

The popularity of GAA radio commentaries helped spread the fame of the games. It drove newspapers to increase their coverage of hurling and football, and attracted thousands eager to see with their eyes what they had heard on radio. Nonetheless, the introduction of radio commentaries had not been without its tensions. Striking the right balance in relationships with all forms of media had always been a concern for sports organisations and the GAA was no exception. There were some within the Association who believed the advent of live radio commentary would ruin attendances at matches. One GAA stalwart had even predicted to P. D. Mehigan that his 'mahogany box' would destroy the Association:

'If they don't take that bloody box out of Croke Park, they might as well close the gates.' Others within the Association, however, understood the potential propaganda value of the new medium – after all, the GAA had from the beginning been acutely conscious of the importance of media profile.

The very establishment of the GAA had been a triumph of propaganda. The idea of the new Association had first been floated in the press by Michael Cusack and Maurice Davin in the summer of 1884. Three of the seven men who attended the founding meeting worked as journalists, and from the very beginning the GAA had a keen sense of the image it wished to present. In the weeks after founding the Association, Michael Cusack secured a weekly column dedicated to the GAA in the popular nationalist newspaper *United Ireland*. Getting that column, wrote Cusack, was proof that 'our dream was not all a dream', rather something real and genuinely possible. Over the following months, the GAA laid out its ideals and its ambitions. Column after column stressed that the GAA would be open even to 'the humbler and more neglected sections of our society'. It immediately stressed its nationalist credentials – and in the context of the bitterly divided politics of the 1880s this was an obvious and important move.

Most importantly of all, the first GAA journalists created vivid images of what it was like to attend hurling and football matches across the GAA. Publishing the rules for hurling and football in 1885 was never going to be enough in itself, so newspaper columns were used to colour in the game sketched out by the rules. GAA members wrote in with their queries on the rules to Cusack and he replied in his *United Ireland* as if he were some sort of Gaelic games agony aunt. In many respects, the story of the GAA epitomises the marriage of sport and media in the late nineteenth century. There were obvious mutual benefits of a sporting world full of heroic men performing almost mythical feats, which were spun by the press and sold to the public. As momentum built around the GAA, the sporting press,

'The crowd swayed backwards and forwards: the priests were sometimes nearly driven off the table. The reporters had from the first to take up a position of defence; they had to bundle their slips into their pockets and to remain, notebook in hand, one eye on the pages before them, the other on the bulky delegates who threatened each moment to fall off the table and onto the Fourth Estate.' – An account from the *Freeman's Journal* of the fiery GAA Convention of 9 November 1887, quoted in T. F. O'Sullivan, *Story of the GAA* (1916), p. 49.

The cover of a book written by All-Ireland winning Tipperary captain Tony Wall, published in 1965. Wall aimed to plug what he perceived was a 'void' in the literature on hurling by suggesting ways in which players might improve their technique and positional play. Hurling was certainly less well served than football as regards books of this sort. In 1916, however, two years after Kerry footballer Dick Fitzgerald had published the first instructional guide to Gaelic football, Tadhg Barry – poet, politician, nationalist and member of the Cork County Board – produced a pocket-sized pamphlet entitled *Hurling and How to Play it*. Dedicated to the 'boy hurlers' of the North Monastery, Cork, the pamphlet opened with advice on choosing a hurley. A 'good hurley', Barry insisted, was 'as essential to good play as a good hurler'. In recent times, autobiographies rather than training manuals have tended to dominate the GAA book market. (*GAA Oral History Project Archive*)

Neighbours gather around the wireless of Christy O'Riordan in Clonmel, County Tipperary, to listen to the broadcast of the 1933 All-Ireland hurling final between Limerick and Kilkenny. (*RTÉ Stills Library*)

The GAA as illustrated news. This view from the (London) *Daily Graphic* of 26 March 1890 focused on the concerns of GAA Patron, Archbishop Croke, about the potential for excessive drinking in and around GAA matches. Editorials in the short-lived *Celtic Times*, the newspaper launched by Michael Cusack, addressed a similar theme, though with no great sense of alarm. On 26 November 1887, the newspaper claimed that the 'large majority of the members of hurling and football clubs are, for all practical purposes, total abstainers. The few weak ones, if indeed there are any, will be encouraged by example, and, with the inevitable exception, cured.'

which had previously relied on a diet of horse-racing, cricket and rugby, began to report GAA matches. Sports coverage was not a major part of the content of newspapers so there was no dedicated GAA page, rather there were occasional columns carrying GAA news. In their reports, journalists were uncertain of the vocabulary of Gaelic games in those first years. Even writing the scores proved problematic. A journalist in the weekly newspaper *Sport* recorded the final score of a Gaelic football match between two Faugh-a-ballaghs teams as one goal and two tries to six tries.

There were problems other than vocabulary, and the relationship between the GAA and the media was complicated from the beginning. From the very first meeting of the GAA, its leading officials complained of the quality and quantity of coverage its affairs received in the national and sporting press. Michael Cusack accused the mainstream press of 'systematic boycotting'. More than ignore the GAA, though, some elements of the press were positively hostile. *The Irish Sportsman*, another weekly sporting newspaper in Ireland, sneered that hurling was 'the swiping game of the savage'. Criticism in the press made GAA men bristle – and this trend, once established, would not easily disappear.

When the GAA began to publish its own annuals in the early years of the twentieth century, they expressed ongoing disappointment at the coverage given to Gaelic games. In 1910, the *Gaelic Athletic Annual and County Directory* claimed that national newspapers 'continue to treat us with as much niggardliness as they possibly can. The minimum of space is doled out to us, and, generally speaking, the matter which they publish appertaining to GAA doings is infinitely inferior, in quality as well as quantity, to that provided concerning foreign branches of sport.' This complaint was not accurate. Once it became clear that the GAA was not merely surviving, but also thriving, a new generation of journalists was employed. After 1900, coverage of the games in the local and national press expanded steadily. Writing on the games was supplemented by the increasing use of photographs, firstly simple team shots, then later shots of players in action. Linked to increased coverage was the fact that Gaelic football and hurling began to draw bigger crowds and, for the first time, hurlers and footballers began to enjoy a certain celebrity.

'What we want to know is this: - Whether the Gaels of Ireland and of London, and of America are content to leave the fate of their mighty association in the hands of a Press, openly hostile or secretly indifferent to its aims, its objects, and its success' – *The Gaelic News*, a short-lived GAA organ, announces its arrival onto the newspaper market, July 1897.

Gaelic Football.

AS IT IS, AND AS IT WAS.

ANYTHING in the nature of even a moderately exhaustive inquiry into the origin and development of Gaelic football would require a much larger space than can be apportioned in this crowded publication. Furthermore, the game is still in a transition stage, and is no more than within sight of its utmost possible development. In fact, is is highly improbable that reference will be made to it as a finished product for many years to come, as the game is constantly being improved and it is becoming more and more of a scientific exercise with each advancing year.

Gaelic football prior to the institution of a disciplinary regime under the G.A.A., seldom amounted to anything more

An advertisement carried in the 1913 All-Ireland football final programme emphasises the quality of Gaelic games coverage available in the local press. It was a view shared by the GAA, which, in contrast, repeatedly denounced the coverage provided by the Dublin-based papers. In 1910 the *Gaelic Athletic Annual and County Directory* declared: 'We might have expected the consciousness of a patriotic duty towards a National movement like ours should have produced some changes in our National dailies at any rate, but apparently they are not troubled with any such consciousness.' (*GAA Museum*)

Reporters scribble notes at the official opening of Kilfane Handball Alley in Kilkenny, May 1930. The visibility of GAA news in the local and national newspapers increased through the 1920s and 1930s, boosted by competition from radio and the launch of the *Irish Press*. (*Kilfane Handball Club*)

'With the attitude of most of the Provincial Press, one has nothing to complain
– these papers are fair, helpful and sympathetic. When things come to the
Dublin Press, things are, however, very different. There things are done –
and done deliberately – to boom the game of the outlander. From the list of
results on Monday morning to the photos in the illustrated portion, it is all
the same – minimize, push down, belittle the games of the Gael. It is time
that stopped definitely and at once or that these papers stop meddling in
Gaelic matters at all.' – **An extract from a letter written by GAA President
W. P. Clifford, and read to the Association's Annual Congress, 16 April 1927.**

GAA correspondents themselves became important figures within the Association.
P. J. Devlin, writing under the pseudonym of 'Celt', brought a distinctive northern
flavour to his work, writing extensively about Gaelic games as part of a wider
project of cultural liberation. Another journalist from that generation was T. F.
O'Sullivan, who also published the first history of the Association, *Story of the
GAA*, in 1916. By the 1920s they had been joined by P. D. Mehigan, whose foray
into radio commentary was presaged by a career as a journalist. He wrote as
'Carbery' for the *Cork Examiner* and 'Pato' for *The Irish Times* and, in time,
published a series of books on hurling, football and athletics.

Newspapers had initially feared that the arrival of radio in the 1920s would
undermine their importance in covering Gaelic games. In Britain there was a prohibition on the broadcast of news and sport on BBC radio before 7 p.m. in order
to protect newspaper sales. Instead, radio coverage drove increased interest in
Gaelic games which, in turn, led newspapers to increase their coverage of football
and hurling. The arrival of the *Irish Press* in the 1930s marked a sea change in
newspaper coverage with extended features on the GAA. Where once GAA coverage
was rooted in the corner of a page, it was now centre stage.

'The popular newspaper has driven out the football ballad which at one
time gave fairly literal accounts of famous matches . . . After the ballad
came the local paper where we were all Trojans in defence and wizards
in attack. I once got a lot of kudos from a report which described me as
"incisive around goal." No one knew the meaning of the word incisive but
it sounded good.' – **Poet Patrick Kavanagh on the changing nature of GAA
coverage, from 'Diary', *Envoy*, No. 9 (1950), p. 80.**

Before radio and television, there was film. Much of the earliest footage of Gaelic games was produced by British newsreel companies. For instance, film from the Tailteann Games festivals of the 1920s and early 1930s survives mostly in the archives of the London-based British Pathé, now managed by ITN. This photograph shows cameramen using the roofs of their cars to get the best angle on the opening ceremony of the Tailteann Games in 1928. (*Irish Independent Collection, National Library of Ireland*)

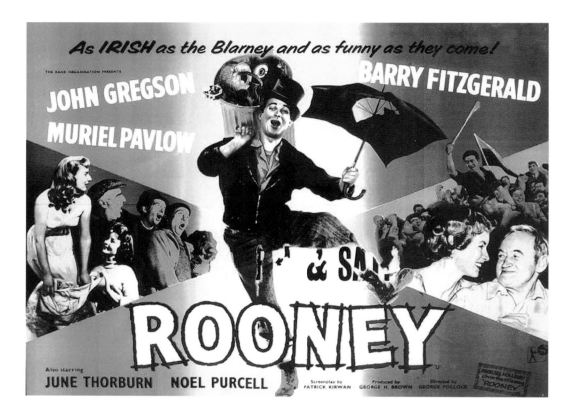

A poster used to advertise the Hollywood movie *Rooney*, released in 1958. The film, a comic classic, followed the fortunes of dustbin man and hurler James Ignatius Rooney as he moves into new digs in Dublin. The adventures of Rooney, played by John Gregson, are played out against the backdrop of the build-up to the All-Ireland final. The film includes scenes shot on the day of the 1957 All-Ireland hurling final between Kilkenny and Waterford. (*Irish Film Archive and ITV Global Entertainment*)

Wife: 'John, is it another one of their rebellions?'

Husband: 'I gather it's the local cricket team.'

Dialogue between an English couple on a train as a hurling team and a pipe band pass by the window of their carriage, from the film *The Rising of the Moon* (1957).

By the mid-1930s more than 350,000 people were attending the cinema on a weekly basis in Ireland. Gaelic games had a central place in what was shown on screens across the country. The first known filming of a GAA match was a 1901 hurling match at Jones' Road – now Croke Park. That film has long since been lost and the oldest known surviving footage is less than half a minute of the 1913 Kerry v. Wexford Croke Cup match. This and other films of Gaelic games in the following decades were shown as newsreels in the country's cinemas. Almost invariably, the films were produced by British companies – notably Pathé – and were accompanied by a plummy voice-over that betrayed ignorance of the games.

By the 1930s Hollywood had taken to the game of hurling. Leading American film-makers came to Ireland to make short films on the game. When MGM made a short, simply called *Hurling*, in 1936, a deputation of GAA officials waited on the Irish Film Censor and attempted to have scenes cut from the film which they deemed objectionable. These scenes – in keeping with most other Hollywood views of hurling at the time – focused on the potential for violence in the game. When Hollywood started making feature films in which the GAA featured, the GAA hierarchy also suffered periodic upset. John Ford's 1956 film *The Rising of the Moon* featured scenes of victorious hurlers travelling home from a match, some on stretchers, others limping, and scarcely a man unscarred. On this occasion outrage came even before the film was released. When Irish newspapers carried reports of the filming of those scenes, the GAA issued a statement declaring their 'deep concern'. Deputations were again organised, this time to Lord Killanin, who was a director of the production company behind the film, complaining of the way the GAA was being ridiculed. Writing in *The Irish Times*, Flann O'Brien lampooned the GAA reaction as 'farcical drool', not least because that same week newspaper reports of a hurling championship match in Clare had described 'literally a procession to the county hospital from the match'. The number of GAA people who paid into these films suggests that the membership of the Association did not hold the same reservations about the films as did their leading officials.

The place of the GAA in Irish cinema was redrawn in the late 1950s when Gael

'The GAA locally when I was young was played on Sunday afternoon. All the local lads used to gather, during the summer months, near the local beach. One of the group used to have a portable radio, which was a rarity, and we used to listen to Michael O'Hehir commentating on the matches Sunday after Sunday. There was no TV sets except one in the parish, and then there were no matches on the TV, except the All-Ireland finals. We used to watch the finals on the TV. The house of the neighbour used to be full of people looking at the final. Planks of timber used to be put up on blocks for seating, so you had to arrive early to get near the TV set.' – **Gerry Harrington, GAA Oral History Project Archive, 2008.**

Linn, the Irish language organisation, began to make short films and weekly news-reels of events in Ireland, with an Irish language commentary. The newsreels showcased Gaelic games, but were effectively rendered obsolete by the arrival of television. The opening of the Irish national television station, Telefís Éireann (later RTÉ), on New Year's Eve 1961, posed a serious dilemma for the GAA. Finding a balance between promoting its games on television without destroying attendances was the conundrum which sports organisations across the world faced repeatedly in the age of television. The GAA opted for a cautious embrace. In its first year of operation, RTÉ was allowed to broadcast the 1962 All-Ireland football and hurling finals, the football semi-finals and the Railway Cup finals for a nominal fee. This arrangement continued through the 1960s and 1970s. Throughout this period the view was prevalent within GAA circles that Gaelic games did not receive from RTÉ the broader coverage it merited, despite the station's statutory obligation to develop national culture. In the 1960s the GAA was particularly irked by the amount of live coverage given to the 1966 soccer World Cup which was played in England.

Throughout the 1980s the number of live televised GAA matches remained low, though there was a significant increase in the showing of recorded highlights, especially on the popular *The Sunday Game* programme. The 1990s brought radical change, however. This change was linked to the revolution led by Sky Sports in the televising of sport, in particular the televising of live soccer matches from England. Faced with a dramatic increase in the amount of soccer being shown on television, the GAA decided it could not stand apart and it allowed for the broadcast by RTÉ of an increased number of championship games. This increase coincided with a new approach to sponsorship, a revamp of the

The age of television: players and guests of the Kerrymen's Association in Dublin gather around a TV set to watch highlights of the All-Ireland football final, 24 September 1962. This photograph was taken following a reception and dinner at the International Hotel, Bray, County Wicklow. Included in the picture, which appeared in *The Kerryman* newspaper, are: Finola O'Donoghue, Killarney; Sheila Geaney, Castleisland; Seanie Burrows, Tralee; Paddy Looney, Killarney; Paudie O'Donoghue, a member of the Kerry minor team from Duagh; and Mr and Mrs Niall Sheehy from Tralee. (*Lensman*)

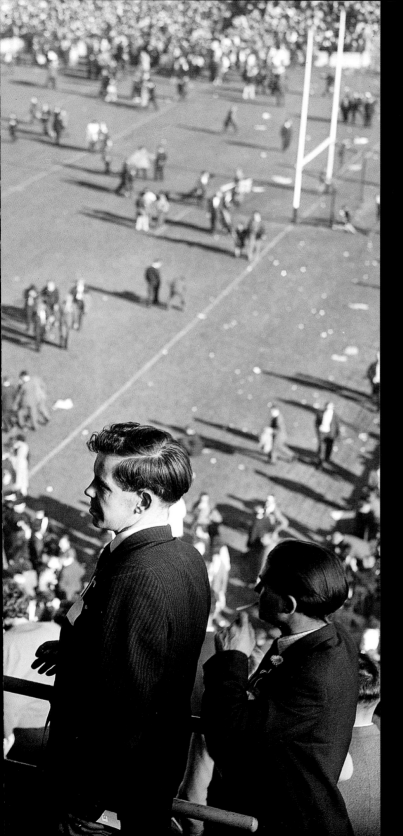

A cameraman films supporters as they spill onto the Croke Park pitch, 1961. Within months of picture being taken, a new Irish television service was launched and the cinema newsreels of Gaelic games were effectively rendered redundant.
(*Fáilte Ireland*)

rtv guide +

PROGRAMMES SEPTEMBER 5 — SEPTEMBER 11

Iris Radio Eireann-Telefis Eireann, September 4, 1964 :: Vol. 2, No. 144 :: Price 6d.

ALL-IRELAND HURLING FINAL

(SEE PAGE 5)

Although the GAA took a cautious approach to the arrival of television, Gaelic games were an integral part of the state broadcaster's schedules. As this cover of the *RTV Guide* (later the *RTÉ Guide*) from 1964 demonstrates, All-Ireland finals were, from the very outset, major television events and coverage came with heavy promotion.

'When the All-Ireland finals in Croke Park were live on television, Ruttledge walked round the lake to watch the match with Jamesie. Jamesie poured whiskey and Mary made tea and sandwiches. The irregular striking of the clocks from every quarter of the house throughout the match served as a cool corrective to the excited commentary. The team Jamesie supported nearly always won, his support completely based on which of the teams he thought most likely to win and provide a triumphant, satisfying ending to the year. Once they lost, it was as if his judgement has been impugned. "No use," he thrust out his hands. "They should have been ashamed to turn out. It wasn't even worth looking at".' – **An extract from the novel** *That They May Face the Rising Sun* **by John McGahern** (2002).

structure of the championship, the redevelopment of Croke Park and a general sense that the Association was thriving. By the turn of the millennium, live television coverage of Gaelic games had become an essential part of the Irish summer. The viewing figures, Sunday after Sunday, were unflagging. In 2006, for instance, despite the fact that Ireland won the Triple Crown in rugby, Munster won the Heineken Cup and the World Cup soccer finals were held in Germany, the most watched sports programme in Ireland was the All-Ireland hurling final between Cork and Kilkenny which averaged more than 750,000 viewers.

This level of audience made broadcast rights a much sought-after commodity. The advent of TV3, an independent commercial station, and of Setanta Sports challenged RTÉ. Setanta had begun operations in 1990, primarily broadcasting Irish-related sports to expatriates. By the end of 2004 it had set up its own dedicated sports channel on cable and satellite television, and started to challenge Sky Sports as a major international pay-TV broadcaster. The former President of the GAA, Jack Boothman, had once told delegates to the GAA's Annual Convention that the GAA could never in conscience sell television rights to any pay-TV channel: 'We are not going to sell our people down the river for money.' Nonetheless, Setanta – which had previously held overseas broadcast rights – was granted the rights to show Saturday-night National League matches. In a television deal agreed in 2007, it retained those rights, while TV3 was given broadcast rights to ten All-Ireland championship matches a year. On top of that, TG4's innovative coverage of club, college and schools matches, as well as in-depth coverage of

CUMANN LÚITH-CHLEAS GAEDHEAL

COISDE CHÚIGE CHONNACHT

Uachtarán: Cathaoirleach: Leas-Cathaoirleach: Cisteóir: Rúnaí:
B. Mac an Adhastair,   P. Ó Laing,   M. Ó Lachtúis,   P. Breathnach,   S. Ó Muilbhigh,
Dún Móir,   Collooney,   Crois Uí Maoilfhíona, Ardsallagh,   Sráid an Caisleáin,
Co. na Gaillimhe.   Co. Sligeach.   Co. Mhaigh Eo.   Ros Comáin.   Caisleán a' Bharraigh,
                        Tel. (071) 71160.   Tel. 40.   Tel. (0903) 6365.   Co. Mhaigh Eo.
                                                                                             Tel. (094) 21920.

22 / 6 / 1981

Liam a Cara,

    I write on behalf of Comhairle Connachta and indeed all GAA, supporters in the west of Ireland to protest in the strongest possible fashion through Ard Comhairle to R.T.E. concerning their apparent unwillingness to ~~confer the honour~~ confer the honour of Match of the Day on our Number one Fixture of the year — the Connacht Football Final Fixed for Castlebar on July 12th at 3/15 P.M.

It will not be sufficient to tell us now that the matter is under consideration because we have good reason to know what their "consideration" has amounted to in recent years.

Telephone: Castlebar (094) 21920
...AS GAEDHEAL
...CHONNACHT
...ch: Cisteóir: Rúnaí:
...   P. Breathnach,   S. Ó Muilbhigh,
...iona,   Ardsallagh,   Sráid an Caisleáin,
                          Ros Comáin.   Caisleán a' Bharraigh,
                          Tel. (0903) 6365.   Co. Mhaigh Eo.
                                                 Tel. (094) 21920.

19...

We wish to remind R.T.E, Also that when they sought permission to televise Provincial Finals LIVE some years Ago Connacht were the first and I think the only Province to Accomodate them. It is an old saying that "eaten Bread is soon forgotten", but on this occasion we trust that Ard Comhairle will use its good services to influence their decision in our favour.

Mise le fíor Meas,

S. Ó Muilbh...

(Runaí)

The relationship between RTÉ and the GAA, or units within it, has often been frayed. In this letter, the Connacht Provincial Committee registers its disgust through the GAA's Ard Comhairle at a decision by RTÉ not to accord 'Match of the Day' status to their showpiece event – the provincial football final.
(GAA Museum)

A photograph showing the audience at RTÉ studios in Montrose during the filming of a programme on the GAA in the 1960s. Pictured in the front row, third from the right, is Seán Ó Síocháin, who succeeded Pádraig Ó Caoimh as General Secretary of the GAA in 1964. (*GAA Oral History Project Archive*)

'The major change is that when you live abroad (as I have for the last 6 years) you can find places with relative ease that can show the games. One can also tune into the local radio stations for league games or any games that are not televised. When Kildare are playing and I'm listening online, I like to also listen in to the local station of the county we are playing. Gives a great insight into how the opposition views us. It's really interesting; sometimes it's like listening to two completely different games! God bless local radio. My favourite quote from KFM – "Balls are dropping in on top of Ken Donnelly like confetti at a funeral". We really enjoy our funerals in the Shortgrass.' – **Enda Gorman, GAA Oral History Project Archive, 2008.**

ladies' football, demonstrates the appeal of every level of Gaelic games to viewers. It continues to irk GAA members in the north that transmission of Gaelic games does not extend across the entire island. Although the BBC offers coverage of Gaelic games, it remains the case that the full run of matches shown on RTÉ and TV3 does not reach all of Ulster due to lack of transmission coverage. Nonetheless, with matches also being streamed live on websites, the GAA has a reach which, even a decade ago, would have seemed unthinkable.

Even as television coverage has reached saturation levels, radio coverage of GAA events has retained iconic status. That status revolves around Micheál Ó Muircheartaigh. Even people with little interest in Gaelic games tune in to hear his commentaries, which are vivid and powerful and entirely unique, flowing between Irish and English, steeped in a deep knowledge of the games and the people

'Life goes on and the grip of the games seems never to loosen. This community within a community seems to endure forever. I see men and boys buried in their graves with their jerseys draped over their coffins. I see families marry into each other and becoming Gaelic town dynasties. I see entire communities consumed by the passion of a season, generations welded together in the love of the game. I see children in my home-place running around in jerseys of Dublin-blue, and no end to the rhythms of our Gaelic seasons.' – **An extract from** *Green Fields: Gaelic Sport in Ireland* **(1996) by** *The Irish Times* **journalist Tom Humphries, one of a new generation of Irish sportswriters that emerged in the 1990s.**

who play them. Coverage of Gaelic games on radio has not been displaced by the arrival of television. Indeed, the opening of so many local radio stations in the 1990s ensured that radio carried more – and not less – coverage of the GAA. The glory of local commentators draws a huge listenership, while many Irish speakers justifiably champion Raidió na Gaeltachta's Seán Bán Breathnach as the finest GAA commentator on the airwaves.

Newspapers, too, dramatically increased coverage of the games, with even the once-frosty *Irish Times* now devoting extensive coverage in dedicated sports supplements to hurling and football. Journalists such as Con Houlihan and Paddy Downey had been an essential reference point for followers of Gaelic games from the 1960s. From the 1990s, a new generation of writers, led by Vincent Hogan, Tom Humphries, Keith Duggan and Denis Walsh, brought a new style to the writing on hurling and Gaelic football; it was a style which owed more than a passing nod to the outstanding tradition of American sports-writing. In keeping with their American colleagues – and, indeed, their Irish predecessors, many of these journalists also published books on various aspects of the GAA. In general, recent decades have seen significant growth in the number of books written on the GAA. The 1980s saw an explosion in club, county and national histories published to mark the centenary of the GAA. More recently, diverse publications have told the story of the Association from almost every conceivable perspective, most obviously through a small library of autobiographies written by players, managers, officials, referees and journalists.

The explosion in media coverage has not been entirely positive. The tabloid press has dipped its toes in the private lives of GAA men and attempted to apply the mores of their coverage of English soccer to Gaelic games. Internet websites, noticeboards and blogs have too often been stained by personal abuse and

'As a cultural entity, hurling was loudly acknowledged to be a national treasure, a golden strand of our identity, uniquely ours, gloriously us. Yet, beyond the rhetoric and the plámás, hurling was willfully neglected in two-thirds of its homeland and half of the counties who took the game seriously were never contenders. Underneath the lipstick and mascara of Munster finals and big days in Croke Park, the hurling championship was pale and sick.' – **An extract from the award-winning book by Denis Walsh**, *Hurling: the Revolution Years* (2005), p. 2.

The proliferation of media outlets since the 1990s has transformed coverage of Gaelic games. Reports and live commentaries of Gaelic football and hurling are now to be found everywhere: on public service and pay-TV and across the spectrum of local and national radio stations. This growth in coverage has led to an overhaul of press facilities at some of the major grounds, but at smaller venues, more temporary accommodation is often installed. This makeshift press box was wheeled into Fitzgerald Park, Fermoy, for a Munster football championship quarter-final match in May 2008. (*Sportsfile*)

ill-informed invective. On a more mundane level, the sheer quantity of requests from across the spectrum of media outlets placed a significant burden on players, team managers and officials. The scale of the GAA media demands a constant flow of content. This, of course, has created opportunities as well as burdens, with ghosted columns and other media opportunities earning for some a significant income, while the organisation as a whole benefited from the revenue gained from rights and sponsorship. The idea that media demands would come to play such a part in the affairs of the GAA would have stunned the founders of the Association, who found it so difficult to secure coverage in its early years.

Part of the everyday of Irish life: a young
girl carries a hurling stick through Mungret,
County Limerick, 1925. (*Irish Picture
Library/Fr. F. M. Browne S.J. Collection*)

Community

'Patriotism begins and ends for most of
us with the parish.' —

Rev B. Doyle, in an address to the Annual Convention of
the Leitrim GAA, *Leitrim Observer*, 27 January 1967.

'Gaelic games in Ireland are now a democratic institution,
    more democratic, probably, than the games of any other country
we can think of at the present moment, for the reason that
    in no other state we know of is a system of National athletics so rigorously
    closed by the aristocratic element as is
        the case here in Ireland.'

For the honour of Ballygeehan, we s...
r utmost to retain Leix Hurling Cha...
a we can do by acquiring the staying...
essary for a player to do his best p...
's hard play.

With these objects in view we wis...
Necessity of commencing to-mor...
eing runs, beginning with one a...
easing the distance by, say qu...
g on the fifth day (Monday ne...
s - three miles.

For the succeeding week continu...
ing, but vary the pace to a sl...
. about six times during eac...
l, the long runs should cease.

For the last week up to Thursda...
ral short runs - bursts of fr...
speed.

f course hurling practice must...

'The social side of the GAA is more important
    than the actual playing of the games,
in my opinion. If the GAA was only about playing sport, it'd never survive.
    Players only make up a tiny
        part of any clubs membership.

On a wild, wet night in the middle of the Second World War, a Meath GAA official cycled thirteen miles from his rural home to a County Board meeting held in Navan. Drenched on arrival, the flow of water from his clothes to the table caused the meeting to be suspended so that the delegate could be taken to a neighbouring bakery, placed in front of an open oven and turned until he was dry. The meeting then resumed, but when its business was completed, the same delegate climbed back upon his bicycle and rode once more through the driving rain across the same thirteen miles of country road to his home.

That story is told by the writer Breandán Ó hEithir in his masterful book *Over the Bar*, which he dedicated to this anonymous figure. It was an acknowledgment of the commitment of thousands of volunteers without whom the Association could not have survived and then thrived in parishes, villages, towns and suburbs across the country. Through the generations, a fundamental strength of the GAA has been its ability to command the devotion of people who commit their time, energy and talents in the service of the games and the community. They have done so at all levels as players, coaches, administrators, family members and supporters.

The extraordinary influence the GAA has exerted on Irish social life is intimately bound up with the decisions taken in its formative years on the kind of structure it should adopt. The ambition from the start was to spread the Association into every corner of Ireland. It aimed to do this by building club organisations around parish units and local community networks. During the summer of 1887 the GAA stressed that its basic unit of operation was one club per parish. The reality was more complex. In the first years, parish boundaries were important but they were not sacrosanct. Clubs also formed around informal alliances which evolved in

'The country was soon humming with interest and activity, the ambitions of the young men were aroused, every parish had its newly formed hurling or football team, prepared to do or die for the "honour of the little villages". Anon the war of the Championships was on! We followed armies of the Gaels many miles along the country roads to the field of combat, where as many as eight or ten teams, gaily clad in their coloured jerseys, struggled for supremacy before our dazzled and delighted eyes! How we cheered our beloved heroes on to victory, and what pride we felt in looking on their stalwart and athletic forms! To play on the "first team" was, indeed, the greatest honour a youth could hope for, and many of us looked forward to the day with swelling hearts.' – Rev James B. Dollard, quoted in *The Gaelic Athletic Annual and County Directory*, 1907–08, p. 19.

farming communities or around a few small townlands. What was clear from the beginning – whatever about the precise nature of the boundaries – was the association between club and place. This stress on the local proved a masterstroke. Residency rules were introduced which restricted the movement of players between teams and these, together with the establishment of a system of internal county-based competitions, helped in the creation of intense inter-community rivalries. This was vital to the success of the early GAA and to the roots it set down. It meant that when clubs took to the field, players were playing for more than personal glory – the reputation of their community was also at stake.

Inevitably, local pride was as often hurt as enhanced. In July 1887, for example, when the footballers of the Geraldines Club from Cabinteely in Dublin crossed into Wicklow to challenge the John Dillons Club of Monaglough, near Woodenbridge, the game was repeatedly interrupted by the former's complaints at the physicality of their opponents play. Finally, unimpressed by the protection afforded by the referee, the captain of the Geraldines led his players off the field and back to Dublin. In front of a large crowd of 3,000 people, the retreat of the Dubliners drew down upon them a wave of derision. The players were the butt of sneers and ridicule and, as one reporter unsympathetically observed, 'they deserved it richly . . . Such absurd individuals I have never seen as the leaders of the Geraldines; their childishness excelled in everything.'

Matches, too, created a sense of spectacle as entire parishes came out in support of their teams. The GAA became a focus of social activity in many communities; it afforded a break from the often humdrum realities of daily life and offered a

A membership card from the Dunmore McHales GAA Club in Galway from 1891. The club had been formed in advance of the 1887 County Convention in Athenry. At a meeting arranged to discuss the formation of a club, Dunmore man P. J. Delaney remarked: 'It is now over three years since the GAA was founded and there are over 800 clubs throughout the land, and it is hoped that in a short time there will be a club in every parish.' Once founded, the club was named in honour of John McHale, a former Bishop of Tuam. Many of the newly emerging GAA clubs took the name of religious leaders or icons of Irish nationalism. (*Micheál Ó Liodáin*)

The social phenomenon of the GAA: from its earliest days, the drawing power of Gaelic games brought communities together in support of their local teams. This extraordinary photograph shows a large crowd watching a hurling match near Borrisoleigh, County Tipperary in the 1890s. (*Timmy Delaney*)

space where people could come together and socialise with those of similar background. The large numbers of women attending matches were from the beginning of the GAA a source of comment in the press, their elegant, stylish dress drawing favourable observation from journalists and, in one instance, comparison with the best of 'Parisian invention'. Club activities centred on the games but were not limited to them. Away from the playing fields, many clubs also ran formal functions, holding annual balls and fund-raising dances and celebrations. A social life developed around clubs and this enabled the GAA to extend its appeal to a wider, non-playing public. Michael Cusack, anxious that such activity would not revolve around drink, suggested that every club should have a room, away from a public house, where members could go and read books and newspapers with a nationalist outlook. Cusack believed the affect on the social tastes of members would be such that they would lose all interest in the attractions of the pub. They did not. Calling for a revolution in Irish sport was one thing, but this was a crusade too far. For all their popularity, pubs were nonetheless only one part of the GAA social experience.

In the early years of the GAA, the social background of GAA players was mainly rural and farming. This was as true for those who joined urban clubs as it was for those from clubs set in rural heartlands: as people migrated from the countryside to the towns and cities, they brought Gaelic games with them and it was not uncommon for entire urban-based teams to be comprised exclusively of country-born players. In Dublin, where the 'Parish Rule' was never applied, non-natives helped to found and fill clubs where the connections among players owed more to the workplace than a shared place of origin or residence. Such, indeed, was the lack of identification with place among many city-based GAA clubs that they were forced to advertise a meeting time and place for their players in the pages of evening newspapers. What every club, urban and rural, had in common was an openness to all social classes. At the founding meeting of the Association, Maurice Davin had insisted that one of its principal objectives was to provide recreation for those effectively shunned by other codes – the poorer sections of Irish society, those 'born into no other inheritance than an everlasting round of labour'. The Association organised itself in such a way as to facilitate their involvement: the cost of membership was relatively cheap and games were played on Sundays, the traditional day of rest for working people. The reality was that people still needed a certain income to engage in organised sporting activity and it is clear that the GAA did not entirely fulfil Davin's aspirations.

Nonetheless, at every level, the GAA defined itself in opposition to the elitism of rival sporting bodies. The Association embraced amateurism, for instance, but

'Gaelic games in Ireland are now a democratic institution, more democratic, probably, than the games of any other country we can think of at the present moment, for the reason that in no other state we know of is a system of National athletics so rigorously opposed by the aristocratic element as is the case here in Ireland.' – *The Gaelic Athlete*, 3 February 1912.

not the exclusive ethos of the 'gentleman amateur', espoused by elite Victorian sporting bodies in England. The difference between the two was crystallised in their different attitudes to money. The Spartan puritanism of English amateurism was absent from the GAA. On the contrary, Gaelic games were awash with commercial activity. Admission fees for games, advertisements in programmes and sponsorships for trophies were common from the outset. This revenue was ploughed back into games, but it was also used to cover the expenses of players. As inter-county competition increased with the introduction of All-Ireland championships for football and hurling in 1887, expenses were routinely paid to players to cover the costs of their travel. More than that, in the early twentieth century, when county teams began to train seriously for one-off, major games like All-Ireland finals, funds were also raised to ensure that they were properly prepared and that players would not suffer financial loss from time off work. The connection between team and place was vital in gathering subscriptions as the burden of fund-raising fell on local clubs and members of their community. Clubs were not always in a position to help out. When the Laois County Board went looking for a contribution from Monadrehid GAA Club prior to the county's involvement in the 1914 All-Ireland final, the latter declined on the grounds that its hard-earned money was being used locally to address a player-welfare issue of their own. With only twenty members, Monadrehid had the previous month paid one of its players 10s a week after he had been hurt in a match. The club came first.

Not everybody approved of the collective system of county team training or the manner of its funding. The Kerry footballer Dick Fitzgerald warned that it was unfair to force special training on players who could afford neither the time nor the expense. Nor was it proper that the public should be asked to cover the expenses they incurred. As early as 1914 Fitzgerald was urging the GAA to stick with its established traditions. The games should be played for their own sake, he wrote, while cautioning against following examples set by rival games. Soccer was a case in point: in 1894, the Irish Football Association, following in the footsteps of its English and Scottish counterparts, moved to legalise professionalism. The GAA

G. A. A.

❧

Hurling Semi-Final for Championship of Munster.

ENNIS: *July, 1914.*

DEAR SIR,

Clare hurlers in the past occupied a proud and prominent position in the Gaelic arena. Unfortunately in recent years, owing to a want of proper training and combination, our representatives have greatly deteriorated, until at the present day we find ourselves occupying a very insignificant position, indeed, in the annals of the G.A.A. General regret, and universal disappointment, is expressed throughout the County at this condition of things, and a hope was expressed on all sides that some steps should be taken to rehabilitate Clare to the conspicuous position she once enjoyed, when her hurlers were second to none in the land. Yielding to the wish thus expressed, a meeting was recently convened, and held in Ennis, of some of the prominent men of the County. As a result of the meeting, an influential Committee was appointed, and they were ordered to take the team, that is going to represent Clare in the Munster Championship, on hands, and to see that they are properly trained and equipped for their fixture at Limerick on the 9th August. In order to properly train the team, the Committee purpose to bring them, the week prior to the match, to Lahinch, so that they may be free from all disturbing attractions, and train in such a manner as will enable them to bring back once more to Clare the high prestige we once enjoyed.

Needless to remark the training of the team will entail considerable expenditure, and in order to defray this expenditure we earnestly appeal to you for a subscription to assist us in the work we have undertaken.

Subscriptions will be thankfully received and duly acknowledged by the undersigned.

Trusting that your response will be spontaneous and generous, and thanking you in anticipation.

We remain,

Yours truly,

James O'Regan, J.P., Sixmilebridge ; P. E. Kenneally, J.P., Ennis ; Dr. Fitzgerald, Newmarket-on-Fergus ; Rev. W. Scanlan, P.P., Tubber ; Rev. M. McKenna, Killimer ; Rev. Fr. McCreedy, C.C., Quin ; Rev. Fr. O'Kennedy, The College, Ennis ; B. Culligan, J.P., Kilrush ; Messrs. P. J. Floyd, P. McNamara, P. Power, J. Callaghan, Dublin ; M. Duggan, Scariff ; W. Moloney, Tulla ; P. O'Loughlin, Ballyvaughan ; D. Healy, Bodyke.

Messrs. STEPHEN CLUNE, Quin ; ⎫
P. KENNY, Ennis ⎬ Joint Hon. Secs.

A circular issued to drive a fund-raising effort in support of the Clare hurling team in 1914. Appealing to local county pride, the circular stresses the importance of raising the status of Clare hurling from its then 'insignificant position'. Later that year, the county won its first ever All-Ireland hurling title. (*Clare Museum*)

BALLYGEEHAN HURLING CLUB,

March 22, 1915.

For the honour of Ballygeehan, we appeal to you to do
your utmost to retain Leix Hurling Championship for 1915.
This we can do by acquiring the staying powers and speed
necessary for a player to do his best for the whole of an
hour's hard play.

With these objects in view we wish to impress on you
the necessity of commencing to-morrow (Thursday) long easy
jogging runs, begining with one mile the first day and
increasing the distance by, say quarter of a mile each day,
doing on the fifth day (Monday next) - at an easy comfortable
pace - three miles.

For the succeeding week continue the long distance
running, but vary the pace to a short sprint of 40 or 50
yards, about six times during each run. On Sunday, 2nd
April, the long runs should cease, also hurling practice.

For the last week up to Thursday, confine yourself to
several short runs - bursts of from 10 to 30 yards at
full speed.

Of course hurling practice must take place each evening
up to 2nd April, and special attention should be devoted
to catching, striking as hard and fast as possible, ground
play and tackling. Long pucking from goal, free pucks

and side line pucks must be practiced.

Some will require training every evening, others will be
best served by every second evening, but each can judge for
himself.

REMEMBER Leix are now All-Ireland Hurling Champions, and
Ballygeehan Champions of Leix (which title you are now called
upon to defend), that your opponents will make a determined
effort to take the honour from you, and that the unbeaten
record of Ballygeehan is at stake. We therefore appeal to
you to put yourself in perfect condition for the coming
contest, so that you may be able to do your share in
retaining for Ballygeehan the hurling honours of Leix.

JOHN W. FINLAY (Ballycuddy House) Captain.
JOHN PHELAN (Ballygeehan House), Hon. Treas. Sec.
JOHN PHELAN (The Castle), Hon. Sec. Treas.

A letter sent to players with the Ballygeehan Hurling Club in March 1915 advises them on training drills required to get themselves in 'perfect condition' for the forthcoming Laois championship. The letter impresses upon the players that they are responsible for defending 'the honour of Ballygeehan'. By fostering a sense of local identity and emphasising the importance of place, the GAA strengthened its roots in Irish community life. (*GAA/Laois/96, GAA Museum*)

Dick Fitzgerald demonstrates the foot pass with Kerry teammate Johnny Mahony. The photograph was published in Fitzgerald's seminal book *How to Play Gaelic Football*, published in 1914. The book lauded the evolution of Gaelic football as a 'scientific' sport and encouraged regular training in helping the improvement of basic skills. Fitzgerald was nonetheless insistent that the game should 'never become the possession of the professional player'. (*GAA Oral History Project Archive*)

was unmoved by such developments. Their players were comfortable with their amateur status and exalted for it. The nationalist press lauded the virtue of players who played only for the honour of their villages and counties, while routinely denouncing professionalism as a debasement of sport. In 1913, for instance, *The Gaelic Athlete* newspaper, a GAA organ, dismissed professionals as the 'very vagabonds and outlaws of the sporting fraternity'.

The amateur nature of Gaelic games was key to their growth. As the inter-county scene expanded from the 1920s onwards, drawing bigger and bigger crowds, the revenues were reinvested in the development of the Association rather than the payment of players. This enabled the GAA to cement its place in Irish life by acquiring new grounds and founding new clubs. The effect was transformative. With the acquisition of fields, many clubs and county boards finally found places to call their own. In the course of a critical phase of growth, the GAA managed simul-taneously to deepen its roots and broaden its reach in Irish society. Between 1924 and 1945, for example, the development of a national network of clubs saw their number double to more than 2,000. Underpinning each of these clubs was a story of massive voluntary endeavour and communities benefited from the availability of organised, healthy recreation and the provision of new places to play and meet.

The GAA certainly brought people together, but its model of inclusivity was not without fault. For much of the twentieth century, the Association opened its doors to everybody, but on a conditional basis. While social class and political allegiances were no barriers to entry, leisure preferences were. The GAA made exclusive demands on its members, banning them from participation in 'foreign games'. The effects of the ban rules were most keenly felt at the local level, within GAA clubs and the communities in which they were rooted. It was here the real

'Why should we put a ban on games? Why shouldn't we be broadminded, and let anybody play any game we are not concerned with? We are concerned only with Camogie. I can understand the reason of the GAA when the ban was first imposed, but Mr. Barry is quite right in saying that this led to endless friction in the GAA. We would be very foolish to impose any set of rules that have no real value, and that would lead to friction and a long series of objections and espionage and all kinds of unpleasant things.' –
The contribution of the Muskerry delegate to a meeting of Cork city and county camogie clubs, quoted in the *Southern Star*, 4 March 1933.

GAA democracy at work: delegates attend the 1945 Congress of the Association at Dublin City's Hall. It is at this annual gathering of representatives that the direction of GAA policy is debated and decided. The 1945 Congress, for instance, saw the re-election of Tipperary man Seamus Gardiner as president and discussion of a wide range of issues, among them the ban on foreign games, grounds development, playing rules and schools. (*GAA Museum*)

Rite of passage: a child grips his father's hand at a hurling game in Clare in the 1950s. This was a typical initiation into the world of the GAA. The family day out at a local club or county game is a tradition that has helped in transferring an interest in Gaelic games from one generation to the next. (*Dorothea Lange Collection, the Oakland Museum of California, City of Oakland, Gift of Paul S. Taylor*)

damage was done. In Galway, for instance, the zealous prosecution of the ban rules led the GAA to abuse its influence in limiting the educational opportunities of those attending, or looking to attend certain schools and colleges. At a time when post-primary education was still the preserve of the few, the GAA in Galway succeeded in 1930 in having the ban enshrined in a local County Council scholarship scheme, which assisted fortunate recipients in continuing their studies. Fr Cogavin, principal of St Joseph's College in Ballinasloe, a school which unusually promoted both hurling and rugby, criticised the move as one likely to hurt, not the schools or colleges, but children from poorer backgrounds. In doing so, it also diminished the GAA. The following year the Dublin County Board passed a motion requesting the city's corporation to enforce the ban in a similar way.

Not alone did the ban alienate sections of the community – north and south – who held an interest in rugby or soccer, it created tensions within the Association itself. The rule crudely cast GAA members into one of two camps: loyal or disloyal. What sustained this type of mentality was a culture that was reflected in organisations across the spectrum of Irish public life. While the ban constituted a distortion of idealism and made an easy target for the GAA's critics, it was outweighed by the Association's other, more positive contributions. A sense of national mission has always been important to how the GAA has understood its role in Irish society. Whether through supporting Irish industry, language, music and culture, or local community initiatives, charities and causes, the GAA appealed to members to imagine their support for Gaelic games as part of a wider social and cultural commitment. During the 1940s, for example, as war-time restrictions led to shortages of food and fuel, the Association looked beyond itself in seeking to instil discipline and a sense of national purpose.

'Volunteers cut grass, put out fertilizer, brush off water from the goal areas, clean up after players, put out flags, line fields, pick up rubbish after people, put out the wheel bin, fix netting and fencing, repair plumbing, put up lights, collect at gates, make lodgements, write cheques, run lottos, raise funds, pay, organise games and trips away, communicate with players and public, absorb grief, attend meetings, attend meetings about meetings, take gear to the laundry, bring it back, apply for planning permission, plan and execute developments, put up bunting, take it down, train, coach, exhort, encourage, drive, hire, dig, backfill, build, drain, delegate, negotiate, volunteer.' – Jerome O'Brien, GAA Oral History Project Archive, 2008.

50 VOLUNTEERS

WANTED

(WITH SHOVELS AND SPADES), in the

GAELIC FIELD, WARRENPOINT ROAD,

On WEDNESDAY EVENING NEXT, at 2.30 p.m.,

(WEATHER PERMITTING)

Lend a Hand to Aid the Good Work.

(SEE COLUMN SIX)

A public plea for volunteers to clear ground for a new Gaelic field on the Warrenpoint Road in Newry, County Down. The driving force behind the development work was a young curate, Fr Esler, after whom the pitch is now named. Páirc Esler is today home to the Newry Shamrocks GAA Club and a regular venue for inter-county games. Voluntary endeavour underpins the origins of most GAA clubs. (*Cardinal Ó Fiaich Memorial Library*)

The business of GAA administration: on a January night in 1960, delegates gather in Annascaul Community Hall for the West Kerry GAA Convention. Meetings in rooms like these were held in clubs throughout the country. (*The Kerryman*)

Bringing it all back home: on returning from captaining Kerry to the All-Ireland football title, John Dowling places the Sam Maguire Cup in the window of his shoe shop in Tralee, September 1955. The amateur status of GAA players ensured that even the most celebrated among them remained grounded in their own communities. (*Kennelly Archive*)

'Idir an dá linn bhí créatúirí bochta eile fágtha aige baile go raibh ainmhithe le aoireacht acu agus gnó le déanamh. B'iontas leis an sagart laghad an phobail a tháinig ag éisteacht le briathar Dé. Bhí an siopadóir ag cnáimhseáil faoin laghad de pháipéirí an Domhnaigh a bhí díolta. Fágadh ba ar an long acre *formhór an lae agus ní ghaibh aon mhótar an slí a chuirfeadh isteach orthu. Bhí an dúthaigh formhór tréigthe agus brait agus dathanna na Gaeltachta ar foluain sa ghaoth.'* – Ár n-aistear go Páirc a' Chrócaigh, sliocht as *Dialann Lucht Leanúna* ar fáil ar líne.

While many members joined the various defence forces, they were further encouraged to assist the crucial labour of cultivating crops and saving turf. The mood of national crisis did not pass with the ending of the war. In 1946, after a summer of bad weather had threatened widespread crop destruction, the country mobilised in support of rural food producers. A massive voluntary effort was summoned and the GAA weighed in behind it. Across all counties and at all levels, fixtures were cancelled to enable members and supporters to volunteer for urgent work in the fields.

The GAA was not the only sports organisation to commit to the national drive to save the harvest, but its involvement was in keeping with the pragmatic patriotism that defined its broad engagement with Irish life. The Association both mined and cultivated a spirit of volunteerism which translated into other forms of community activism. Peadar Kearney from Clogherhead in County Louth was typical of many whose community service began with the GAA, but extended beyond it. A part-time farmer and a rent collector for Louth County Council, Kearney's playing days never stretched past his years in school. Yet he spent a lifetime entrenched in the GAA, serving at all levels of administration – club, county, provincial and national. Within his own locality, Kearney was a singular influence on the development of the Dreadnots GAA Club and was responsible for securing from the Land Commission the ground on which the club built its permanent home. In doing so, Kearney was forced to face down opposition from local farmers who were anxious to acquire for themselves the same tract of prime agricultural land. Because of Kearney and his determination to provide a recreational outlet for the younger members of the community, the public good triumphed over the private interest. Like many other volunteers across the GAA, Kearney applied these same qualities of passionate public engagement and community-mindedness to other projects. A member of the local development association, he was instrumental in establishing a credit union in Clogherhead and also helped ensure that the area benefited from rural electrification, securing the extension of a scheme which transformed the experiences of ordinary people throughout the Irish countryside.

That countryside was nevertheless home to a falling population. Through the 1950s, the land of Ireland emptied with mass emigration and this cut deep into the GAA experience, embedded as it was in rural community life. The Association responded by trying to divorce its fate from that of a decaying agricultural economy. For a start, it made common purpose with a range of rural voluntary organisations which, in line with the prevailing Catholic social teaching, aimed to regenerate rural life through community action. The GAA shared with groups like Muintir na Tíre a commitment to the parish as the key unit of social organisation, to the role of the volunteer and the principles of community participation and self-reliance. The two organisations were also joined in the belief that the best way to

Irish rural decline was balanced by urban growth. Many GAA people who migrated to Dublin helped to found new clubs and fill the ranks of established ones. This photograph shows Muiris Prenderville and Senan Griffen, walking past the Grand Central Cinema on O'Connell Street, on their way from work to hurling training in the early 1940s. Born and raised in Cork, Prenderville moved to Dublin to work in the Department of Defence in December 1936. His assimilation into city life was eased by his involvement with the Civil Service GAA Club. Many years later, Prenderville acted in a voluntary capacity as secretary to the influential MacNamee Commission, which in 1971 issued a report recommending the overhaul of GAA administrative structures. (*GAA Oral History Project Archive*)

'We think too much in terms of victory and defeat and too little in terms of the social impact the games make – the pageantry, the excitement, the sense of pride and moral uplift which a sporting, manly game can engender in a whole community (and don't forget the disappointment, the distaste, amounting to disgust which the bad game, the rough and unsporting game can engender).' – Seán Ó Síocháin, 'The Club's place in the social structure of the Parish', quoted in the *Leitrim Observer*, 9 December 1967.

combat the flight from rural Ireland was to improve the quality of life of the people who lived there. For the GAA, this would entail the provision of playing fields in every parish in the country, as well as adequate facilities around them. As an example of what could be achieved, the Clann Éireann Club in Lurgan, County Armagh, rallied the support of members to build a youth club hall to serve their community in 1954. The first facility of its kind, the new hall was a monument to voluntary endeavour. As one newspaper reported: 'Teachers left their schools and brought their pupils along after hours to lend a hand, chemists and dentists mixed mortar and businessmen trimmed the costs – not for their own reward, but for a great cause.'

Significantly, the GAA's response to rural decline was not simply to set itself against an inexorable trend. The Association was equally intent on adapting to the new demographic realities. By the 1960s, Ireland was becoming an increasingly urban-based society. Villages developed into towns and cities spilled out into sprawling suburbs. The GAA met the challenge of growing urbanisation by recasting itself as a community-development organisation fixed on providing an expanded range of social activities. Drawing on the model of Clann Éireann, the GAA pushed the idea of building social centres that would be linked to existing or emerging clubs. These centres ensured that the GAA club was both the sporting centre of the community and its social focus. The benefits were obvious: players would no longer be as inclined to drift away from the GAA on retirement, families would be included more fully in the social life of the club and members of the wider community would be brought together for social events held under the umbrella of the GAA.

Social centres were particularly important to the spread of the GAA in Dublin. Through the 1960s and 1970s, as the institutional and occupational city-centre clubs went into decline, new clubs developed in the capital's rapidly expanding suburbs. Social centres added to the GAA's physical foothold in many of these areas,

'You can't expect wives to be football widows all their lives. When our centre is completed wives will be able to talk to other wives in the ladies room or else play on our 18 hole pitch and putt course which will be opened next March while the children can play on the swings in the playground while the husband is watching or playing the match.' – **Interview with Marcus Wilson of St Vincent's GAA Club in Dublin on the development of community facilities from** *Gaelic Weekly*, **26 October 1968, quoted in William Nolan (ed.),** *The Gaelic Athletic Association in Dublin, 1884–2000*, **vol. 2 (2005), p. 535.**

but they also helped to attract people through their doors. Kilmacud Crokes and Ballyboden St Enda's on the southside of the city were examples of clubs that developed premises offering a range of services and activities – sporting and social – which proved popular with residents in newly-built housing estates. Alongside playing fields, facilities were provided for tennis, billiards, card games, ballad sessions, parties, meetings and more. These multi-purpose complexes acted as social glue – they bound people together and helped forge communities from the bricks and mortar of suburban sprawl. The lessons of this were relevant not just to Dublin. In 1971, the report of a special commission on the GAA stated that all clubs into the future would need to cater for the 'social, recreational and sporting needs of its members from early youth to late middle-age.' A system of grants had by then been put in place to assist clubs in the funding of major physical infrastructure – dressing rooms, function rooms, catering and bar facilities – though, in many cases, voluntary labour helped keep costs down.

Raising money for clubs has taxed inspirational minds for decades. On becoming secretary of the Clonakilty Club in Cork in 1960, Tim Downey helped drive the development of a new club pavilion. As with any such building programme, the biggest headache was raising the money. To solve the problem Downey bought a bingo machine from an amusement arcade in Kinsale and began a series of bingo nights at Lowney's Cinema to raise money for the club. The success of the bingo, which was still running at the beginning of the twenty-first century, not only helped cover the cost of the 1960s' pavilion, but allowed for a further redevelopment to be undertaken in the late 1980s.

Community fund-raising reinforced the idea of the club as vital to the social fabric of Irish communities. Over the decades, the fortunes of those communities reflected upon the GAA experience in different parts of the country. In Northern Ireland, the violence of the Troubles brought GAA clubs into the firing line of

228 A.G.M

Minutes of Tenth Annual General Meeting held at the South County Hotel on 10th November 1964 at 8 p.m.

Attendance Mr. M. Burke, Chairman, presided and there was an attendance of ninety two.

Chairman's Address The Chairman welcomed Very Rev. S. Clune P.P. Mount Merrion and Very Rev. B. Harley P.P. Kilmacud, Brothers Rossiter and English, Oatlands and Bro Cornelius Obelisk Park. He paid tributes to the work being done for the games by the Brothers at Oatlands and Obelisk Park & by the De La Salle Brothers at Mt Benildus. He said that there were a great number of boys to cater for and he appealed for the support of parents in promoting games for the boys. The G.A.A. Club should serve as a means of bringing people in the area together. The lands at Glenalbyn had been purchased to provide playing fields for our players and also to provide a site for a Community ✕ Centre. The playing fields would be used exclusively for G.A.A. games and games permitted by the rules of the association. The Community Centre would be open to all those interested and would be controlled by an organisation to be called the Glenalbyn Social and Recreation Federation ✕ Plans had been lodged with the County Council and it was expected that the Centre would be ready by the end of 1965. The project had the full approval of the G.A.A. authorities. In conclusion the Chairman thanked all those who had helped in any way during the year.

Minutes The minutes of the fifth annual general meeting were taken as read on the proposal of Mr. B. Meredith seconded by Mr. J. Sweeney.

Secretary's Report The Secretary's report was approved on the proposal of Mr. P. Coffey seconded by Mr. B. Battersby.

Lending their weight to the club cause: members of the Roche Emmets GAA Club in Louth – Pat Murphy, Brendan O'Callaghan, Vincie Kirk, Hughie Grant, Benny McConnon, Sharon Treacy, Pat Treacy and William Treacy – remove goalposts from Treanor's field as the club prepares to move to new facilties in 1983. The club had enjoyed the long-term use of a field belonging to local GAA enthusiast Jack Treanor, but secured a field of its own just a few hundred yards away in the townland of Rathduff. The first game was played on the new field, Páirc de Roiste, in June 1983. (*William Treacy*)

More than just a sporting organisation: a Belfast GAA club attracts a large crowd for a night out in 1981. (*Andersonstown News*)

The modern face of the GAA: a view from the splendid new bar and function room at Donaghmore Ashbourne GAA Club in County Meath. Between 2002 and 2006 the population of Meath increased by 21.5 per cent. Anticipating such growth, the Donaghmore Ashbourne Club started - in 1998 - to plan for future needs. Almost a decade later, in December 2007, the club opened the doors of its new facilities near the centre of Ashbourne. The development includes new playing pitches and a new clubhouse, with space for ten changing rooms, function and meeting rooms, a bar and a 40 m x 25 m indoor arena with an artificial playing surface. (*Fred Re*

*'Ba suarach an tír í Éire marach na ceannródaithe a bhí agus atá ag tabhairt
leath a saoil go deonach d'fhonn áiseanna a chur ar fáil don aos óg agus
d'fhonn an cultúr gaelach a chothú.'* – Joe Steve Ó Neachtain, quoted in
Comórtas Peile na Gaeltachta 2006 – Clár Oifigiúil (2006), p. 63.

political conflict. Because they afforded a popular space for members of the
nationalist community to meet and socialise, GAA clubs and their members
found themselves targeted for attack. Clubs in the rest of the country endured nothing as traumatic, but through the recession of the 1980s, high emigration threatened
the viability of many, particularly in western counties. When economic slump
was replaced by spectacular growth in the 1990s, new challenges presented
themselves. Emigration gave way to immigration and the GAA was faced, for the
first time, with the challenge of attracting different nationalities into the
Association. The results were mostly positive. The GAA acted as a pipeline to
Irish communities and their social networks and the assimilation of many
immigrant children was certainly eased by their involvement in Gaelic games in
schools and clubs.

Challenges abounded. As Irish society transformed in the 1990s, the effects of
economic boom raised a series of issues that struck at the GAA's core values. How,
for instance, would the ethos of 'voluntarism' and 'community' survive in an age
of increased consumerism, changing work patterns, developer-led housing sprawl
and long commutes? For all the competing pressures, the GAA continued to
inspire a massive voluntary input. A study published in 2005 showed that the
Association accounted for 42 per cent of all those who volunteered for sport in
Ireland, more than twice that of its nearest competitor. It also underlined the
extent to which the GAA was as much a social movement as a sporting organisation.
The Association's appeal transcended social class and, uniquely in the Irish sporting
context, it could claim a higher number of non-playing than playing members.
The growth of the GAA demanded that certain roles within the Association –
notably that of some administrators – be made full-time, salaried positions. Overall,
the evidence pointed to a broad-based organisation in robust health, yet there was
a growing unease that the ties that bound everyone together – players, mentors,
members – might be in danger of unravelling. The anxiety centred entirely on the
place of the inter-county players within the Association and fears of a rising
professionalism.

Concerns over threats – perceived and real – to the amateur status had been a

'My favourite memory of that day is meeting my father after the game in the Davenport Hotel . . . The whole experience made me think back to our childhood days when my father was always encouraging us to play and talk hurling. He brought us everywhere to games. When we were young fellows we always had hurls in our hands, pucking stones over walls. Bringing in the cows from school we brought our hurls with us. Even when we went to foot or clamp turf in the bog, the hurleys were constantly by our sides.' – Johnny Dooley reflecting on Offaly's 1994 All-Ireland triumph, quoted in Seamus McRory, *The All-Ireland Dream* (2005), p. 70.

constant throughout the twentieth century. From the 1980s onwards, illicit payments to managers at club and county level were an open secret, but they drew more condemnation than actual sanction. The sense that the amateur ethos was being eroded from within was reinforced through the 1990s, though the focus shifted from mentors to players. As the GAA's coffers filled with new revenues from big sponsorship and television deals, inter-county players began to lobby for improved conditions and financial rewards. The establishment of the Gaelic Players' Association (GPA) in 1999 signalled a shift in the relationship between elite players, and both officials and the wider membership. Despite the legitimacy of many of its initial grievances, the emergence of the GPA, with a membership restricted to inter-county players, gave rise to concerns about its ultimate objectives. A tendency to equate respect for players with monetary return, allied with a propensity for threatening strike action, sat uneasily with those who viewed the GAA as ostensibly egalitarian, voluntary and community-driven.

The response of the GAA has been to marry concessions with a reaffirmation of core values. It invested more in player welfare and loosened rules to allow players to benefit more from commercial opportunities around their sport. Wrong-footed

'The GAA is totally unique on this planet. It has two driving forces. First, it's about place . . . about where you're from; who you are; your community; and its place in the world. Second, it's about "we" . . . people working voluntarily for some greater good; for a value; an ethos; for something that's worthwhile; for community betterment.' – Mark Conway, Tyrone, quoted in the *Irish Independent*, 5 December 2007.

by a political promise made in the run-up to a general election, it acquiesced with GPA demands for a system of state grants for elite sportsmen to be extended to inter-county hurlers and football. A line remains drawn at pay-for-play and the GAA has stressed repeatedly its commitment to its inheritance of voluntarism. That inheritance is visible in cities, towns, suburbs, villages and open countryside. To travel through Ireland today is to be reminded of the scale of the GAA's voluntary achievement: the national patchwork of playing fields – many newly floodlit – the dressing rooms and the clubhouses stand as brilliant, living monuments to community spirit.

Canon Hamilton, Bishop O'Brien and Archbishop Kinnane attend the 1949 Tipperary county senior hurling final. (*Martin Burke*)

Religion

'I shall be happy to do all that I can, and authorise you now formally to place my name on the roll of your patrons.' —

Thomas Croke, Archbishop of Cashel, writes to Michael Cusack on 19 December 1884 in support of the Gaelic Athletic Association, *The Nation*, 27 December 1884.

'A lot of the villages depended on the local teachers
who would be free at 3 or 4 o'clock, and the parish priest
or local clergy and they generally would fill up the car and bring the team.
You could bring a whole team and a sub in four cars, which
wouldn't be seen or heard of or put up with nowadays.'

'In the Limerick City of my youth there was no shortage of sports.
There were Catholic sports and Protestant sports and some we couldn't place.
Nationalists, patriots, Catholics played the native games:
Gaelic football or hurling. Women played camogie, a kind of field hockey.
All were played under the aegis of the Gaelic Athletic Association, a stern organisation
in Dublin that forbade its members to play
or even attend foreign sports...

The 1958 All-Ireland football final between Dublin and Derry was a unique occasion. Derry were appearing in the All-Ireland final for the first time and were seeking to become the first team to bring the Sam Maguire Cup north of the border. The redevelopment of the Hogan Stand meant a reduced capacity and, so great was the crowd (around 70,000), the gates had to be closed more than an hour before the throw-in. The thousands locked outside relied on a public relay of the radio broadcast to hear the game. Those inside saw the game started with a ritual that had become central to big GAA matches – a member of the Catholic hierarchy throwing in the ball. In recognition of Derry's achievement in reaching the final, the honour was given to Dr Neil Farren, Bishop of Derry from 1939 until 1973. Having thrown the ball between the opposing players, the bishop headed swiftly for the safety of the sideline and eventually took his place with the other dignitaries in the stand.

The bishop throwing in the ball on All-Ireland Sunday symbolised the relationship that had developed between the GAA and the Catholic Church after the partition of Ireland and the establishment of the Irish Free State in 1922. It is unsurprising that two organisations of such importance in independent Ireland should have sought to share a mutually beneficial rapport. The nature of that rapport was shaped by the same forces that shaped the wider society. The Catholicism of the southern state was reflected across the operations of the GAA. For all that the Association's constitution proclaimed its non-sectarian nature, the overt Catholicism of its symbols ensured that the GAA was perceived as an organisation for Catholics. After all, the men who stood for the Catholic hymn, *Faith of our Fathers*, on All-Ireland Sunday and who knelt to kiss the bishop's ring on the field of play were invariably Catholic.

The Bishop of Cork and Ross, Dr Cornelius Lucey, starts the Munster senior football final replay between Cork and Kerry at Páirc Uí Chaoimh, 1976. By then a dying tradition, the sight of a bishop throwing in the ball was, in previous decades, a singular feature of big GAA match days, symbolising the close relationship between the GAA and the Catholic Church. (*Irish Examiner*)

Soft seats and great views: members of the clergy get priority treatment along the sidelines at the opening of Fitzgerald Stadium in Killarney, 1936. The ground was officially opened by Dr John M. Harty, Archbishop of Cashel and Patron of the GAA, and blessed by Dr O'Brien, Bishop of Kerry. (*Irish Independent Collection, National Library of Ireland*)

This Catholicism was found at every level of the GAA. As an organisation, the GAA was centrally involved in the Eucharistic Congress of 1932, the most public display of popular piety in Irish history. The Association agreed to play no major games during the period of the Congress, gave the use of Croke Park for one of the week's ceremonies and provided 3,000 stewards for the public masses that were staged in the Phoenix Park. The patronage of the GAA was also reflective of its relationship with the Church. A succession of bishops from the archdiocese of Cashel and Emly were invited to become patrons of the GAA. Indeed, it was suggested that any potential occupier of the Bishop's Palace in Thurles was obliged to have a genuine interest in Gaelic games. For example, Archbishop John Harty became a prominent figure within the GAA, serving as patron from 1928 until his death in 1946. Harty was presented with a crozier worth £150 by the GAA to mark his acceptance of the position of patron. His first act as patron was to pass on the GAA's congratulations to the Pope on the signing of a treaty between the Vatican and the Italian government. The Pope's subsequent expression of gratitude was later inserted into the minutes of the GAA's Central Council.

On a local level, the most obvious identification between the Catholic Church and the GAA was the notion of one-parish, one-club. Rooting the GAA to the geographical structure of the Catholic Church, of course, was a matter of convenience, not one of religious devotion. It was a decision which was shaped during the first All-Ireland championships in the 1880s, when it became clear that numerous clubs were essentially pulling players from wherever suited them in order to win matches. Parish boundaries – in time – offered the most straightforward boundaries between local clubs. Nonetheless, the establishment of clear boundaries did not always inhibit clubs in their search for talent with which to win matches.

In some parishes, the Church played a prominent role in GAA affairs; in others, it played little or none. In general, it was considered a boon to a club to receive into the parish a priest who would help with the running of the club. Like every other voluntary organisation, GAA clubs and county boards were invariably delighted to get whatever help they could. All the more so when it came from a

'A lot of the villages depended on the local teachers who would be free at 3 or 4 o'clock, and the parish priest or local clergy and they generally would fill up the car and bring the team. You could bring a whole team and a sub in four cars, which wouldn't be seen or heard of or put up with nowadays.' – **Honora Kavanagh Martin, GAA Oral History Project Archive, 2008.**

Adopting the Catholic Church's parish structures helped GAA clubs to build identity, engender local passion and drive support for various initiatives. Church-gate collections were a popular way for clubs and counties to raise revenue. This poster, issued by the Donegal County Committee, offers GAA members and supporters the opportunity to 'help in a personal way to bring the first All-Ireland to Donegal'. The payback would be a long time coming – it was not until 1992, thirty-eight years later, that the county would claim its first All-Ireland senior title. (*Donegal County Archives Service*)

figure of stature within the community – and one with flexible working hours who was uninhibited by the constraints of raising a family. Men such as Fr Tom Scully – who trained Offaly to reach the All-Ireland football final in 1969 – were dedicated to the GAA and it was a dedication rooted in a love of the game. In this respect, just as many priests were involved in the GAA, so it was that many more had no interest or involvement. Most usually, it came down to a matter of personal taste.

The involvement of priests in the GAA was not without its constraints. It was perceived within the Catholic hierarchy as being one thing to oversee a club or run a team, but entirely another to join the fray in the field. This perception of how a priest should behave – or at least be seen to behave – was rooted in the 'devotional revolution' which took place in the second half of the nineteenth century. Wholesale reform of the Catholic Church was led by Cardinal Paul Cullen in the three decades after the Famine in the 1840s. A prime focus for this reform was the behaviour of Catholic priests whose principal vices were considered to be drunkenness, lust and avarice. In reaction against this, the hierarchy of the church sought to redefine the engagement between the clergy and their flock. The new definition did not include playing football and hurling. This had implications for any priest who wished to play for a club and it also had implications for those studying to join the priesthood. Martin White, who won All-Irelands for Kilkenny in the 1930s, remembers being a student at St Kieran's in Kilkenny in the 1920s when there was a clear divide between ordinary students and ecclesiastical students: 'A lot of those chaps that were there, they went for the priesthood afterwards. On account of that they were lost to hurling. Once they went across to the ecclesiastical side they could hurl away over in the fields but they didn't play for a team after that. That was kind of a strict rule at the time. Once you went into the Ecclesiastics, that finished you hurling outside, you didn't play with a team outside.'

In spite of the rules that were supposed to restrain them, for some priests Gaelic games were a calling that was impossible to ignore. There are many cases of priests playing football or hurling under assumed names and against the instructions of their seminary masters or their bishop. In 1959 Fermanagh won the All-Ireland junior championship. On the team sheet that was published in the *Fermanagh Herald* was one Sean Maguire. For those who had been at the game and who knew the players, they would not have readily called Maguire to mind. He was in fact Fr Ignatius McQuillan. A teacher in Derry's St Columb's College, McQuillan played under an assumed name. McQuillan acknowledged later that his bishop, Bishop Farren who had thrown in the ball at Croke Park a year earlier, knew that he was playing under an assumed name but chose to ignore the issue. For

Students hurling in St Kieran's College, Kilkenny, *c*. 1952. The college remains one of the country's best-known hurling academies. At the time this photograph was taken, the majority of those attending the school were there on a full-time boarding basis. *(Bickew Collection, NUIG)*

The priest as player: Gaelic sports were a feature of recreational life at the Irish College in Rome. This photograph shows a seminarian during a puck around in the college in 1957. Five years later, in March 1962, when a group of Aer Lingus hurlers travelled to Rome to play a team drawn mostly from the Irish College, it was the first time since 1910 that a team from Ireland had travelled to play a match on the continent of Europe. (*Archives, Pontifical Irish College Rome*)

McQuillan his new name caused confusion. As more people became aware he was a priest, they were never sure whether he was Fr McQuillan or Fr Maguire. The error was compounded when he flew home from a holiday in France to play against Kerry in August 1960. The *Irish Independent* reported that 'Maguire' was flying in to play for Fermanagh. Such dedication, which was repeated across the country by various priests, at different levels, was central to the success of the GAA in the twentieth century and created an organic link between the Church, its community and the members and followers of the Association.

Although it was not until the 1920s that the relationship between the Association and the Catholic Church flourished, clerics had been centre stage in the GAA from the outset. In December 1884 Archbishop Croke sat in his study at the Bishop's Palace in Thurles and wrote a sensational letter to Michael Cusack, by way of return to Cusack's invitation to become patron of the newly formed GAA. Croke's letter is more a manifesto for cultural change and national independence than a mere acceptance slip. Although the GAA was established with the clear intention of redrawing the Irish sporting world, Croke did not insult games such as tennis and cricket, describing them instead as 'very excellent … health-giving exercises', in their own way. He merely pointed out that they were 'not racy of the soil'. At its crescendo, the letter lamented a form of Englishness characterised by 'effeminate follies' and 'degenerate dandies', and proclaimed that if Irish people did not set about reviving their own national pastimes, 'we had better, and at once, abjure our nationality, clap hands for joy at the sight of the

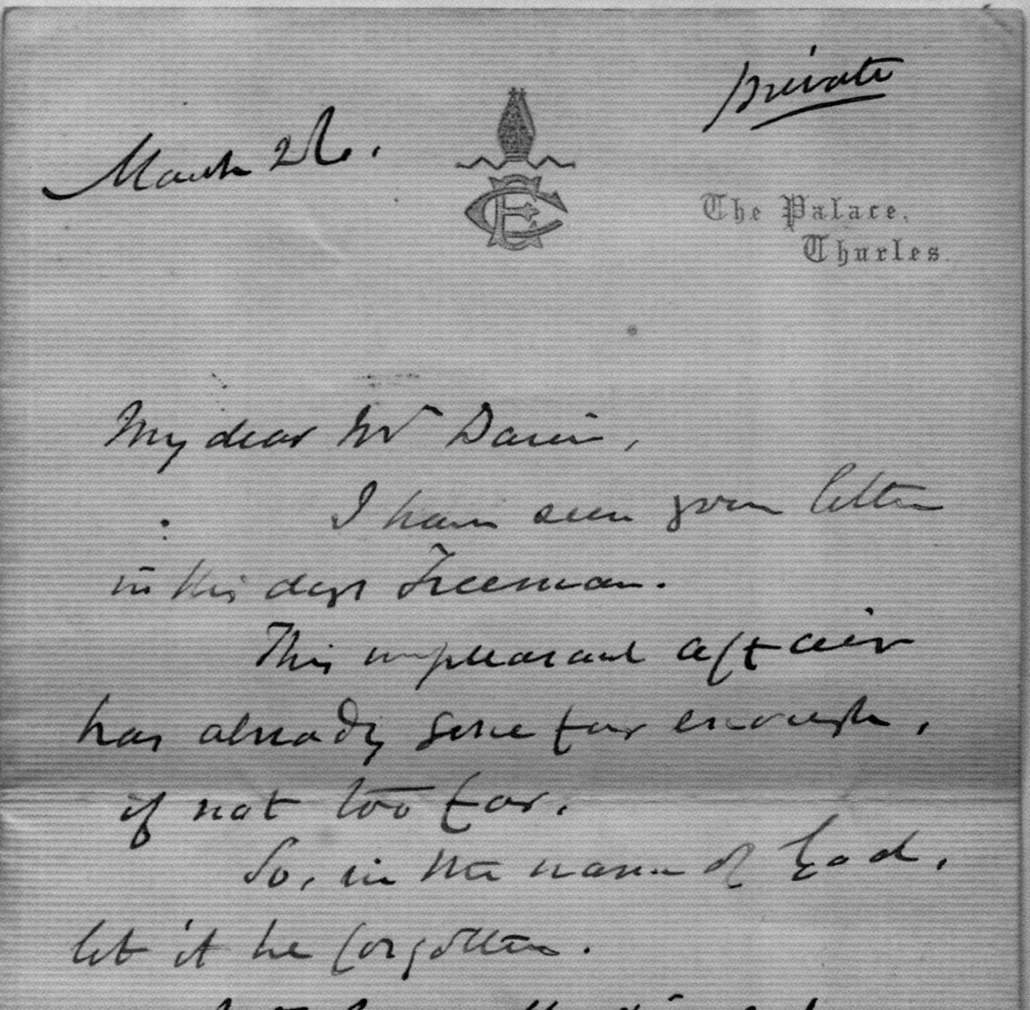

March 26.

The Palace,
Thurles.

My dear Mr Davin,

    I have seen your letter in this day's Freeman.

    This unpleasant affair has already gone far enough, if not too far.

    So, in the name of God, let it be forgotten.

    Mr Cusack did not weigh his words sufficiently: but we all know he would not deliberately insult me.

    Yrs faithfully

    + T.W. Croke.

Mr M Davin —

A major dispute arose in the GAA in early 1886 around intemperate remarks made by Michael Cusack about Archbishop Thomas Croke, Patron of the Association. In an effort to quell the dispute, Croke wrote to GAA President, Maurice Davin, suggesting that the controversy over Cusack's remarks was unnecessary.
(GAA Museum)

'A good deal of struggling and a great deal of confusion followed. The reporters had to jump up on the benches to save themselves. No blows were struck but some of the priests were hustled about and sticks were wielded ominously, and things looked extremely threatening.' –

Account from the *Freeman's Journal* of the 1887 Annual Convention, 9 November 1887, quoted in T. F. O'Sullivan, *Story of the GAA* (1916), p. 49.

Union Jack, and place "England's bloody red" exultantly above the green'. With this in mind, he called on nationalists to rally to the GAA.

Croke's support for the GAA should not be taken as evidence that the GAA and the Catholic Church enjoyed a harmonious relationship from the beginning, however. It should be remembered that Archbishop Croke was a singular figure within the Catholic Church in Victorian Ireland and his outspoken support for the GAA was a source of considerable disquiet amongst other members of the hierarchy, who believed the GAA was a mere front for republican separatists. For example, Croke became embroiled in a public spat with Bishop Coffey who had refused the GAA in Kerry his patronage for a GAA tournament in his diocese and who condemned the GAA as an association run by Fenians. This battle between Fenians and clerics for control of the GAA was so heated that it almost destroyed the organisation before it had properly established itself. In the course of that row there were numerous disputes, the most dramatic of which was at the GAA's Annual Convention in November 1887 when priests and IRB men wrestled each other for control of the top table. Sticks were brandished, punches thrown and an IRB man (thought to have been Anthony Mackey, granduncle of the future Limerick great, Mick Mackey) was reported to have roared, 'We'll pulverise the priests'. Even if events rarely got that heated, it remained the case that, before the establishment of the Irish Free State, the relationship between the Catholic Church and the GAA was strained by the prominent presence within the GAA of leading republicans. The clergy was caught in a bind between not wanting to facilitate an organisation that might be misused by republicans and not wanting to cede complete control of that organisation to those same republicans. Clerical involvement in the GAA reflected this uncertainty, falling and rising by place and by time.

Throughout its history the GAA has had high-profile members who were Protestant. The most obvious of these is Sam Maguire, after whom the trophy for the All-Ireland football championship is named. The GAA has made much of its Protestant members, but the reality is that Protestants have been greatly under-

Secret.

S. W. DIVISION.

Co. of _Kerry_

Tralee 22nd April 1895.

I beg to forward
the annexed extract on
the above subject, and
to state that Dr. Coffey's
pronouncement on the
Gaelic association, and
its Connexion with Secret
Societies. have caused
a good deal of uneasiness
to the heads of that org-
-anisation in this County.

the parents of a good
many young men. around
here. who are members of
the G. a. a. are most
anxious to have them
sever their Connexion
with that association
since Dr. Coffey's pronoun.
-cement on the matter.
the Dist. Inspector

Submitted
behoves have
thought the
published account
of the proceedings
at the Thurles
Convention in
1890 (I think)
1887
places the question
of the Connection
of this association
with Secret Societies
beyond doubt.

Saw the above
25.4.95

early relationship between the GAA and the Catholic Church was marked by a mixture of harmony
ord. This Crime Branch report details the repercussions arising from the refusal of Dr Coffey, Bisho
y, to give permission for a football tournament organised for Killarney on the grounds that the GAA
nected with secret societies. The allegation was refuted by, amongst others, Dr Croke who stated
Association was 'purely an athletic body and that alone' (CBS 9854/S, National Archives of Ireland)

The Palace.
Thurles.
Co. Tipperary

22nd April 1949

Mr. Patrick O'Keefe
General Secretary, G.A.A.
31 North Frederick Street,
Dublin.

My dear Mr. O'Keefe,

Once more on behalf of the Trustees of Maynooth College I offer you and the Gaelic Athletic Association our deep thanks for the magnificent subscription of £5,612 -12-0 from the Association to the Maynooth College Fund.

For my own part, words can hardly express how much I appreciate this most generous action of the Gaelic Athletic Association. The material value of the subscription to Maynooth College is very great; but even more precious in my eyes is the splendid indication which it affords of the happy union between the Hierarchy and clergy of Ireland and its manhood as represented by the Gaelic Athletic Association. That happy union is a most important factor in promoting both the interests of religion and the well-being of our Gaelic games.

May I say that I also deeply appreciate the gesture of the Gaelic Athletic Association in selecting me as the medium through which to make this subscription? It forges another link in the chain which has bound so closely the Association to the See of Cashel ever since Most Rev. Dr. Croke wrote that letter long recognised as the Association's charter, and it will be a further stimulus to me to strive to walk, however haltingly, in the footsteps of my illustrious predecessor.

With renewed expressions of thanks, and wishing you and the Gaelic Athletic Association every blessing,

I remain,
Yours very sincerely

+J. Kinnane
Archbishop of Cashel.

represented in the Association. In the north this has been the product of the bind between religion and political allegiance, and in the south it was the product of a range of different factors. Ostentatious involvement of the Catholic Church in GAA affairs was a partial explanation, but there were others, not least a divided education system.

Across Ireland, the schools which dominated hurling and Gaelic football were, for the most part, run by the Catholic Church: St Jarlath's in Tuam, St Kieran's in Kilkenny, St Mel's in Longford, North Mon in Cork, the Carmelite in Moate and the Sem in Killarney. By contrast, Gaelic games were not a significant presence in non-Catholic schools. And, as if to remind us that there is no neat explanation of the relationship between religion, education and sport in Ireland, the most prestigious schools run by Catholic priests gave their allegiance to rugby football and not to Gaelic games.

During the first decades of the GAA, the most famous school to pledge its allegiance to the Association was Patrick Pearse's school, St Enda's, which opened in 1908. It provided a bilingual education in Irish and English, lessons in Irish folklore and history and, in the context of sport, the embrace of hurling as the

The GAA both facilitated and participated in displays of popular piety. Almost thirty years after GAA volunteers helped with the organisation of the Eucharistic Congress in 1932, Croke Park was the venue for a massive celebration Mass to mark the Patrician year. The service, held on 25 June 1961, was attended by both the Taoiseach and the President of Ireland and was preceded by a procession into the ground of priests, bishops, archbishops and cardinals, as well as the Papal Legate and his officials. (*GAA Museum*)

Dominican College, Sion Hill, from Blackrock in Dublin celebrate after defeating Dominican College, Eccles Street, Dublin, in March 1930. (*Cumann Camógaíochta na nGael*)

ideal game for Irish boys. Pearse's execution after the 1916 Rising led to the school being closed down. It was reopened later in 1916 by a former pupil, Frank Burke, who remained true to Pearse's educational and sporting curriculum. Beyond St Enda's, numerous schools run by Christian Brothers in Ireland were devoted to Gaelic games. This was as true for primary schools as it was for secondary schools. Christian Brothers' schools, such as Marino and Artane, dominated the competitions run by Cumann na mBunscol, which was founded in 1928 in Dublin. These schools produced a remarkable conveyor belt of players who went on to star at every level of Gaelic games. The ritual of playing Gaelic games at school is the fondest school memory for many, though for others the insistence on play created a backlash, which damaged the Association.

More recently, the place of the religious in education has greatly diminished – schools are now dominated by lay teachers and the presence of Gaelic games in Irish schools has been transformed. Leading this transformation is a small army of full-time, part-time and voluntary coaches who have brought a programme of coaching and skills games to schoolchildren across Ireland. The importance of a teacher who is dedicated to promoting Gaelic games remains crucial, however. Teachers have traditionally played a key role in establishing the GAA in areas where it had little or no presence. Arriving as single young men, with the status and respectability of their profession, embracing the GAA presented an entry-point into the homes of the local community. The links between teachers and clubs are many and are found across the country. Mount Sion, in Waterford, began as a school club founded by two teachers, Brothers O'Connor and Malone. Sean O'Heslin, a teacher in Ballinamore, County Leitrim, led his local club to five senior county championships in the 1930s, and the club was eventually renamed after him. Tomás de Bhaldraithe, former President of the Irish National Teachers' Organisation, arrived in Freshford, Kilkenny, in 1948, as the new principal of the local school. He promoted hurling in the school, and by 1951 Freshford had won their first schools championship; something they repeated throughout the 1950s.

Traditionally, too, teachers lived in the area where they taught, allowing them to take sports training in the evenings after school, with both school teams and local teams. This vital link between the teacher and the GAA club has been eroded in recent years with improvements in transport and the increased distances people are willing to commute for work. However, the importance of a teacher positively disposed towards the GAA in a locality is a recurrent theme in oral testimonies about local GAA life. John Stephen O'Sullivan, a retired teacher himself, recalls that he 'went to a secondary school where football was not played and where the headmaster would have regarded football as an absolute waste of time, when we should be studying and therefore during that time I lost touch with football to a great extent'.

Just as in primary and secondary schools, the GAA has a long tradition in third-level education. For almost a century, university competitions have been a core part of the GAA calendar. The Sigerson Cup for Gaelic football (1911), the Fitzgibbon Cup for hurling (1912), the Ashbourne Cup for camogie (1915) were dominated for much of the twentieth century by the old universities. In 1987 a new trophy, the O'Connor Cup, was added for ladies' football. A remarkable change in Irish education since then has seen an explosion in the numbers of students who attend third-level education. This dramatically rebalanced third-level competitions, which have broadened to include institutes of technology and training colleges. With scholarships now on offer in many institutions, the profile of the GAA in the third-level sector has never been higher. There is little doubt that involvement in Gaelic games in third-level institutions is one of the ways that students adapt to a new life away from their home areas and clubs. Sharing a common interest with fellow students eases the process of integration into a wider and more diverse community.

All of this is part of the wider changes in Irish society, which have shifted the relationship between the GAA, the Church and the education system. Society has become more secularised and Church authority has weakened. This has, in part, been due to a series of scandals and revelations, not least the report of the Ryan Commission. As a result, the symbols of Catholicism have become a diminished presence on major GAA occasions. Echoes of the past live on, however.

A Gaelic football match at St Patrick's College, Carlow town, 1947. At the time the college served principally as a seminary. (*Irish Picture Library/Fr. F. M. Browne S. J. Collection*)

A revolution in Irish education occurred in the late 1960s. With the introduction of free secondary education, the numbers in secondary schools greatly increased. Irish education continued to be dominated by religious-run schools and while many espoused a GAA sporting ethos, others did not. This photograph shows supporters from Carmelite College, Moate, at a schools match in the mid-1970s. (*Westmeath Examiner*)

A musician entertains crowds as they make their way home from a hurling match at Croke Park, 1964. Busking remains a tradition around GAA grounds across the country.
(*Magnum*)

9

Music, Parades
and Culture

'Spotless in the midst of the speckled.' –

This was how Michael Cusack described Maurice Davin, the
greatest Irish athlete of his generation, in a column written
for the *United Ireland* newspaper a week before the two men
combined to found the Gaelic Athletic Association. It was
envisaged from the start that the Association would be more
than a sporting organisation and that it would include a
strong social and cultural aspect.

'At the close of the day the band of the local branch
of the Gaelic Athletic Association turned out and played some popular airs.
After about 15 minutes they returned, and were in the act of playing
the final tune opposite their bandroom before dispersing, when,
without one word of warning, they were set upon by a body of police, who knocked
down the leader of the band, rushed their members about,
and caused non-instruments about the streets.'

'If Gaels cannot play football in the
Torrid Zone, they can march in the cool
of the evening, in their hundreds, with bands playing and banners flying,
like a well drilled and well disciplined regiment of soldiers.

On the first Sunday in June 1964, GAA followers in Cavan were faced with an almighty dilemma. As the local paper – the *Anglo-Celt* – reported, Cavan Gaels had to choose between the opening of the new pitch at Cornafean, where they could watch Cavan play Galway in a senior football challenge, or else they could head for the Tanagh Field Day in the grounds of the Sacred Heart College at Dartrey, Cootehill. For all that the paper devoted extensive coverage to the Cavan senior footballers, it favoured the Tanagh Field Day as the better day out, one which promised 'music, song, dancing and a bumper list of athletic contests'. The bands included the Emerald Girls' Pipe Band – renowned as the world champion Ladies' Pipe Band and for having led the St Patrick's Day parade in New York on two separate occasions – and the De La Salle Boys' Band from Dundalk. There were also the All-Ireland band competitions which, the reporter opined, you could only fail to enjoy and feel your chest swell if you were 'stone deaf'. There was a full singing and dancing competition schedule (over twenty events), and athletics and cycling contests. The whole day was to conclude with a tug-o'-war event, while to ensure that patrons made it that far, a range of catering and refreshment facilities was provided (with proceeds going to the Mission funds).

While the event was not one organised by the GAA, the roots of athletics, and the All-Ireland model of competition for music and dancing, lay with the Association. Indeed, in the first years of the GAA, the events of the Tanagh Field Day would have been fused with those of the pitch-opening at Cornafean. From the very beginning the GAA offered Irish people a day out with a difference – a unique cocktail of sport and drink and music and pageantry, which mixed the local with the national. Bands and their music became central to GAA tournaments,

A conductor leads the choir at the opening ceremony of the Tailteann Games in the 1920s. In the early years of the Association, music and pageantry were an integral part of GAA events, with marching bands helping to lead crowds to the grounds where the games were played. (*Irish Independent Collection, National Library of Ireland*)

'If Gaels cannot play football in the Torrid Zone, they can march in the cool of the evening, in their hundreds, with bands playing and banners flying, like a well drilled and well disciplined regiment of soldiers. The discipline of the football field, the soldier-like costumes, the firmness of tread and elasticity of frame, the consciousness that they are discharging a national duty when aiding in averting the physical deterioration of our race, and the elevating character of the musical entertainments of the disciples of Robert Emmet are having a marked effect on most of the members of this branch of the Gaelic Athletic Association. There is a robustness about most of their proceedings surrounded by a halo of nationality.' – *The Celtic Times*, 25 June 1887.

and advertisements for tournaments almost always listed the names of the bands that would be attending. At GAA matches in the 1880s patriotic songs such as 'God Save Ireland', 'The Wearing of the Green', and 'O'Donnell aboo', were supplemented by popular tunes like 'When the Room's Going Round About 'Tis Time to Gang Way'. But some of the bands who attended stepped beyond the expected and even included in their programme some operatic selections. Observers (somewhat wishfully) believed the music added up to the perfect way to promote feelings of friendship and good fellowship amongst the players, while offering delightful entertainment to spectators between contests.

The band which became most associated with the GAA was the Artane Boys' Band. Formed in 1872, it drew its members from the boys of the Artane industrial school on the northside of Dublin. The Artane Boys' Band gave its first performance at a GAA tournament on 14 June 1886. It became such an integral part of major GAA events that it was even sent to New York in 1947 to play before the Cavan–Kerry final of that year. The Artane Boys' Band was the public face of the Artane school, a place where sexual abuse of, and violence towards, boys by Christian Brothers was a chronic problem over many decades. From the late 1960s, the band began recruiting from beyond the industrial school. Later it changed its rules to allow girls to join, resulting in changing its name to simply the Artane Band.

Across the country, meanwhile, brass, pipe and marching bands provided the soundtrack of the GAA. Whether marching from train stations or from some changing-point in town, the GAA parade immediately established itself as a raucous Pied Piper, drawing spectators towards the field of play. In the beginning, it was crucial to developing a sense of occasion in every town where a GAA match was staged. For example, when the Kanturk Brass Band led 'the great

A ticket for a Gaelic Ball organised by Armagh Harps GAA Club, December 1890. Many GAA clubs in Ireland and abroad ran dances as social events and fund-raisers. (*Gaelic Games in Armagh CD, Cardinal Ó Fiaich Memorial Library*)

Soundtrack to the GAA: a brass band leads the Tipperary hurling team through the streets of Nenagh on their return from a tour of the United States in 1926. Music accompanied the team wherever they went. On their departure from and return to Cobh, they were met by the Cork Volunteers Pipers' Band. When the players finally made it back to their home county after two months' travelling, another band struck up the airs of 'Gallant Tipperary' and 'Star-Spangled Banner', together with a series of Irish national airs. (*GAA Oral History Project Archive*)

Across the generations, bonfires and lit sods of turf have greeted victorious teams returning to their home place. Some teams returned on trains, some in cars, while others marched on foot through the streets of their villages and towns. This photograph shows Kerry footballer Mick O'Dwyer, the Sam Maguire trophy strapped to the roof of his car, making his way to Valentia after winning the All-Ireland title in 1959. (*Kennelly Archive*)

'At the close of the day the band of the local branch of the Gaelic Athletic Association turned out and played some popular airs. After about 15 minutes they returned, and were in the act of playing the final tune opposite their bandroom before dispersing, when, without one word of warning, they were set upon by a party of police, who knocked down the leader of the band, pushed its other members about, and kicked their instruments about the street. This unjustifiable violence they followed up by attacking the crowd more savagely, sparing neither sex nor age, and inflicting very serious injury on several persons.' – **James Carew MP informs the House of Commons of an incident at a GAA tournament in Naas, County Kildare, quoted in** *Hansard*, **22 December 1888, vol. 332, cc 1010-43.**

and eager throng' down the Main Street of Charleville, County Cork, and out to a field on the edge of town in the spring of 1887, it was a clarion call: 'Over the hedges and across the fields from all directions, the people poured.' In time, of course, the parade no longer led players through the towns, instead it was reinvented inside stadiums to pull players around the sidelines in front of cheering spectators and to provide the half-time entertainment.

Parading was, by the time the GAA was founded, a long-established feature of Irish life. And, just as the GAA used parades to draw people to its games, so it, in turn, began to be represented at a wide range of political, religious and cultural parades. GAA members marched in the great political funerals of the late nineteenth and early twentieth centuries for nationalist icons such as Parnell and O'Donovan Rossa. Members also paraded in the centenary celebrations for 1798 and in the various anniversary parades that took place over the years to mark the 1916 Rising. The GAA has been represented in St Patrick's Day parades in Ireland and across the world. Its representatives have marched down 5th Avenue in New York and through the streets of Dublin; and every town in Ireland has witnessed the sight of local club players riding down the main street on the back of a lorry or tractor.

Of course, the most joyous of all GAA parades is the homecoming revelry. Perhaps the most remarkable feature of these homecoming celebrations is the endurance of the tradition of lighting bonfires to welcome home conquering teams. The lighting of bonfires is a tradition steeped in Irish history, dating back, at least in myth, to St Patrick's lighting of a fire on the Hill of Slane. Throughout much of Irish history and particularly during the land agitation of

Brickey GAA Club joins the St Patrick's Day parade through the streets of Dungarvan, County Waterford, 1977. GAA clubs have a long association with St Patrick's Day celebrations across the world. In 2009, to mark its 125th anniversary, the Association led the St Patrick's Day parade in Dublin. (*Waterford County Images*)

A parade through Drogheda town prior to the Under-14 Street League final between Marsh Road and Bóthar Brugha, 1954. The tradition of parading teams through the streets continues as part of the annual Féile na nGael and Féile Peile na nÓg competitions. (*Richard Gerrard*)

'The GAA is supposed to be Irish, well the members of it play Gaelic football and hurling. But that is all they know about the GAA. When they go home from a match they go off to a dance or perhaps their own club is running a dance to clear their expenses. What's Gaelic about that, after winning their way through all the matches during the year, what honour is that when they organise and support foreign dancing which brings them back to a lower degree than when they started.' – **Letter to the Editor of the** *Meath Chronicle*, **14 January 1939**.

the nineteenth century, the lighting of bonfires at prominent points on the landscape was used to send messages of warning and celebration across vast tracts of countryside, as well as conveying a community's symbolic power and control over a certain territory. The use of bonfires by celebrating GAA communities, then, can be viewed as their way of spreading news of their success to everyone in the parish, while also sending a visual representation of their strength and prowess on the field to their neighbouring, vanquished rivals. Today, much of this symbolic meaning is forgotten, but the bonfire-lighting culture survives as one of the most important homecoming traditions.

The GAA has also used parades to make a cultural point. During the Irish Language Week parade in 1910, a selection of GAA hurling and football teams marched behind the Glencullen Brass and Reed band and the Athlone Pipe Band, carrying placards proclaiming 'The GAA wants no soldiers or shoneens', and 'Irishmen be Irish – Play your own games'. The Irish language had held a prominent place in the GAA from the very beginning. Michael Cusack was a passionate promoter of Irish and he regarded English as an acquired language. Cusack had joined the Society for the Preservation of the Irish Language in 1882 and later became honorary treasurer of the Gaelic Union. Meetings of the Union were held in his home on Gardiner Place in Dublin before he had even established the GAA. At GAA meetings Cusack, despite the lack of comprehension from many of his fellow committee men, insisted on frequently using Irish. He argued simply that a nation without its own language was not a nation at all. For Cusack, the promotion of the Irish language was at least as important as the preservation and promotion of native sports. He agreed with Douglas Hyde, the founder of the Gaelic League, who warned in 1892, that unless the forces of British cultural imperialism were challenged, 'we shall find ourselves toiling painfully behind the English at each step following the same fashions, only six months behind the

'There appears to be a general apathy in the GAA towards An Ghaeilge, which gives me cause for concern given the influence the Association has. The lip service high officials afford to the language is akin to that of a politician promising the world to gain votes.' – **Letter to the *Irish News*, 4 January 2008.**

English ones'. In that same lecture – 'The necessity for de-Anglicising Ireland' – Hyde had lauded the work being done by the GAA. Cusack, for his part, returned the favour by contributing in Irish to Gaelic League meetings. The GAA subsequently worked closely with successive Irish language organisations, including Foras na Gaeilge, Gael Linn and others. The close relationship between the Association and the language (at least at official level) has been evidenced by the joint publication of *An Camán* with the Gaelic League, by Pádraig Ó Caoimh's passionate promotion of Irish during his period as general secretary, by Seán Ó Síocháin's role as a trustee of Gael Linn and by Liam Ó Maolmhichíl's position as chairman of Foras na Gaeilge.

Finding ways to increase the use of Irish at GAA events – on and off the field – has been problematic for the Association from the very start. Every generation has produced its own booklet of Irish terms for use on the field but, for all their merit, the impact has been minimal. Beyond the annual playing of Comórtas Peile na Gaeltachta – played between GAA teams from Gaeltacht areas – Irish is not in widespread use on the playing fields of the GAA. Various rules in the GAA's *Official Guide* stipulate the use of Irish in correspondence and official documents (and these have traditionally been a rich source of successful objections by teams who have sought to reverse defeats by exploiting technicalities). For many, however, the presence of Irish has simply been distilled into the opening lines of the speech made by almost every GAA captain who is presented with a trophy: '*Tá an-athás orm an corn seo a ghlacadh* . . .' Although the tokenism of that phrase can grate, its presence at least acknowledges a relationship between the GAA and the Irish language. And, of course, when speeches such as those by Joe Connolly on receiving the Liam McCarthy in 1980 and Dara Ó Cinnéide on receiving the Sam Maguire in 2004 are spoken wholly in Irish, it elevates them beyond the ordinary.

Through its Irish Language Officers, its Coiste Náisiúnta na Gaeilge and through funds raised for Irish language bodies by the Oireachtas tournament, to mention a few initiatives, the GAA has sought to offer practical support for Irish language

P.a. on G.A.A. file.

THE G.A.A AND THE LANGUAGE.

Dr.Douglas Hyde in an address at Limerick on June 6th 1909 said

"I always thought that one of the influences that actuated Michael Cusack was the feeling that when he was promoting Irish games, he was promoting the spirit of Irish Nationality; and I may say that, second to the Gaelic League itself, the work of the Gaelic Athletic Assiciation in keeping alive that most vital and important feature in the life of the nation - its sports, its pastimes - has tended more than anything else to keep alive the fact that we are in Ireland and part of Ireland".

In 1910 Captain Otway Cuffe, Kilkenny, presented a silver shield, weighing 56 lbs. to be competed for between six of the leading hurling teams in the country, for the benefit of the Irish College at Ring. The final match, won by Tipperary, was held at Jones' Road, Dublin on April, 9, 1911, and the gate receipts, £230, were handed over to the College.

In a letter to the G.A.A. in June, 1912 Dr.Hyde wrote "One society is improving the intellect; the other the physique of Ireland. Neither of them is complete without the other. The Gaelic League recognised this from the first. Has the Gaelic Athletic Association recognised it equally? Well-developed Irish brains in well-developed bodies is the true ideal of the Gaelic League. Well-developed bodies with well-developed Irish brains ought to be the ideal of the Gaelic Athletic Association".

A newspaper article in 1927 referring to the objects for which the G.A.A. was founded stated

A Department of An Taoiseach memorandum from the 1930s on the relationship between the GAA and the Irish language. As the extracts used in the memorandum make clear, Douglas Hyde believed that the objectives of the GAA and the Gaelic League, the movement he helped found, were largely complementary. In 1938, however, Hyde would fall foul of the GAA – he was removed as Patron when, as President of Ireland, he attended an international soccer match in defiance of the Association's ban on foreign games.

mion-Caint báipe

(Phrases of the Game)

Compiled by an t-ataip u. mac Domnaill)

Ʒaċ aoinne cun a áit ḟein.
Goh-eenga　　cun a ought hain.
Every man　to his own place.

Mirneaċ, a ḃuacailly!
Mish-nock, a woo-kalee !
Play up,　　　boys !

Dioíḃ i ʒcóir.　　ḃḟuil riḃ ʒo léir i ʒcóir.
Bee gee igore.　　Will shiv gu lair igore.
Get ready.　　Are you all ready.

Támuiḋ.　　Tarraing uirri a Ṡeaʒain.
Thawmweed.　Tharring erry a hyawn.
Yes.　　　Draw on it Jack.

Duaile ap a ḋtalaṁ í.　　Tóʒ ruar í.
Booil er a dholov ee.　　Thogue soos ee.
Hit it on the ground.　　Take it up.

ná bí a tóʒaint i ʒcoṁnuiḋe.
Naw bee awe thogant goonee.
Don't be always lifting it.

The GAA regularly published lists of Irish language expressions and terms, which it hoped would encourage the everyday use of Irish in the conduct of GAA affairs. This extract is taken from a rulebook published for the Dublin Schools League in 1917, a competition open to minor, juvenile and schools teams in the city and county. The rules stated that it was 'compulsory' for all teams and clubs to assist in the spread of the language. The league organisers retained the power to withhold trophies from teams whose members 'did not show a knowledge of the Irish language'. (*GAA Oral History Project Archive*)

'Cé mhéid Gaeilge a bheadh á úsáid sa tír seo muna mbeadh sé mar aidhm, mar atá, ag Cumann Lúth-Chleas Gael an Ghaeilge a úsáid agus a choimeád. Éinne a bhí mar rúnaí ar aon chumann den Chumann Lúth-Chleas Gael chíodh sé an méid úsáide a bhí ann den Ghaeilge, fiú amháin liostaí na n-ainmneacha do gach cluiche, an áit ina rugadh agus a tógadh na himritheoirí, dáta breithe agus mar sin de. Tá ár mbuíochas tuillte acu gur lean siad den Ghaelachas agus den Ghaeilge a choimeád agus a úsáid.'
– Denis Lyons, speaking in Dáil Éireann, *Dáil Debates*, 22 November 1984, p. 535.

activities. If the impact of these initiatives could be measured through the number of new speakers brought to the language, the record is not one of success. There are those within the GAA whose love of Irish is as central to their lives as is their love of hurling and football. However, the sincerity of their pro-language initiatives is smothered by the disinterest of much of the wider membership. Ultimately, the problem with spreading the use of Irish within the GAA replicates the problem experienced in wider society: sporadic enthusiasm, which is undercut by popular disinterest.

As well as including a commitment to promote the Irish language, the GAA's *Official Guide* also carries a commitment to foster Irish music and song and other aspects of Irish culture. As early as 1887 suggestions were put forward for the establishment of an annual competition for 'jig and reel dancing, recitations, essays and poems in Gaelic, songs in Irish, words set to old melodies, playing on the pipe and harp, etc'. Eighty years later this suggestion was recast in the formal creation of a cultural competition – Scór – in 1969. The birth of Scór offered a practical platform for clubs to promote Irish culture in a meaningful and enjoyable manner. A key attraction is that it brings people into clubs who are not necessarily interested in the sporting side of the GAA. Scór is organised on the same All-Ireland lines as the Association's sporting competitions with clubs competing in categories such as céilí dancing, ballad singing, recitation, storytelling, novelty acts and question time. Beginning at club level, Scór works through a series of county and provincial championships until a national final is held in early summer.

Scór does not have a prominent presence in many clubs, however. Several counties do not enter the annual event, while others, especially the Ulster counties, are strong in their commitment. The importance of Scór, for those who do compete, is obvious and is reflected in the seriousness with which the competition is embraced. In 1995, for example, the Corofin club became the first ever Galway

The introduction of the Scór talent competition in 1969 coincided with the recasting of the GAA as a community development organisation. Clubs developed new social centres and broadened the range of activities available to members. Scór reached out to retired players, but it also made GAA clubs attractive to those with little interest in playing the games. This photograph shows members of a Leitrim ballad group which competed at the Scór finals in 1971. The group members are (l-r): Geraldine Dooner, Eileen Crossan, Marian Canning, Brid Duignan and Áine McGirl. (*Leitrim County Library*)

winners of the All-Ireland Scór set-dancing competition, considered by many to be the blue riband event. Recalling the moment when the first place for Corofin was announced, the report in the *Tuam Herald* noted: 'Corofin had won on merit. Their moment of glory had come at last, and they were immediately surrounded by hundreds of supporters not only from Corofin or Galway but from the entire

'The adjudicators probably are influenced by the reaction of the audience, and the reaction of the audience would probably be louder for something that has popular appeal but mightn't be of great quality, whereas something which appeals to someone's quieter emotions wouldn't get the same reaction from the adjudicators.' – John Stephen O'Sullivan, a member of Rathmore GAA Club in Kerry, a participant and former secretary of his club's Scór committee, GAA Oral History Project Archive, 2008.

Scene:	Road outside pub.
Characters:	2 men – Paddy native, Michael returned emigrant.
	2 girls – one inside bar, another passerby.
	Two men talking outside pub, girl inside washing glasses.
Paddy:	How are you, Michael? Welcome home.
Michael:	Thanks Paddy. How are you keeping. Did you get married yet?
Paddy:	Oh! The devel a marr. What about yourself?
Michael:	No fear Paddy, I don't believe in it.
Paddy:	Why don't you believe in marriage, Michael? Sure a fine looking fellow like yourself must have plenty girls.
Michael:	I have plenty girls alright, but why marry one when you can have them all.
Paddy:	I don't know about that. I was never much good to chat the girls. You could get around them alright – I'm kind of shy.
Michael:	I'll tell you what there is a girl coming up the road now – watch me in action and you will see how its done.
Paddy:	If you can make a date with this one, you are a good one alright.

Extract from Scór script, *The Emigrant Returns*, by Benny O'Connell, *c.* 1980s, GAA Oral History Project Archive.

province, who were delighted with their success.' Such glory, a driving force that sits alongside the joy of taking part, is familiar to Scór competitors, young and old, at all levels of competition, whether in the local club or on the national stage.

Far beyond the confines of Scór, music has a prominent place at many GAA gatherings. Some of this is formally arranged: the singing of the national anthem before important matches, the music of the parade and the half-time recital. Much more of it is informal: banjo players busking on the streets leading to grounds, songs sung in pubs before and after matches. Many of the verses and airs have their roots in the song-collecting renaissance of the late nineteenth and early twentieth centuries. Central to this are the county songs – the 'national anthems' belted out by partisans of one county or another. Some of these tunes may be of questionable artistic merit, but this has done nothing to undermine their anthemic attraction to those who sing them. These songs rarely refer to the GAA, rather they are ballads which are a public announcement of place through song and which unite people from across the county, proclaiming the shared ties that bind them to their home place. County songs usually reference key landmarks in the geography of a county, not least 'Slievenamon' in Tipperary and 'The Banks of My Own Lovely Lee' from Cork.

Other songs, which detail events from the GAA's history, have been passed

The informal musical culture of GAA life: the Dunne brothers from Limerick, one of whom was blind, were familiar faces at social events in the southwest of Ireland in the 1950s. They busked at fairs, markets and matches. This photograph shows them playing for spectators attending a hurling match in Clare. (*Dorothea Lange Collection, the Oakland Museum of California, City of Oakland. Gift of Paul S. Taylor*)

A dance organised by the Offaly Association in Dublin in the early 1990s. After the Second World War, county associations offered a social network for country people based in Dublin and in cities across Britain and the United States. Social events were often rooted in the calendar of GAA fixtures. (*GAA Oral History Project Archive*)

'Here's to the boys of Lios na Caolbhaí –
No bolder or better in Ireland were seen,
For wrestling or goaling or taking a spree
There's no match for the brave boys of Lios na Caolbhaí.' –

An extract from the anonymously penned ballad 'The Kickers of Lios na Caolbhaí', which describes a game of football played between two teams on the Dingle Peninsula in 1888.

from generation to generation. Great teams and matches, whether local or national, have been commemorated in verse. Many of these songs, such as 'The Kickers of Lios Na Caolbhaí', survive from the early decades of the GAA (and some even pre-date the GAA), and locate themselves in an emergent sporting culture that resisted the dominance (both political and cultural) of Britishness. These historical songs are also valuable in demonstrating how parish and county rivalries emerged. The recording of such rivalries inscribes them with significant meaning, and the repetition of the song recreates not only the historical moment, but also the rivalry, which continues to the present.

Other songs recall the great players, such as 'The Gallant John Joe', which commemorates the life and achievements of Cavan legend John Joe O'Reilly. One of the most famous GAA songs is about an event that never happened. The Cork group Galleon produced a vinyl single in the weeks before the 1982 All-Ireland football final which celebrated Kerry's five-in-a-row of All-Ireland victories. A late Offaly goal denied the Kerry men their historic moment and denied Galleon the

'And I dreamt I'd hold the medal
So precious in my hand
With all the people round me
And the ghosts up in the stand
Then on Monday evening
We'd bring the cup back home
The bonfires would be blazing
All along the road

'Maroon and White Forever', a song by The Folk Footballers, released in a 1998 album, *The First Fifteen*.

The coffin of the celebrated Cavan footballer John Joe O'Reilly is carried to his final resting place in Killeshandra, 1952. An army officer, O'Reilly played for Cavan from 1937 until his death in 1952. He was thirty-four years of age. For many who never saw him play, John Joe O'Reilly lives on as a presence celebrated in song. (*Cavan County Museum*)

truth of their song. In addition to those songs generated and sustained by the followers of the GAA, there are also a range of songs produced commercially. Bands such as The Saw Doctors have a number of songs that refer to the GAA in their repertoire, and a related group, The Folk Footballers, produced a whole album about Galway football, *The First Fifteen*, to coincide with the county's appearance in the All-Ireland final of 1998. This was one more old tradition reinvented for a new era.

His record's a proud one without blemish or stain
Since he played his first football with famed Cornafean
Till he's laid in his cold grave where the wild flowers grow
A true son of Breifne is the gallant John Joe.

He led Cavan to victory on that memorable day
In the final against Kerry in New York far away
The next year in Croke Park when our boys beat Mayo
Once again they were led by the gallant John Joe.

In each corner of Breifne there's sorrow and pain
Such a true-hearted sportsman we'll ne'er see again
New players may come and old players may go
But we'll ne'er have another like the gallant John Joe.

– An extract from 'The Gallant John Joe', by Tommy Gilronan.

A sliotar-maker at work in the early 1950s. This photograph was taken by George Pickow, an American photographer who came to Ireland with his wife, the singer, musician and folklorist Jean Ritchie, in 1952. Over the course of eighteen months, Pickow compiled a series of photographic features on aspects of Irish life, including the traditional crafts of sliotar- and hurley-making. (*Pickow Collection, NUIG*)

10

Hats, Flags and Rosettes

'They went down to the beach and collected roots of seaweed and shaped them into a ball.'

Caitlín Ní Giolla Bhríde, Gaoth Dobhair, describes how her neighbours made handballs in Pat Holland, *100 Years of Handball: Handball, Donegal and the World* (2004).

'The manly out-door sports of the future will be
largely confined to the hurling field and to the football field, if we are
not content to run after bits of paper, instead of
stretching our legs after a greyhound. Men of all
classes must turn to the hurling field.

We played hurling twice a day at school.
The Master would pick two teams. Hurleys were heavy and if it broke
you had to mend it and band it. The ball was generally
homemade and very heavy. The core was made of twine tightly bound. The out
side was made of pure leather by cutting out two pieces in the shape
of the figure eight and sewing it together with hemp.

When Kildare reached the 1998 All-Ireland football final, whole sections of Croke Park looked as though they were covered in blankets of snow. Men and women of all ages sat resplendent in their Lilywhite jerseys. On the terraces, too, the brilliance of the white jersey eclipsed the maroon worn by the Galway supporters. It was a most striking image, confirmation that the style in the stands at GAA matches had changed dramatically through the 1990s. Where once men and women wore their Sunday best, people of all ages now sported replica county jerseys. Alongside the county jerseys, a new range of leisurewear was developed: fleeces, raingear, polo shirts, T-shirts. From the start of the 1990s, wearing county colours to social events was the clearest statement of where you were from. In the new millennium, from teenagers at the Oxegen music festival to holidaymakers in the south of Spain, the county jersey has become ubiquitous.

This level of commercial activity in the sale of sports clothing places GAA supporters in the same domain as followers of English soccer, American football or, at the global level, the Olympic Games. For counties, sponsorship of jerseys and deals with jersey-makers has netted tens of thousands of euro every year. The growth in media exposure has lent momentum to this process. And, as with much else, what happened first for counties was then adopted by clubs who understand the potential to derive revenue. Club jerseys are now commonplace in towns and villages across Ireland. Dedicated websites selling a range of T-shirts, bearing slogans such as 'Hendrix was a hurler' and 'On the sod', find a ready market. The wearing of replica jerseys has spun out, in turn, to the sale of retro jerseys. Websites sell jerseys recreated from past eras – the Dublin jersey of the 1920s, Kilkenny in the 1930s and many more.

Armagh supporters display their allegiance on All-Ireland football final day, 1953. On big match days, GAA grounds become a riot of colour as spectators turn out with hats, scarves and flags of their clubs and counties. However, it is only with the casualisation of fashion in recent decades that replica jerseys have become a popular form of dress among supporters. In 1953, as can be seen here, the crowd were more formally attired, dressed in their Sunday best. The match, played between Armagh and Kerry, attracted a record crowd to Croke Park at the time. A total of 85,155 people squeezed into the stadium, with thousands more turned away at the turnstiles. (*Fáilte Ireland*)

'The manly out-door sports of the future will be largely confined to the hurling field and to the football field, if we are not content to run after bits of paper, instead of stretching our legs after a greyhound. Men of all classes must turn to the hurling-field. Although we are generally believed to be a drinking people, our passion for fun and manly sports is infinitely stronger than our passion for alcoholic liquors. The money hitherto spent in the public house may now be spent in purchasing a national hurling uniform.' – *The Celtic Times*, 26 November 1887.

The range of GAA ephemera and collectables on sale reflects the rich material culture of the Association. Jerseys, initially, were not worn by many teams, with the players taking to the field wearing their everyday clothes and with only sashes or hats to distinguish them from their opponents. This quickly changed. The passion in the Victorian era for distinctive sporting clothing was almost immediately adopted by GAA teams. Kilmoyley in Kerry is a case in point. In their first county final, played against Kenmare (then known as The O'Connells) in 1889, the Kilmoyley players wore saffron jerseys, long pants and multicoloured woollen caps knitted by wives, girlfriends and other female supporters. Early GAA jerseys were usually cut in the same style as the rugby jerseys of the period. It also took several decades for clubs and counties to adopt standard colours. For example, the Thurles team that represented Tipperary in the 1887 All-Ireland hurling final wore a green jersey with a galaxy of stars woven as a crest. In the twentieth century, however, blue became the colour of the Thurles team.

Long before a merchandising market bloomed in the purchase of replica jerseys, the sight of hawkers selling 'hats, flags and rosettes' outside GAA grounds was a familiar one.

'Their attire was as characteristic as their appearance. Their "reefers", cutaways, Ulster and Inverness capes were of the soft, warm national frieze. Most of them wore knee-breeches and all carried blackthorns or furze sticks that would more than prove a match for the hickory or locust of "one of the finest". Mr John Cullinane, their advance representative, sported a small blackthorn tree which, to use his own words, was "historical, as it worked through the Mitchelstown riot".' – **Description of the 'American Invasion' athletes from the** *New York Herald*, October 1888.

Wexford supporters buy their hats and rosettes on the walk to Croke Park on All-Ireland hurling final day, 1965. Today, as in the past, hawkers selling their wares are a familiar sight on the roads leading to GAA grounds on match days. (*Fáilte Ireland*)

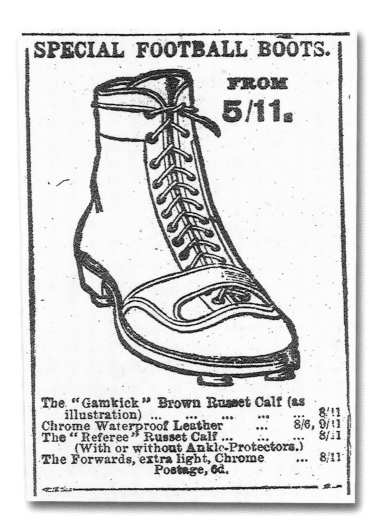

An advertisement for football boots published in the *Carlow Sentinel*, 1908. The practice of wearing specialist footwear developed gradually over time: when the first All-Ireland hurling final was played in April 1888, both teams – Thurles and Meelick – lined out in bare feet. (*Carlow County Library*)

Many supporters bought, and countless others made, rosettes and crêpe-paper hats in their county colours. Hugh and Sarah Coughlan from Tallow spent their spare time making paper hats in the 1940s and 1950s to sell to Waterford hurling fans. They recalled that their time was filled with the 'making and selling of the blue and white of Waterford . . . Crêpe paper hats and the blue running down your jaw if it rained, no refunds mind you'. In time the paper hat gave way to the oversized sombrero. All the while, that most distinctively Irish of sporting phenomena – the woollen headband – grew in popularity. Its presence was not limited to foreheads, but was also wrapped around wrists, hung from necks, and tied to car mirrors and travel bags.

The development of the GAA's activities, and the sheer number of people involved, created a growing market for sporting goods. The need for the players of the GAA to access equipment for their games ushered in a trade in sporting goods that kept many a sports supplier in business. Newspaper adverts for various pieces of equipment began appearing regularly from the 1880s. By the 1920s these were an almost daily occurrence. Naturally, prices and styles changed over the years. In 1923, the 'Celt', an Irish made football boot – all leather with six studs – was available for six shillings and sixpence, while jerseys, in either green and amber, green and white, or black and amber, could be had for two shillings and sixpence apiece. The design of the jerseys featured lacing at the neck and was longer than we would be familiar with today. Shorts, or what were then referred to as 'football knickers', were one shilling and eleven pence, and a match ball with a solid leather cover and a Moseley rubber bladder could be bought for anything from nine shillings all the way up to twenty-three shillings. In time, of course, design changed dramatically – heavy cotton shirts have been replaced by lightweight synthetics, and heavy leather boots that went up the ankle have been substituted for low-cut, lighter boots modelled on the advances made in boot technology in the soccer world. Soccer boots, made by European and American multinational bootmakers eventually overwhelmed any prospect of native Irish bootmakers thriving. The 'Celt' did not survive, nor did other Irish boots such as the Blackthorn and the Gola.

The archaeology of Ireland includes old hurleys and horsehair hurling balls, dating back through the centuries, having been preserved in bogs. In the early years of the GAA the equipment used by hurlers emphasised the sense that hurling was a sport caught between old traditions and new developments. 'Sceilg' (politician and author John J. O'Kelly) recalled that on Valentia Island, the hurls would be cut from furze stumps or whatever wood was available in the nearest ditch. By contrast, in Dublin, the journalist and hurler P. P. Sutton wrote of his beautifully

An advertisement for the Kerry Knitting Company, included as part of the programme for the Kerry v. Wexford All-Ireland football final in 1913. GAA newspapers and programmes were filled with advertisements for Irish-made prizes, sportswear and general athletic equipment. In January 1912 *The Gaelic Athlete* newspaper argued that, as members of a national organisation, it was incumbent on Gaels 'to support the products of their own land, and thereby increase the prosperity of their own country'. (*GAA Museum*)

A group of boys stand ready to collect a batch of newly made hurleys, 1958. The need to ensure a reliable and cheap supply of hurleys was an ongoing challenge for GAA administrators and encouraged, in later years, efforts to develop an alternative hurley from man-made materials. (*Frank O'Brien/The Kerryman*)

'When the cows are casting their hair, they pull it off their backs and, with their hands, work it into large balls which will grow very hard. This ball they use at the hurlings, which they strike with a stick called comman, about three and a half feet long in the handle. At the lower end it is crooked and about three inches broad and upon this broad part you may sometimes see the gamesters carry the ball, tossing it forty or fifty yards despite all the adverse players.' – John Dunton, *Teague Land or A Merry Ramble to the Wild Irish* (1698), p. 3.

grained, nicely varnished, corded-handled hurleys. Sutton also had access to shops selling sliotars, while Sceilg recalled they used to make their sliotars from cattle hair rolled hard into a ball and steeped in gutta percha. He also claimed to have heard of a whale's eye used as a sliotar. Sometimes, old and new traditions met on the same field. In December 1887, a match in Carrick-on-Suir, County Tipperary, saw hurlers use everything from 'the polished and painted camáns to the less pretentious fir-bush crooks'.

Some hurleys simply did not work. During the American Invasion of 1888, a series of hurling exhibition matches drew huge praise in the local press and were reported as creating 'a veritable hurricane of excitement and applause'. The matches seemed to be anything but exhibitions. For example, in the match in the Manhattan Grounds, there were at least a dozen hurleys broken. Not long into the tour, the hurlers were running out of hurleys and had to get some made for them by the veteran Fenian, Bob Kelly. Unfortunately, the only wood available was hickory. The clash of the hickory did not have quite the same ring to it and in the first skirmish most of the newly made hurleys broke into matchwood.

Deciding the type of sliotar to use in hurling matches also created problems. When Michael Cusack invited teams from Tipperary and Galway to play a match in the Phoenix Park in Dublin in February 1886 there was a dispute over the type of ball that should be used. The Galway men viewed the ball used by the Tipperary men as being too big and too soft. They favoured a ball which was smaller and harder. A key aspect of the modern sports revolution was the standardisation of the equipment used precisely to prevent such disputes. The size and weight of the ball were standardised. In time, handmade ash hurleys also became the standard. The shape and style of the hurley – though regional variations remain – evolved in tandem with changes in the way hurling was played. This has led to the adoption of a stick with a wider, flatter *bas* than that used by those who played hurling in the 1880s. Footballs, too, have evolved, with the brown lace ball being replaced by the lighter white ball, which is of considerable benefit on a wet day.

The art of hurley-making is another matter again. The growth of hurling under the GAA has seen dedicated hurley-makers establish themselves across the country. Family businesses, handed down through the generations, have each developed a style of their own. These businesses develop relationships with clubs and individuals which are based around much more than commerce. The touch, weight, balance and intangible sense of confidence that is vital to any hurler looking for a new hurley brings a uniquely personal element to the purchase. The store a hurler places in finding and keeping a hurley that feels right is underlined by the repeated repairs which are often undertaken.

While hurley-makers continue to make some hurleys by hand, many more are now machine-cut and mass-produced. The poor quality of the early mass-produced hurleys was problematic, feeding the belief that handmade hurleys were far superior. Improved technology has redressed that imbalance, but an enduring problem for hurley-makers remains the supply of good-quality ash. In 1940 a motion was passed

The size and weight of modern sliotars is set out in the GAA rule book. Regular testing ensures that all

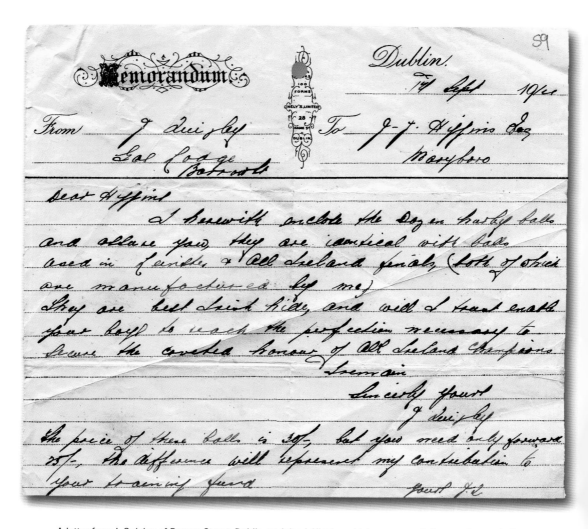

A letter from J. Quigley of Barrow Street, Dublin, to John J. Higgins which accompanied a consignment of sliotars to the Laois hurling camp prior to the 1914 All-Ireland final. Made of the best Irish hide, these sliotars, states Quigley, would help the Laois hurling team 'reach the perfection necessary to secure the coveted honour of All-Ireland Champions'. Quigley reduced the cost of the order by way of a contribution to the team's training fund. (GAA/Laois/59, GAA Museum)

by the GAA's Central Council that a scheme be put in place by the government to plant more ash, a challenge still being met today by the state agency, Coillte. Not everyone believed that such pampering was necessary, or even a good idea. As one delegate told the GAA's Annual Congress in 1940, 'when I was growing up they cut their hurleys from the ditches, and they could still do the same'.

In the last decades of the twentieth century, sports across the world, which used wooden equipment, were revolutionised by the introduction of modern, man-made compounds. Tennis and golf are two of the most obvious examples of this. In hurling, an attempt was made to introduce hurleys made from synthetic materials. The Dutch piping manufacturer, Wavin, which had a huge manufacturing plant in Ireland, made a range of plastic hurleys. Although much of the impulse behind the experiment was to reduce the cost of the hurley and to address

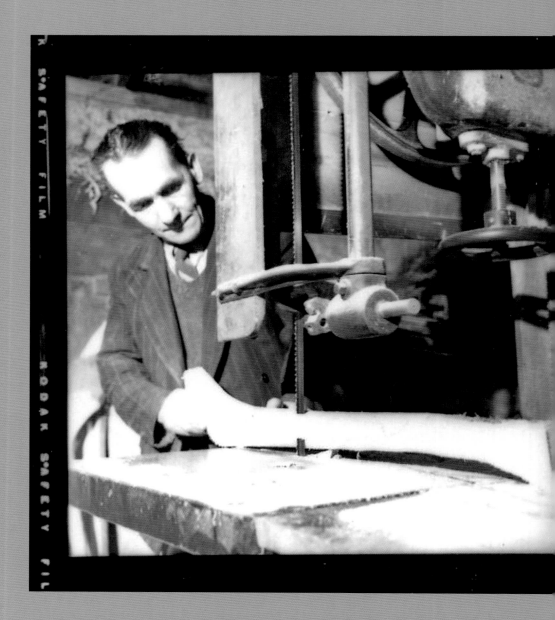

Crafting a new hurley in the early 1950s. By the early twenty-first century, approximately 350,000 hurleys were being produced each year, the ash supplied, for the most part, from countries across Eastern Europe, along with Germany and Britain. (*Pickow Collection, NUIG*)

> 'The revival of hurling is heavily handicapped in comparison with that of football. The implements for playing it are far more expensive and more difficult to procure, while the practice necessary to attain any degree of proficiency with the camán is vastly greater than that required for football. As regards football, all that is required to play it is a ten- or twelve-shilling ball, and without more ado a whole parish may indulge in the game to their hearts' content.' – **Journalist P. P. Sutton, writing in** *Sport*, **25 June 1887.**

the problems caused by dependence on scarce ash, it did not succeed. Ash hurleys remain unchallenged – although 80 per cent of the ash used to make those hurleys is now imported from across the world. In the 1990s a partnership was formed between the Irish Guild of Ash Hurley Makers and Coillte, who began to examine possible locations from where ash could be imported. These new locations include England, Denmark, Sweden, Poland, Romania and Slovakia. The other 20 per cent of hurleys are still being produced with Irish timber and Coillte (who have undertaken an ash-planting scheme) hope that Ireland will again be self-sufficient within ten years.

The major trophies of the Association embrace traditional art forms: the Sam Maguire, for example, is based on the Ardagh Chalice. Other trophies are named in honour of leading personalities in GAA and Irish history. For example, the National League trophy, the Croke Cup, commemorates the Association's founding patron; and the Connacht senior hurling trophy, the Flaherty Cup, is named after M. J. Flaherty, from Galway who was a well-known local player with the Liam Mellows and Ballinasloe clubs. While the receipt of medals and trophies by winning teams became standard, this was not always the case. Funds were not always available to supply these most basic of mementos. Such was the financial state of the Ulster Council during the First World War that Antrim and Monaghan withdrew their claims for their hurling championship trophies in 1916 and 1917. In a resolution passed at the Ulster Council's Annual Convention in 1917, they requested that the winners be awarded a set of jerseys and the runners-up be awarded a set of hurleys.

In general, the value of GAA memorabilia has increased dramatically. In the 1920s the Wills cigarette company began producing cards, featuring the leading players of the day, for collection. In addition to the player cards, at least one cigarette company offered people the chance to collect coupons from their cigarette packets. When they had a sufficient number gathered, they sent off the coupons and

John Brophy 19 Michael St Nenagh

OFFICIAL PROGRAMME]   [PRICE—TWO PENCE.

National League Hurling
AT THURLES,
On Sunday, 6th Nov., 1927.

TIPPERARY V GALWAY.

JUNIOR FOOTBALL FINAL—NORTH V. SOUTH—AT 1.30 P.M.

Here's to the pastime our ancestors loved
And here's to the sports that we follow;
Here's to the comrades whose spirit we've proved,
And here's to the fun of the morrow

Special Trains will return as under :—

To Galway and all Intermediate Stations ... 6 30 p.m.
 " Waterford ... 7 0 "
 " Nenagh ... 6 45 "
 " Cashel ... 7 15 "

LIBERTY PRINTING WORKS, THURLES.

Among all GAA collectables, match programmes are the most popular and widely circulated. Programmes vary from single sheet documents with team lists to lavish colour booklets, filled with photographs and special features. This is the front page from a programme issued for the National Hurling League meeting of Tipperary and Galway at Thurles, 1927. Leagues in hurling and football had been introduced the year before as a secondary competition, a winter complement to the summer championship. (GAA Museum)

A presentation of medals at the Tailteann Games at Croke Park. When the ancient festival was revived in 1924, it attracted competitors from across the world in a broad range of disciplines, sporting and non-sporting. Over 5,000 competitors took part and 1,000 medals were awarded, all of them designed by Tyrone-born sculptor Oliver Sheppard. One side of the medal featured a depiction of Queen Tailte in traditional Celtic costume, with the inscription 'An Bhainríon Tailte.' On the other side, the centre was left blank for the name of the medal winner, but the edge was decorated with intricate Celtic knotwork and depictions of ancient sportsmen, scribes and artists. (*INDH 881, National Library of Ireland*)

received a football in return. Sean Scollon, originally from Leitrim before later emigrating to America, recalled his mother saving these coupons for him and the excitement that greeted the arrival of the football. The joy proved short-lived – after a day of exertion on the nearby meadow the leather had fallen away from the ball and all that remained was the bladder.

While the balls did not endure, the cigarette cards, throwaway items when first produced, are now desired by specialist collectors and regularly appear at memorabilia auctions. Such auctions and collectors' fairs are dominated by one item above all others: the match-day programme. When first produced in the 1880s such programmes were simple black-and-white documents, rarely more than a folded-over sheet of paper, which featured some advertisements and the team sheets. The desirability of these items to collectors was evidenced in 2008 when a programme, made of a single folded page, from the 1915 Wexford–Kerry final sold for €2,600. At the same auction another item much beloved of collectors, game tickets, also realised a high price: a single ticket from the Bloody Sunday game of 1920 fetched €7,500. The money paid for medals also soared. Medals for the first All-Ireland championships were not actually presented in the 1880s. Instead, they were awarded retrospectively around 1913. The gold medals had '1887' on the front and the recipient's name on the back. The medal of one of the Limerick Commercials' star players, Malachi O'Brien, was bought in November 2005 for €26,500 at Sothebys of London.

Other GAA ephemera is even more rare. In response to the presence in Irish shops of a range of games based around soccer, an attempt was made in the 1970s to develop a GAA alternative. The result was 'Páirc', the first GAA board game, finally released in 1985. It did not take off. Several decades passed before a further attempt was made with the introduction of 'League Leader'. Officially authorised by the Association, 'League Leader' is a Monopoly-style board game available in both football and hurling formats. The evolution in entertainment which brought the advent of consuls and a culture of video gaming based around computers and television screens also drew in the GAA. Other sports – notably soccer through FIFA World Cup – were repackaged for play on consoles. First released by Sony in 2005 for use on its PlayStation, 'Gaelic Games Football' featured commentary by Micheál Ó Muircheartaigh, with instructions in both Irish and English. It allowed players to play a single game or to play out a full GAA season, including the National League, provincial and All-Ireland championships. The graphics of the game allowed competitors to solo, hand-pass, shoot and tackle in one of eleven photo-realistic stadiums including Croke Park, Semple Stadium and Casement Park.

Dressed up and ready for the big game: a group of Tipperary supporters from Boherlan/Dualla, Cashel, Clonoulty and Cahir set off for Dublin on the day of the 1945 All-Ireland final. When these supporters got inside the gates of Croke Park and joined the crowds that had travelled from other parts of the country, they helped create a spectacular backdrop to the game. The *Munster Express* reported that: 'All around, the arena was one huge sea of faces, with the Tipperary and Kilkenny colours showing up everywhere, as enthusiastic supporters displayed coloured caps, flags and even coloured umbrellas'. (*John Devane*)

Connolly Street in Kilkenny is festooned in black and amber in the run-up to the county's appearance in the 2008 All-Ireland hurling final. Kilkenny hurlers, managed by Brian Cody, set a new standard for the game in the first decade of the twenty-first century, contesting seven All-Ireland finals between 2000 and 2008, winning six. With Gaelic games rooted in a sense of place, a good championship season for a local club or county frequently brings with it the colourful make-over of housing estates, villages, and towns. (*Edward Dullard*)

'. . . knickers, jerseys and caps of Irish make are to be obtained, which for quality and price will compare very favourably with the imported, and it is really criminal carelessness on the part of any club to allow its team to be fitted out in anything of foreign make.' – *The Gaelic Athlete*, 13 January 1912.

Players could choose from any of the county teams, including London and New York. In 2007 the football game was revised, and Gaelic Games Hurling was added.

Overall, the material culture of the GAA is rich and diverse. With each passing decade the nature of that material culture will change. Today's must-have replica jersey will be tomorrow's retro issue. Fashions change, technology transforms equipment and children's tastes and interests shift. This shift produces a market in memorabilia and, like many sports, the GAA has thrown up a whole series of collectables for its fans. Social change, sporting change and the judgment of history separates valuable memorabilia from mundane attic-fillers. The turn of the wheel of history continues to recast the value of the GAA's material culture.

Tuition time: schoolgirls are shown
how to hold a hurling stick at an Irish
Fair, held at the Gaelic Athletic Ground
at Whitefoot Lane, Catford, south
London, 21 July 1935.
(*Getty Images*)

Women and the GAA

'Prejudice and opposition had to be combated. Small blame to the girl who carried her stick neatly wrapped up in brown paper to the nine acres for her first practice.' —

Seán O'Duffy, writing in August 1928 about the first camogie practice matches played in the Phoenix Park, Dublin, in the early years of the twentieth century, published in an unidentified newspaper, preserved in the *Seán O'Duffy Collection*, Cumann Camógaíochta na nGael.

'The introduction of ladies' football and the expansion of camogie,
has been the single most influential factor in the GAA.
With these games, and particularly football, the active membership
of the GAA increased spectacularly, and a whole new surge of able
and dynamic members began to participate
in all levels of club activity.'

'This national game of ours, of which the Cardinal is Patron,
cannot by any stretch of the imagination
be called unwomanly or any way
unsuited to the dignity of our sex'

'Perfume took over from embrocation as the prevailing odour in the dressingrooms yesterday when Offaly hosted Kerry.' That was how the *Evening Press* opened its report on what it described as the first ever inter-county ladies' football match, played in Tullamore, County Offaly, on Sunday 29 July 1973. The reporter observed that the game had initially been seen as a joke and that some diehards had turned up merely to mock the idea of women playing Gaelic football. In the end, however, those same diehards had been converted: 'Two dedicated teams quickly earned their admiration, and some of the combined movements proved that these girls have little to learn from their male counterparts.'

The game in Tullamore confirmed the momentum that was gathering around ladies' football. During the 1960s women had begun to organise themselves into teams – and then into clubs – in Offaly, Waterford, Tipperary and other counties. Initially, the women's game was played as seven-a-side matches organised in conjunction with local carnivals and festivals. By the early 1970s, the game had evolved to the establishment of leagues and then local championships in Cork, Waterford and Tipperary. The logical step was the establishment of an association for ladies' football. When that happened, the symbolism of the moment was stark. On Thursday evening, 18 July 1974, a small group of men and women gathered in Hayes' Hotel in Thurles, County Tipperary. Ninety years had passed since the Gaelic Athletic Association had been founded under the same roof. The upshot of the meeting was the establishment of the Ladies' Gaelic Football Association. Over the following decades, that Association entirely revolutionised the way in which women played Gaelic games. The rules of football were modified to allow for the ball to be picked off the ground and to restrict the level of physical contact. An All-Ireland championship was established and ladies' football was extended across every county in Ireland.

Life before camogie: this photograph shows members of the Dillon family and friends playing croquet on the Clonbrock estate, County Galway, in the 1860s. More of a sedate pastime than a competitive sport, croquet was a fashionable game among wealthy Irish women in the late nineteenth century. (*Clon 435, National Library of Ireland*)

The belated establishment of an Association to organise Gaelic football for women was a reflection on wider society and on the place of sport within that society. It is a simple fact that man walked on the moon before woman played football in Croke Park. In sport, the past holds a tight rein on the present and, when it comes to women, the sporting mould shaped by the Victorian world was never properly broken. It was not just that the sporting organisations which came to dominate the twentieth century were set up for men, but for a very definite type of man. Sport, it was proclaimed, was what made boys into men, the perfect academy for learning the virtues of courage, vigour, strength and stamina. To be good at sport was to be naturally male. *Sport*, a weekly sports paper, noted that playing organised sport was crucial to discourage effeminacy in an age of 'gentleman's corsets' and men writing 'maudlin poems in praise of each other'.

When Michael Cusack and Maurice Davin founded the GAA, they pledged to open its doors to men of all classes. It never seems to have occurred to them that women, too, might wish to play. This inability to see women as athletes did not stop Cusack from noticing that women turned up in their droves to football and hurling matches in the 1880s. It was simply assumed that a woman's enduring role would be as part of the scenery, rather than at the heart of the action. In his newspaper columns, Cusack eulogised their native beauty, particularly the women of Tipperary. According to Cusack, Tipperary women turned up at hurling matches, dressed in their 'gala attire to flash looks and smiles of approval on their rustic knights'. Cusack noted that those women were 'amongst the most earnest admirers of the play'. Indeed so much taken was one of them with the dexterity and skill of the play that she expressed her regret they were not eligible for election as members of the GAA, because, she said, 'if they could not play itself, they could decorate the jerseys for the boys'.

Clearly, there were many men and women – rich and poor – who considered women's involvement in sport to be decorative. Wealthy women, who might have been expected to lead a sporting movement for women, held other priorities. It was considered vulgar to have a robust fitness. Naturally, the very abstinence from activity made women more prone to illness. And the less women did, the less they appeared able to do. Science fed the belief that men and women were complementary opposites. In the 1880s the notion was still current that excessive sporting activity could diminish a woman's capacity to have children. Women were considered only to have a fixed amount of energy and wasting it on sporting activity deflected them from fulfilling the roles of wife and mother. For example, in 1887, the Chairman of the British Medical Association said: 'In the interests of social progress, national efficiency and the progressive improvement of the human race, women should be denied education and other activities which would cause constitutional overstrain and inability to produce healthy offspring.' Even the visionaries of continental sport believed women had no place in the world of sport. The founder of the modern Olympic Games, Baron Pierre de Coubertin, argued that women's sport was 'against the laws of nature', and that 'the eternal role of woman in this world was to be a companion of the male and mother of the family, and she should be educated towards those functions'. While women were eventually allowed enter the Olympics, it was initially in a limited way. Only in 1928 were track and field events allowed and even then there were only five events and the longest was 800 m.

As a corollary to this, many attempts by women to organise sport for themselves were belittled, trivialised, or simply ignored. The general tendency of the Victorian sporting world was to patronise and to parody the sporting female, as evidenced in a newspaper column suggesting that 'when a woman throws a brickbat, the great problem seems to be not how to hit the target, but how she can avoid knocking her brains out with her elbow'. In time, of course, the boundaries began to shift. Wider change in Irish society brought change to the female sporting world. By 1900, women were appearing in far greater numbers in secondary schools, in teacher training colleges, in universities and in the civil service. Independent

'I suppose Camogie is the only new outdoor game that has emerged from the Irish Revival? It's not new either, says you, it's only the feminine form of Hurling. Even so, it's a new departure due to Gaelic League. Cuchulainn played Hurling. There is no record of Mrs and Miss Cuchulainn playing their version of it.' – Editorial on 14 October 1945, published in an unidentified newspaper, preserved in the *Seán O'Duffy Collection*, Cumann Camógaíochta na nGael.

women sought their own place in the world and sport played a significant part in shifting the perceptions of what a woman was capable of doing. This shift involved a leap over the sideline and onto the playing field. In Ireland, far from waiting for the men to receive them into the GAA, women moved to form their own clubs to allow them play hurling.

The initiative was framed by the involvement of women in the Gaelic League, which had been founded by Douglas Hyde in 1893. As well as its primary endeavour of promoting the Irish language, it was also charged with the promotion of all aspects of Irish culture. In 1898 members of the Gaelic League in Navan, County Meath, had come together and established a ladies' hurling team. The immediate inspiration behind this move was the playing of an exhibition match amongst themselves as part of a local commemoration of the 1798 Rebellion. The game was played at the Hill of Tara, a site resonant with historical allusions.

No further advances were made until 1903, and again a branch of the Gaelic League was involved. In Dublin the Keating Branch had fine hurling and football teams for its male members. In 1903 a group of women members, including many who had travelled from various parts of Ireland to work in Dublin, determined to play the game of hurling. Led by Máire Ní Chinnéide, who was a graduate of the Royal University (a forerunner of the National University of Ireland), the group devised a code of rules based on hurling but amended in ways that were considered to make the game more suitable to women. Both hurls and sliotars were to be smaller and lighter than those used by the men, and the pitch was shortened so that its dimensions were to stand between 60 and 100 yards in length and between 40 and 60 yards in width. The number of players per team was twelve and amongst the rules was one which cited as a foul the deliberate stopping of the ball with the long flowing skirts then fashionable amongst early players. The game which carried these rules was renamed 'camogie'.

In that summer of 1903, the women of the Keating Branch began their practices,

A camogie team at practice in 1904. By the end of that year, five teams were contesting a league competition in Dublin, which was won by Cúchulainns. The capital was both the birthplace and early stronghold of the new game. (*Cumann Camógaíochta na nGael*)

firstly in Drumcondra Park, and later in the Phoenix Park, where many hurling matches were played immediately before and after the founding of the GAA. The extent to which these women were pioneers attempting to go against public opinion is shown by the fact that many of the women hid their hurls under their coats as they travelled to the game in an attempt to deflect ridicule from the wider populace. A second camogie club, Cúchulainns, was founded in Dublin in early 1904. This allowed for the staging of the first recorded camogie match, which was played at the Meath Agricultural Society Grounds (later redeveloped as Páirc Tailteann) in July 1904. The final score saw Keatings claim victory by a single goal to no score.

So successful were the early attempts to establish camogie that by the end of 1904 there were five teams playing in an organised league in the city. There was also a club active in County Down, and the game was even played in Glasgow in 1904. The progress was sufficient to allow for the formal establishment of An Cumann Camógaíochta, with Máire Ní Chinnéide as president, at 8 North Frederick Street in Dublin on 25 February 1905. The impetus that followed saw more clubs established around Dublin. The game spread tentatively to the south with the foundation of a club in Cork, and spread north with Louth, Monaghan, Fermanagh and Antrim becoming involved. That the game was played in areas where hurling was not well established emphasises the importance of the Gaelic League to its development.

Progress was slow and the organisation stagnated. In 1911, led by Seán O'Duffy of the Crokes Club, An Cumann Camógaíochta was relaunched in Dublin. Eleanor, Dowager Countess of Fingal, was appointed president at a meeting attended by thirteen Dublin clubs. Accepting the position the Countess wrote: 'I will be delighted to do anything I can to help what I consider a splendid work, for I believe if we could make the boys' and girls' lives in Ireland more happy and cheerful we would keep many more of them at home. I will gladly be president of the Association and do all I can to further the objects for which it is being founded.' The idea that the game offered a great opportunity to improve women's

'The following notice of motion, put forward by the Gráinne Mhaol Club, London, was, after a brief discussion, unanimously carried: - "That a clause be added to the rules requiring that players wear skirts not less than eight inches from the ground".' – An unidentified newspaper report of 17 April 1912 on the first Annual Convention of An Cumann Camógaíochta, held in the Oak Room of the Mansion House, Dublin, preserved in the Seán O'Duffy Collection, Cumann Camógaíochta na nGael.

Action from an inter-varsity camogie match between University Colleges Cork and Galway at Victoria Cross, Cork, 1 March 1916. The Ashbourne Cup, played out between Irish universities, is the oldest camogie competition. The trophy was donated in 1915 by Edwin Gibson, Lord Ashbourne. (*Irish Examiner*)

health was stressed in the newspapers: 'This healthy game, which suggests a blend of hurling and hockey, was introduced a few years ago in Dublin and it provoked some most interesting contests between local clubs. Only a little organisation should be needed to preserve it as a means of recreation for many hundreds of indoor workers in Dublin.' This time a determined effort was made to establish the game on a nationwide basis and by the middle of 1912 there were camogie matches regularly played in each of the four provinces. The game was dominated by single women, who were students, graduates or out at work. The first official inter-county game was played in that summer of 1912 when Dublin defeated Louth by 2-1 to 0-0 at Jones' Road. Then, in the 1915–16 season, the oldest camogie competition, the Ashbourne Cup, was established as an inter-varsity competition.

The politics of the Camogie Association were nationalist. A letter from Cáit Ní Donnchadha and Seán O'Duffy (who later fought in North King Street in the 1916 Rising) to the *Evening Telegraph* newspaper outlined the broader vision which underpinned the game:

Notwithstanding the excellence of certain foreign games, it is obvious that the country at large, and the city of Dublin in particular, would be strengthened and purified by our women cherishing and practising games of native origin and growth. The energy displayed by so many Irish ladies in advocating women's rights proves that active forces are still to be won over to national objects. I would respectfully suggest to those ladies to devote portion of their organising energy and resources towards ameliorating the lot of their less fortunate sisterhood, who toil in vitiated shops, stores, warerooms, etc. and whose social life needs brightening. We want something to supplement the ballroom and the skating-rink. We want to organise the womanhood of Ireland into one grand body, whose sole object, under that of national emancipation, would be the raising of the sex from the slough of a false and foreign occupation. The realisation of such an ideal would naturally give rise to a more independent and more self-respecting race. When we have secured national freedom – which is the goal of all true Irish women, no matter how they may differ in trivial matters – let us have our own national pastime as an essential element of our existence as a nation.

By 1920 a record number of teams were competing in the Dublin colleges leagues, camogie was prospering in the universities and more counties were organising. It

Delegates at the Annual Congress of Cumann Camógaíochta na nGael at Jury's Hotel, Dublin, 2 March 1936. The same congress was informed that efforts to establish an all-Ireland organisation had succeeded. Included in this picture are (l–r): Seán O'Duffy, Director of the organisation; Agnes O'Farrelly, Honorary President; Máire Gill, President; and Áine Ní Riain, Secretary and Treasurer. (*Cumann Camógaíochta na nGael*)

remained a constant struggle to raise the profile of the game, however. Well-received matches played at the Tailteann Games – footage of which was shown in cinemas across Ireland and overseas – helped boost support. Nonetheless, the game was continuously undermined by a chronic lack of funding, which largely explains several abortive attempts to establish an All-Ireland camogie championship. Camogie was not helped by a series of internal disputes. Such were the divisions and the lack of cohesion that, while some clubs played under camogie rules, others insisted on playing by the hurling rules used by men. Once again, it became necessary to relaunch. Cumann Camógaíochta na nGael was reborn at a special convention held at the Gresham Hotel in Dublin on 25 April 1932. It was then that camogie truly began to establish itself as a national sport. It was in that year that the first All-Ireland championship – won by Dublin – was started, though the final was not played until the summer of 1933. By 1935, camogie was being played by 10,000 players on 423 teams in 28 counties.

Almost immediately, the association again tore itself asunder. A proposal from Dublin clubs to lift the ban on hockey players playing camogie led to a bitter split. The motion was passed, but only after Ulster counties withdrew from the association. A rival 'National Camógaíocht Association' was established, drawing support from counties in every province. For several years, the associations ran in parallel lines. Mediation from leading GAA officials brought unity which proved short-lived when a dispute involving Cork brought even more destruction. That dispute centred on whether male officers should be represented on camogie committees. Again, rival associations were established and 'official' and 'unofficial' All-Irelands were run.

'Girls! Jump to it! Your teachers will help and encourage you to end the playing in Ireland of what Archbishop Croke once described as "foreign, fantastic games," and to popularise the only game for Irish girls; hurley's little sister – Camogie.' – An extract from the article 'Hurling: As played by the Girls' by Seán Piondar, *Ireland's Own*, 5 August 1933.

'This national game of ours, of which the cardinal is Patron, cannot by any stretch of the imagination be called unwomanly or any way unsuited to the dignity of our sex.' – Prof Agnes O'Farrelly, Honorary President of the Camógaíochta Association, February 1944, from an unidentified newspaper report, preserved in the *Seán O'Duffy Collection*, Cumann Camógaíochta na nGael.

Only in the early 1950s was unity restored. This unity proved enduring and established the foundation for the long-term development of camogie. The All-Ireland championships grew in popularity. By the 1960s the association had a formidable structure in place, with club, county and inter-collegiate competitions well established. The 1960s saw the end of what might be considered the most successful career of all in Gaelic games. In 1961, the Dublin player Kathleen Mills won the last of her fifteen All-Ireland senior medals when Dublin beat Tipperary in the All-Ireland final by 7-2 to 1-4. That final was played on Mills' thirty-eighth birthday and was her last in Dublin colours. She had first played for the county in 1941 and her medal haul included six in a row between 1950 and 1955.

Along with ladies' football – with which it now fell into competition – camogie progressed slowly through the 1970s and 1980s. Both games developed their championship and league structures, extended underage structures and improved coaching. For all this development, neither game was accorded the respect or progression that was merited. Their story is that of the passionate few dedicated to providing women with sporting opportunities. It was not until the 1990s that significant growth was experienced, particularly in ladies' football, which grew at an extraordinary rate. This growth was characterised by the success in developing the elite inter-county level of the game in tandem with a huge surge in grass-roots participation.

The reasons for the growth are several and largely straightforward. Financial investment, allied with the simple fact of working hard and coaching in clubs and

Cumann Lúit-Cleas Saeðeal, Teoranta

Teac an Crócaiş,
bótar Cluan Life,
Át-Cliat.

PHONE: 72095.

Meitheamh 25adh, 1941.

To:

Miss J. McHugh,
23 Rockmount Street,
BELFAST.
and

Miss Ryan
41 Parnell Square,
DUBLIN.

A Chara,

At the last meeting of my Council members expressed
the wish that an effort should be made to bring both
parties at present controlling Camoguidheacht in this
country, together.

After a discussion the members asked me to try and
do so. I am now writing you to know if there is any use
in my going ahead with such a proposal.

If you agree you could discuss the matter with some
of your members and let me know. On hearing from both
sides that they are willing to discuss the matter, I shall
write you further.

As I will be going on holidays on Saturday next for a
few weeks there is no immediate hurry but I trust, however,
that you will consider the matter seriously in the interests
of Camoguidheacht generally.

Mise, le meas,

Ð o Caoimí
RUNAIDHE.

In 1939 camogie divided over the issue of a ban on hockey players playing the game. With rival organisations claiming the allegiance of members, the GAA acted as mediator between the two sides. This letter from GAA General Secretary Pádraig Ó Caoimh to Cumann Camógaíochta na nGael offers his assistance in helping to heal the rift. (*Cumann Camógaíochta na nGael*)

Cualacht Camoguiochta agus Luith Chleas
na mBan Ghaedheal

A Chara,

Representatives of both bodies having come to an agreement at a Meeting in the Gresham Hotel, on Sunday 26th October, that in the interests of the national game of Camoguidheacht there should be only one body in control of the organisation. With that object in view it was decided:

(1) To hold a special Congress on Sunday, 7th December, in the Gresham Hotel, Dublin, commencing at 11 a.m.

(2) Representation for this Special Congress to be as laid down in Rule 1, page 42, Camoguidheacht Guide. The present affiliation of the two bodies to be taken as official; the representation to inclide members of the two outgoing Central Councils.

(3) That as a difference of opinion exists between the two bodies as totthe definition of the word club in the above Rule, that the special Congress define exactly what is a club.

(4) That Congress be summoned jointly by the Secretaries of the two bodies. Professor A. O'Farrelly to preside, assisted by the officers of the two bodies.

Agenda For Special Congress.

(a) Formal ratification of agreement.
(b) Election of officers.
(c) Definition of Club as referred to in paragraph 3 above.
(d) Finance and property of the Association.
(e) Question of right of Officials to vote. Ruling on this matter.
(f) Date of Ordinary Annual Congress.

Sinne, le meas,

SINEAD NIC AODHA,

AINE NI RIAIN.

'Camogie made school bearable. We watched the clock and waited for the bell to ring at four o'clock. Then it was up the field until six. It did not matter how many turned up. We all threw in our hurleys and two teams were picked by pulling out hurleys in either direction.' – **Mary Moran, GAA Oral History Project Archive, 2009.**

'In 1998, RTÉ decided to provide live coverage of the women's All-Ireland in Croke Park. It was a decision that was to have seismic consequences. Suddenly, women's football became the classic example of a revolution that was televised'. – **Harry McGee,** *Sunday Tribune*, **20 July 2003.**

in schools, began to reap dividends and the games developed in areas of the country where they had not previously been played. The general rise in interest in Gaelic games through the 1990s was an undoubted help to the development of the women's game. This, in turn, helped the game spread and as more clubs and counties began to compete for honours the games prospered. This prosperity was facilitated by the availability of the GAA's pitches and clubhouses throughout the country, a ready-made network onto which could be grafted a growing association. As the more traditional elements within the GAA came to accept women playing football, barriers to the growth of the Ladies' Gaelic Football Association fell away. The extent of the progress is not confined to Ireland. Clubs are now organised in most continents and the numbers of new clubs continues to grow.

After more than 100 years in existence, camogie – now played by teams of fifteen-a-side on a pitch the same size as that used by men – could boast a record 515 affiliated clubs. Ladies' Gaelic football enjoyed an even more spectacular expansion since its foundation in 1974. Unlike camogie, women who start playing Gaelic football in their late teens can quickly become adept at the game. This accessibility has allowed Gaelic football to gather a momentum crucial to all progress. By the end of 2008 there were 132,000 players and around 1,100 clubs. By any standards this is an extraordinary number. To put it in context, there are merely 70,000 registered women soccer players in England.

Although the development of camogie and ladies' football has enjoyed support from the GAA, it remains a singular fact that both games are run by organisations which are distinct from the GAA. Tentative steps have occasionally been taken to move towards a merger of the various bodies, but these steps have never gathered

Sounds from the sidelines: camogie supporters at a Colleges final in Coolock, Dublin, c. 1940s. Schools and colleges were key to the progress of the sport and, through the 1940s and 1950s, more colleges began to play the game and new competitions were introduced. (*Cumann Camógaíochta na nGael*)

'Mr Camogie': Seán O'Duffy shelters
UCD goalkeeper, Kitty McGrath,
during the Ashbourne Cup final,
February 1946. Mayo-born O'Duffy
was a tireless promoter of the sport.
At the time, the involvement of men in
official roles was a divisive issue within
the sport. O'Duffy was nevertheless a central figure in camogie's development and
the All-Ireland senior championship
trophy is named in his honour.
(*GAA Oral History Project Archive*)

Coisve Camóʒuıᵷeaċca Co. Áċa Cliaċ

Secretary's Address:
6 Fergus Road, Dublin 6.

February, 1968.

A Chara,

Since the formation of the Dublin Camogie Board, its members have enjoyed many happy hours and made lifelong friendships on our grounds in the Phoenix Park. In the beginning we had one pitch; a second pitch was acquired in 1932 and, in the Summer of 1967, two further pitches were formally opened. During all that time, the same pavilion has served the many generations of camogie players who have come and gone. We are now faced with the problem of providing a new pavilion to cater more adequately for our present and future needs, a project which, inevitably, will involve us in high financial commitments.

Our only sources of revenue are Club Fees, our annual Flag-day and gates (rarely substantial) on the occasions of County Semi-Finals and Finals which, thanks to the co-operation of the G.A.A., are played on enclosed grounds. In spite of our limited income, the Board has managed over the years, to maintain the grounds, do essential repairs to the pavilion, provide a room for its weekly meetings, provide trophies for the numerous competitions in the ten grades from Senior to Juveniles and field a County Team second to none in good play and sportsmanship, without going into debt or seeking outside help.

The present committee and members of the Board have been working for some time on a fund raising campaign. We feel, however, that many of our past members as well as friends of camogie in Dublin would like to be associated with our efforts to enhance the prestige of the association by providing reasonable amenities for our players.

As it would be virtually impossible to contact everybody concerned we should be grateful if you would inform any of your friends who might be interested. All subscriptions, large and small, will be gratefully accepted and officially acknowledged.

beıꞃ buaᵷ ıꞃ beannaċc.

Mise,

Caitríona de Léis,
Runaꞷe Oıꞃıʒ.

Subscriptions may be sent to the Secretary or any of the following:

CAMOGIE BOARD OFFICERS

Miss E. McCarthy, 11 Airfield Road, Rathgar, Dublin 6, *Chairman.*

Mrs Mollie (Fitzgerald) Murphy, 11 Glenbeigh Road, North Circular Road, Dublin 7, *Treasurer.*

The Dublin Camogie Association appeals for subscriptions to redevelop long-standing facilities at Phoenix Park, 1968. From the very beginning, the Phoenix Park served as the focus of camogie activity in the capital. Finding suitable playing grounds was a constant concern not only for administrators in Dublin, but throughout the country. (Cumann Camógaíochta na nGael)

meaningful momentum. Within the GAA, itself, women continue to be grossly under-represented at high official levels. No woman has ever trained or been a selector with a county team, and no woman has refereed GAA matches at the top level. In part, of course, this is a failure on the part of women who have not forced themselves into such positions. It is also a failure on behalf of the GAA who have not actively created such possibilities. It would also be wrong to consider that the growth in camogie and ladies' football has brought an equal playing field for women involved in sport. It remains a singular feature of modern sport that women's sport is undervalued in relation to men's. The evidence of this is everywhere: from coverage in the media to the level of sponsorship deals. Although there continues to be change in Gaelic games, room remains for considerably more. After all, the bald truth of attendance at the All-Ireland finals every year is stunning: when men play football and hurling, Croke Park is full; when women play there, 40,000 seats stay empty. The mould shaped by the Victorian world has never properly been broken – overt discrimination may have disappeared, but its remnants live on.

'It built up such a social network, it was brilliant because when everyone left after university it was like, oh who do I text now to go out and go to the cinema or go wherever? So it built up a really good network and we had Scottish girls, English girls, even girls who had no connection, no Irish heritage at all.' – Fiona McConnell speaking about her involvement with ladies' football in Liverpool, GAA Oral History Project Archive, 2008.

OFFALY ASSOCIATION (LONDON)

Affiliated to the Council of Irish County Associations

17 Downhill Road, Catford, London SE6 ISU
Telephone : 01-697 1147

President: Mr. O. Brannigan   Chairman: Mr. K. Devery
Secretary: Mr. D. Egan   Treasurer: Mr. P. McHugh

Our Ref: DE/PG。

Your Ref:

15th February 1975。

The Secretary。
Offaly Association。
163 Botanic Road,
Glasnevin,
Dublin 9。

Dear Sir,   <u>re: Your proposed visit to London</u>

        We thank you for your recent communications in respect
of the above.

        We are delighted to learn of your interest in a London
visit, and are grateful to you for arranging your trip to
coincide with our bank-holiday weekend, i.e。 May 23rd-25th,
the occassion of our Annual Dinner & Dance。

        You can be assured of our co-operation in making this
venture a success for all concerned. The idea of hurling
and football matches being arranged is welcomed, as an
Offaly Sports Day had already been contemplated. Despite
our very limited involvement in sport we are confident that
we will be fairly represented by Offaly teams in both
games for the occassion。 We are enthusiastic about the
idea of a ladies football match, but of course since this
sort of venture is unknown in London, we doubt if we could
provide a suitable opposing team. Hence, we would be
anxious to know if you feel there might be enough lady
footballers amoung the visitors to provide an exhibition
game, with both teams drawn from your party.

        For reasons of co-ordination may we respectfully
request that you deal only with this association in respect
of any sports activities.

                                        /continued.....。

All correspondence must be addressed to the association

A sports day organised by the Offaly Association of London includes ladies' Gaelic football as part of its showcase of events. The novelty of this endeavour is apparent in the admission by the hosts that the game was unknown in London. The ladies' match went ahead as a seven-a-side exhibition with Offaly providing the two teams. A feature of the sport's expansion in the subsequent decades was its popularity among Irish immigrant communities. (*GAA Oral History Project Archive*)

Action from an early ladies' Gaelic football game. In counties such as Waterford, Laois and Monaghan, which experienced little success in men's Gaelic football, the ladies' variant thrived. (*Westmeath Examiner*)

Players from the Donaghmoyne Club in Monaghan celebrate their victory over Moville from Donegal in the Ulster club final replay, November 2008. The growing strength of the ladies' game has been reflected in the rise in club numbers. By the end of 2008, ladies' Gaelic football could claim a playing population of 132,000, drawn from 1,100 clubs. (*Pat Murphy, Sportsfile*)

The fortunes of ladies' Gaelic football were transformed with the introduction of live television coverage of its games. 'Once we got TV onside, people could see that it was a good team sport to play', Helen O'Rourke, chief executive of the sport, remarked in 2003. This photograph was taken to promote TG4's coverage of the 2008 All-Ireland finals at Croke Park. Featured are the senior and intermediate captains from the competing counties (l–r): Angela Walsh, Cork; Niamh Kindlon, Monaghan; Angela McDermott, Tipperary; and Louise Henchey, Clare. (*Brendan Moran, Sportsfile*)

A home from home: spectators avail of the perfect vantage point at Gaelic Park, New York, c. 1950. As the list of fixtures on the scoreboard shows, Irish county loyalties were frequently recreated on American soil. (*Pickow Collection, NUIG*)

Exile

'A little corner of Ireland abroad.'

Jerome O'Brien comments on the place of the GAA beyond
Irish shores, GAA Oral History Project Archive, 2009.

'It would prove a difficult task to bring

together at short notice a more splendid assemblage of specimens

of manhood than the half hundred clear-complexioned

and clean-limbed, stalwart, bright eyed muscular, strapping and fine-looking

young fellows who were grouped on the deck of the Steamship

Wisconsin yesterday.' – The New York Herald reports on the arrival

the GAA's American invasion party in September 1888,

quoted in of the GAA, 1994: 7, 77.

'It's like I've two lives over here.

I go to work and I talk soccer

and rugby all day because that's all that any of them know

about. The rest of my life is hurling then. Talking GAA and

meeting GAA people. That's what's kept me happy in London.'

On the first Sunday in September 1980, Joe Connolly from Castlegar stood on the steps of the Hogan Stand in Croke Park and looked out over a swarm of jubilant supporters. Galway had just won their first All-Ireland hurling title in fifty-seven years and Connolly, as captain, approached the microphone to deliver a speech that transcended sport. A native Irish speaker, he spoke not from a prepared script but from the heart, and his words were directed as much towards an audience across the seas as towards the crowds in front of him. Connolly spoke of the honour of captaincy and his pride in his sense of place. He acknowledged those Galway people who could not make it to Croke Park, those who were scattered in America and England and who, he imagined, must have been crying tears of happiness at that moment. The speech was not the longest ever delivered by an All-Ireland winning captain, but it was certainly the most memorable. In making a connection between events at Croke Park and the world of the Irish diaspora, his words struck an emotional chord and offered a reminder of how GAA life at home and abroad has been shaped by the wider experience of emigration.

It has been that way from the start. Almost a century before Connolly delivered those words in Croke Park, a steamship arrived in New York after a nine-day voyage from Cobh in Cork. On board was some of the best Irish sporting talent and a cargo of 200 hurleys bearing green labels on which were inscribed the words 'Gaelic American Invasion'. It was 1888. The GAA was only four years old and its ambitions had already outgrown Ireland. The invasion party reflected the sporting diversity of the early GAA and comprised a mix of fifty top athletes and hurlers. Over the course of a month, the plan was for the athletes to engage in athletic competitions against their American counterparts and for the hurlers to play a series of exhibition matches in cities along the northeastern seaboard of America. They were there to showcase their talents and their traditional games, but ultimately to raise money. The primary purpose of the tour was to raise £5,000 which was to be used to restage the Aonach Tailteann, an ancient Irish athletic and cultural festival, which was supposed to have taken place at the Hill of Tara during the centuries before the Norman invasion.

America had been the obvious destination of choice. The country had been a focus of Irish emigration throughout the nineteenth century, particularly in the wake of the Great Famine of the 1840s when the numbers of Catholic Irish ballooned in the big urban centres of New York, Boston, Chicago and beyond. America, too, had a long attachment to Gaelic sports: reports of hurling in New York reached back as far as the 1780s and as the numbers of Irish in America increased across the following century, so too did the prevalence of pre-codified versions of Gaelic games.

The Invasion tour, led by Maurice Davin, gave the GAA an early opportunity to cement links with these Irish-American communities and to demonstrate the great progress they had made in reviving traditional pastimes. They were well received. Wherever the touring party went they were feted and fed by local members of the GAA, as well as by Irish societies and groups such as the Ancient Order of Hibernians. But that was as good as it got. The Invaders found themselves caught in the crossfire of a bitter dispute between rival American athletic bodies, which deprived the Irish athletes of local opposition in a number of cities. This loss of international competition inevitably took from the appeal of some of the organised events, but so too did bad weather and the counter-attraction of an American presidential election, then in full stride. With the exception of Boston, the antic-ipated large crowds never materialised. The effect was to plunge the tour, and the GAA, into financial crisis. Instead of providing a vehicle for fund-raising, the

'. . . as stalwart and manly a lot of men as one could wish to see. They have taken the town by storm and have conquered the hearts of everyone.' This was how *The Globe* newspaper of Boston described the Invasion team's arrival in New York in September 1888. This picture of the touring party was taken at an unknown location. (*Pat Walsh*)

'The nearest approach to Irish fair squabbles in this country arises from the Gaelic football games and the hurling matches . . . About three hundred spectators witnessed the game yesterday, and about one-third of this number carried hurleys . . . The players threw their whole souls as well as their muscles into the game, and the quaint and many-colored costumes, darting across the field, gave the appearance of a wrecked rainbow. The hurleys, which were lifted over the shoulders of the players and swung at random with full force, sometimes came in contact with the pates and shins of the members of the opposing team, and many a sore head and bruised limb was carried home.' – A *New York Times* report on a game of hurling at Wallace's Park, Ridgewood, Long Island, 19 December 1892.

touring party became a drain and a loan of £450 from Michael Davitt, provided as a security in advance to cover any unforeseen expenses, was required to cover the cost of the team's return trip to Ireland.

Not everybody returned. Around twenty of the fifty athletes, smitten by the excitement and promise of America, opted to remain permanently in the United States. What Ireland lost, America gained. For all the damage the Invasion caused to the GAA at home – saddling it with debt and forcing the abandonment of the 1888 All-Ireland championships – it gave a great boost to Gaelic games in the United States. It helped to enhance the profile of the GAA and, in the decades that followed, GAA clubs were established and games were played across the United States. For those who played and watched them, Gaelic games not only provided an opportunity to enjoy healthy physical activity; they also helped maintain a connection with Ireland, affording a space to meet and socialise with people of a similar background and experience. The GAA created, in essence, a home away from home. County loyalties frequently re-formed on American soil, with GAA teams taking the names of Irish counties and drawing their players predominantly from these areas. This practice was particularly common in New York where county societies played a prominent role in the affairs of the Irish community and where, by the early twentieth century, football and hurling games were increasingly organised as part of their recreational remit. There were, however, other factors influencing which teams players joined. Often work loyalties were more important in choices made. In addition, younger siblings who followed older family members to America, often joined the team of their family. Ties of kinship, friendship and economics combined to create a bond more powerful than any simple allegiance to county identity.

Those American GAA clubs that did not bear the name of an Irish county invariably took theirs from the pantheon of popular nationalist historical personalities or organisations. This again was standard practice in Ireland, yet it underlined the links that the Association in America maintained with the broad cause of Irish nationalism. To support the GAA was to strengthen a sense of Irishness among immigrants and, by extension, to advance the nationalist movement. For that very reason, the Association enjoyed the support of a range of nationalist organisations, which identified with its cultural mission and saw it as a fertile recruiting ground. Ultimately, though, it was the games and the social world around them that remained the GAA's central attraction. By the early twentieth century, in cities across America, rival clubs were facing each other in championships played in front of large crowds. The efficient organisation of these competitions and the enforcement of rules was greatly helped by the inauguration of various governing bodies, among them the 'Gaelic Athletic Association of the United States', founded in New York in 1914. Many years later, the New York GAA Board reflected that the emergence of this body 'was to New York what the Thurles meeting was to Ireland'.

As it was in America, so it was in Britain, Australia, Argentina, Canada and South Africa. In fact, wherever significant numbers of Irish people travelled or settled in the late nineteenth and early twentieth centuries, Gaelic games were played. Levels of organisation varied by region as did the numbers involved. This, and problems with the availability of proper equipment, made it difficult to replicate perfectly the Irish version of the games. Playing Gaelic games on foreign fields occasionally demanded a measure of local improvisation. When, for example, the first official hurling game was played in Argentina in 1900, the two Buenos Aires-based teams – Almagro and Palermo – lined out with nine players each owing to a shortage of hurley sticks. This would prove an ongoing problem for Argentina's small hurling fraternity as sticks had to be imported in the holds of ships, a method of transit which, given the distance to be covered, dried out the ash, rendering it brittle to the point of being useless.

No such problems were encountered in Britain. As the nearest of the GAA's international outposts, it was also the one which enjoyed the most frequent contact with home. In 1896, anxious to increase interest in Gaelic games in England, the GAA's Central Council sanctioned the sending of teams of athletes and hurlers to London. When the two hurling teams, drawn from counties in Leinster and Munster, arrived at Euston train station, they were met by three pipe bands who

ESTATUTOS

DE LA

FEDERACIÓN ARGENTINA

DE HURLING

—✷—

BUENOS AIRES
Imprenta Gadola · Rivadavia 775
1918

A rule book for the Irish Argentine Hurling Federation, 1918. References to recreational forms of the game date from the 1880s, but a network of Catholic Irish-Argentine schools aided its diffusion in the early twentieth century. Hurling was key in promoting a distinctive Catholic Irish identity in Argentina. (*GAA Museum*)

Díbírteaca ó éirinn

HURLING   CLUB.

YOUNG IRISHMEN ! Rally to the Standard of the G.A.A., and support our National Pastime.

Practices, Sefton Park, Saturdays, 3.30 p.m.

FURTHER PARTICULARS FROM

Hon. Sec., 78 Duke-street, Liverpool.

ANNUAL MEETING, WEDNESDAY, 21st MARCH, 8 p.m.

A plea for young Irishmen to play hurling, carried in a concert programme published by Conradh na Gaeilge in Liverpool, 14 March 1906. In cities across Britain, Gaelic games were part of a range of social and cultural activities that served the interests of Irish immigrants, providing support and bolstering their sense of ethnic identity. (*Máire Bhreathnach Collection, Cumann Camógaíochta na nGael*)

marched the players, hurleys raised like rifles on their shoulders, through the neighbouring streets to promote a match and a sports meeting organised for Stamford Bridge the following day. That match would come to be recognised as the first ever inter-provincial fixture and it clearly had a galvanising effect. Later that year, the London County Board was founded and soon after, in 1900, England was designated a GAA province for organisational purposes.

The GAA in London, like elsewhere, proved a magnet for Irish nationalists. In the early years of the twentieth century, membership of the GAA frequently overlapped with that of other Irish cultural and political organisations such as the Gaelic League and the Irish Republican Brotherhood (IRB). Among the prominent members in club and county board circles were London-born businessman Liam McCarthy, and Cork-born Sam Maguire who had moved to London in 1897 to take up a job in the Post Office. Both combined GAA commitments with IRB

'We set off in the mail train to Dublin on Friday evening, sailed from Dun Laoghaire that night and arrived in Liverpool the next morning. We hadn't a bite to eat from the moment we left Cork to the time we arrived in England, not even a cup of tea to drink. When we got to our hotel in Liverpool there was no reception for us . . . We played our match at the Waterloo pitch in Bootle on Saturday and then we went down to London to play the second game at Hearn Hill. After that match we had to tog-in on the tube train as we made our way out of London.' – **Cork's Eugene Coughlan, who in 1927 travelled as part of the Cork team which attempted to promote hurling among Irish exiles in Britain, quoted in Tim Horgan,** *Cork's Hurling Story* **(1977), p. 57.**

Formation Provincial Council for Britain.

Mr. McGrath reported having attended the Conference called for London for the formation of the Provincial Council, representatives were present from London, Liverpool, Portsmouth and Wales. Mr. Jas. Collins, London, was elected President, Mr. Jas. Ryan, Liverpool was elected Treasurer, Mr. C. McGough, London was elected Secretary.

Owing to the present financial position of the Co. Boards in London and Liverpool financial assistance would need to be provided to enable the Prov. Council to function.

Mr. McGrath suggested either the voting of £100 or the sending over of the Cork and Tipperary Hurling Teams to play Exhibition Matches at Liverpool and London, the Central Council to provide the travelling facilities, the Local Committees to undertake and be responsible for Hotel arrangements.

After discussion it was decided to arrange for the Cork and Tipperary teams to visit Liverpool on June 4th and London on June 6th the proceeds of both matches after deducting local expenses to go to the Provincial Council.

The President mentioned he had been informed by Mr. McGrath that no replies had been received from the Secretary to correspondence sent from London, The Secretary stated he had not received any communication from Mr. McGough to which he did not reply.

Mr. J. J. Buckley, Secretary Cork Athletic Grounds, applied for permission to run a tournament to raise funds for further equiping the athletic grounds, the Counties to be invited to compet were Dublin, Kilkenny, Wexford, Limerick, Tipperary and Cork, the Permit was granted,

llege Committee.

A letter was read from the Secretary Leinster College

20 May 1926: on the day of their arrival in the United States and in front of thousands of curious onlookers, the Tipperary hurlers were feted at New York City Hall. En route to the reception, the players changed into their jerseys and togs while crossing New York Bay on board a ferry. The welcoming party, pictured here, included 'Baron' John J. Hanly, Monegea native and Broadway millionaire; Tom Delaney, a prominent Tipperary man then based in New York; Governor Billings of the State of Vermont; and James J. Walker, the New York Mayor of Irish descent to whom the visitors presented a hurley. (*Tipperary County Library*)

Saturday, May 15th: 'Not much sleep last night when Nealon and Kennedy called on their rounds with notebook and pencil, asking if we jazzed with the Germans, thereby suspending ourselves from the GAA, and if we took the meat sandwiches, thereby excommunicating ourselves from the Catholic church.' – **Extract recalling the passage of the Tipperary hurling team on board the SS** *Bremen* **to America in 1926, quoted in Thomas J. Kenny,** *Tour of the Tipperary Hurling Team in America, 1926* (1928), p. 17.

activism, and both, ultimately, would lend their names to All-Ireland championship trophies. Maguire, the younger of the two, had been recruited into the IRB in 1902 at a time when he was an influential member of the Hibernians Gaelic football team, then on course to win four consecutive London championships. He rose quickly through the ranks of the IRB and became head of its London district, taking responsibility for the recruitment of new members. One of those was Michael Collins, another Cork exile, who was serving as secretary of the Geraldines GAA Club in London at the time of his recruitment in 1909.

For Michael Collins, the GAA in London provided a political launch-pad. For countless others, however, it remained simply a means to enjoy sport, or the concerts and dances that were run as club fund-raisers, in the company of other Irish people. This social world was upturned by the convulsions of the Great War and it was not until the mid-1920s that the GAA properly re-established itself across Britain. A Provincial Council of Britain was established in 1926, but by then teams from England and Scotland had already participated in the Tailteann Games, which had been revived in Dublin by the newly founded Irish Free State in 1924, three decades after the GAA's abortive efforts of the 1880s. Held on three occasions between 1924 and 1932, the Tailteann Games helped to showcase the GAA's international dimension, but their contribution to the overseas development of Gaelic games was eclipsed by that of touring county teams which visited Britain and the United States throughout the late 1920s and 1930s.

The most ambitious of these tours was that undertaken by the Tipperary hurling team in 1926. Over a two-month period, the team crossed the great expanse of the United States, from the east coast to the west and back again. A diary kept by one of the travelling party, Thomas J. Kenny, documented the games played, the sights seen and the people met throughout the tour. The diary was later published as a book and what shines through its pages most is the players' sense of wonder at the scale of it all: the size and bustle of the cities and the vast, uninhabited spaces of open country. Six of the players were sufficiently enthralled with America to emigrate to New York once the tour ended. Comparisons with the Invasion tour of 1888 were inevitable and Kenny was moved to wonder whether there would ever be a day 'when there will be room and work for every Gael in his own country'.

Tours by different county teams continued through the years of the Great American Depression, ending with the outbreak of the Second World War. Soon after, once the United States joined the fighting, GAA activity effectively ground to a halt – immigration stopped and troop mobilisation soaked up many eligible footballers and hurlers among the Irish-American community. By the time the war had ended, the GAA in America was severely weakened. Searching around for ways to rejuvenate the Association, an outlandish suggestion was made to stage a major event like an All-Ireland final on American soil. This idea was first floated by John 'Kerry' O'Donnell, a leading figure in the New York GAA, and picked up by Canon Michael Hamilton, chairman of the Clare County Board. It was Hamilton who presented the case for holding an All-Ireland final in New York to delegates attending the GAA's Annual Congress in 1947. In a powerful speech, he appealed overwhelmingly to sentiment: the memory of the Great Famine was invoked as Hamilton spoke of the isolation of exile and the delight that thousands of Irish would take at the opportunity to watch their county in an All-Ireland final, most likely for the last time. Legitimate concerns over costs and logistics were drowned out in the wave of emotion aroused by the Canon's rhetoric. The motion passed, but months of negotiation and planning by GAA officials from Ireland and New York would follow before the 1947 All-Ireland football final was eventually staged at the Polo Grounds, home of the New York Giants baseball team. Despite the failure to fill 20,000 of the 54,000 seats in the stadium (not least because of heavy rain on the eve of the game), the event was an organisational triumph for the Association. Not only did it succeed in raising the profile of Gaelic games and improving participation across America, it also generated a profit, which the GAA used to set aside a grant of £2,000 – substantial for the time – for an 'International fund' to be used for the promotion of the Association in the United States.

After the war, the GAA at home and abroad once again served as an effective barometer of Irish economic performance. When the Irish economy stagnated and emigration increased, clubs in Ireland haemorrhaged members and struggled to field teams. This was a particular problem throughout the 1950s when soaring emigration ravaged entire families and communities, especially in rural areas, the very heartlands of the GAA. The extent of the exodus was borne out by the figures:

The Los Angeles Gaelic Athletic Association

Aided by the Catholic Wives and War Mothers and the Eire Four Province Club

118 East 119th Street   Telephone PLeasant 22287   Los Angeles 3, California

Los Angeles Breakfast Club - - - 3201 Los Feliz Boulevard - - - Sunday, 22nd - - - 2 P.M.
Net Proceeds to Provide Recreational Equipment for War Wounded at Sawtelle Hospital

President
Harry McDermott

First Vice-President
Joe Finneran

Second Vice-President
Mrs. Julia Collins

Corresponding Secretary
Frank Donnelley

Financial Secretary
Kathleen Collins

Treasurer
Joe Kerr

Chairlady
Hospital Visitation
Mrs. Michael Snee

Manager
Pat Murphy

Publicity
George Groe

**Members
on Speakers Committee**

HONORABLE THOS. P .WHITE
Judge Dist. Court of Appeal

HONORABLE FRANCIS J. WHELAN
Spec. Atty. U. S. Dept. Justice

HONORABLE JOSEPH SCOTT

Pres. Catholic Wives & War Mothers
MRS. CATHERINE D. MEIER

Pres. Four Eire Province Club
MARY CAVANAGH

Pres. Catholic Radio Guild
DAN DORAN

Chairman of the Day
JAMES GRATTAN

Working Vice Chairman
GEORGE DAVIS

July 2, 1945

Honorable Eamon deValera
Premier of Eire
Dublin, Eire

My dear Mr. deValera:

     As President of the Southern California chapter of the Gaelic Athletic Association and on behalf of the Association, I wish to extend to you the congratulations and felicitations of our body upon your dignified and estimable conduct of your high office during the troublous times that have occurred since the outbreak of the war in Europe. Viewed objectively, your administration of the affairs of state for Eire has been dispassionate, wholesouled and based upon the principles of justice.

     Eire's contribution of twelve million dollars to aid the starving and homeless people of Europe, as reported in the press, carries on her glorious tradition of devotion to Christian principles of mercy and charity. Those with Irish blood in their veins throughout the world can again be proud of their heritate.

     You may be interested to know that for years the Southern California chapter of the Gaelic Athletic Association has been carrying on what we believe to be a very good work. As citizens of the United States we have taken an active part in promoting the qualities that go to make better citizens -- the development of the mind and the body as well. At the same time we have ever been interested in Eire's success in meeting its problems as one of the nations of the world.

     We look forward to an even brighter future for Eire, fully cognizant of the fact that with you and your fellow officers in charge of the ship of state that hers will be a brilliant part in the eventful days to come. We would be honored to have this message read in the Dail.

     On behalf of the Gaelic Athletic Association, Southern California chapter, I remain

Respectfully yours,

Harry McDermott

HARRY McDERMOTT, President

You Also Serve When You BUY WAR BONDS

A letter from the Southern Chapter of the Californian GAA congratulates Éamon de Valera on the neutral stance his government adopted during the Second World War. By slowing immigration and diverting many eligible men into the armed services, the war seriously weakened the GAA in the United States. Yet, as the list of officers and members included on this document illustrates, the Association continued to command widespread support. The prominence of women in the administration of the Californian GAA is notable as is the assistance from various Catholic and Irish voluntary organisations. (D/Taoiseach, S 13852, National Archives of Ireland)

RADIO REVIEW
CINEMA AND THEATRE WEEKLY

VOL. 2

R.E., BBC, AFN AND EUROPEAN PROGRAMMES, SEPTEMBER 13-19

No. 76

SEPTEMBER 12th, 1947

Registered at the G.P.O. as a Newspaper.

Price 2D PRICE IN SIX COUNTIES AND GREAT BRITAIN 3D

ALL SET FOR ALL-IRELAND

Says Micheal O hEithir From New York

BAIL O DHIA ORAIBH GO LEIR A CHAIRDE !

Hello everybody, wherever you may be, may I send you greetings from New York, where the sights of many skyscrapers, the glamour of famous Radio City and the hustle and bustle of enormous crowds is enough to knock anybody off their balance.

From 8 p.m. to 10 p.m. (Irish time) on Sunday, September 14, Radio Eireann will be relaying from New York the 1947 All-Ireland Football Final between Cavan and Kerry. The commentator will be Micheal O hEithir, who sends greetings in this article to the listeners at home.

KERRY

Kerry line-out, not announced as we go to press, will be drawn from the following :

D. Kavanagh, Lieut. J. Keohane, P. Kennedy, P. B. Brosnan, T. Brosnan, B. Garvey, D. O'Keeffe, G. O'Sullivan, F. O'Keeffe, Teddy O'Connor, T. O'Connor, W. O'Donnell, E. Walsh, J. Lyne, D. Lyne, E. Dowling, M. Finucane, S. Keane, S. Terhan, T. O'Sullivan.

However, as I am on the eve of fulfilling a life-long dream—to broadcast from America, I cannot help looking back on the many thrills and incidents which have been the happy (and sometimes not so happy) lot of yours truly in the ever-interesting and changing life of a sports commentator.

In 1938 I went through the ordeal of a broadcast test when still a schoolboy, but more terrifying still was the day of my first effort on the air. Mullingar was the venue and August 14 the day. Oddly enough, the actual broadcast was not a source of worry, but as I made my way home to Dublin from the Westmeath town I was very confused. "What kind of a fool had I made of myself? Would I ever be able to look anyone in the face again?"

These thoughts were flying through my mind as we sped homewards, but on arrival there reporters, photographers and friends were waiting, and from their remarks I gathered that all was not as bad as expected.

Thus started a life of variety and interest.

All Weathers

At Thurles the microphone was on the sideline, and in sweltering heat, the sweat poured profusely as I covered a Munster Final; at Wexford the snow-covered field made football almost impossible, but the commentator shivered in a draughty watchman's hut converted into a broadcasting box;

at Croke Park the thunder cracked and the box rocked as Cork and Kilkenny fought out a thrilling hurling final as war clouds broke over Europe in September, 1939;

rain made visibility almost impossible at The Maze as the B.B.C. took coverage of the Ulster Derby and relayed my commentary to the race-goers present as well as to the listening public, while the numerous thrills of Grand Nationals and Cheltenham Gold Cups for the B.B.C. and the glamour of Horse Shows at Ballsbridge and Balmoral have all played their parts in the life of this broadcaster.

But I would not change for all the tea in China, nor would I like an indoor radio job instead of my outdoor commissions.

Any broadcaster will tell you the ordeal of speaking to an unseen audience, yet I have always received great satisfaction from letters received from listeners who have listened and enjoyed. Picture the lonely exile listening to some event that helps him to relive his life in Ireland or the invalid whose only connection with the world of sport is the radio — letters from these people always make one feel that all the work and

effort put into a broadcast is really worth while.

By the way, may I take this opportunity to thank all those people who sent messages of good wishes for the American trip?

Open the Window

Of course all letters are not "pats on the back." "Let us hear the band better, by leaving the window open at Croke Park," wrote many listeners, not realising that the window is always wide open. Then, on the more humorous side, the followers of some teams hold me responsible for their defeats and have actually blamed me for making players miss scores. What a life!

Please do not run away with the idea that I am complaining. Far from it, for all your letters, suggestions, etc., are welcome. I know none of us is perfect in our job and I am always anxious to hear from people with suggestions that might help to make things more interesting for listeners.

And so, as I prepare for the Polo Ground game at New York, may I express the wish that you will enjoy my effort to bring the thrills and glamour of the U.S.A. Final to your home. It will be a great day for the Irish over here, and I trust the radio will make it so for the folks at home.

Good luck, God Bless agus slan agaibh go leor.

Listeners who are tuned to Radio Eireann on Sunday at 7.20 p.m. will get the right atmosphere for the match, with the forty-minute feature, "Background to the G.A.A." This programme, which immediately precedes the relay from New York, has been compiled chiefly from data provided, among others, by Irish author Patrick Purcell.

CAVAN

Cavan team will be picked from the following players, who are at present in New York :

W. Doonan, B. Kelly, T. Sheridan, J. J. Cassidy, I. McGovern, T. O'Reilly, E. Tiernan, V. Gannon, B. O'Reilly, P. Sneed, P. J. Duke, J. J. O'Reilly, S. Deignam, C. McDyer, P. Brady, M. Higgins, J. Stafford, P. Donoghue.

CAVAN

KERRY

Michael O'Hehir prepares Irish radio audiences for his landmark broadcast of the 1947 All-Ireland football final between Cavan and Kerry from New York's Polo Grounds. Although championship matches continue to be played on American soil, this remains the only All-Ireland final to be staged outside the country.
(*GAA Oral History Project Archive*)

'I lived in New York, so Gaelic Park was like the church to us almost, we went there every Sunday, year after year after year. Actually I met my wife in Gaelic Park. You go there to hurl or football. There was a dance, there was a dinner, there was so much going on in Gaelic Park, and any given Sunday if there was any kind of a final, semi-final, you had close to 10,000 people there. Even all the Irish-American people used to go there; in fact, I shook Robert Kennedy's hand in Gaelic Park.' – **Jimmy Fahey, GAA Oral History Project Archive, 2009.**

for want of work and a better life, more than 400,000 people left the country over the course of a decade. This was mostly a flight from the land and it accelerated the demise of agriculture as the mainstay of Irish economic life. In 1954 GAA General Secretary Pádraig Ó Caoimh insisted that the GAA had a vital role to play in arresting this process of decline and stemming the flow of emigrants. According to Ó Caoimh, many of the country's clubs could, and should, work to brighten the appeal of rural living and, in doing so, weaken the pull of the great American cities. For all its great influence, the GAA was no match for the forces – social and economic – which drove the phenomenon of emigration in the 1950s. The departures continued unchecked. Young men and women continued to leave and the pages of local newspapers filled with stories of GAA teams losing players, sometimes several at once.

Many of these players, though lost to their home place, were not lost to the GAA. For many among this new wave of emigrant, the very existence of voluntary organisations like the GAA helped to soften somewhat the trauma of their exile. GAA clubs and events held an obvious attraction: they offered key points of contact, places where new emigrants could go to meet other Irish people, and find a job or a place to stay. It is obviously impossible to quantify the role played by the GAA as a welfare resource for emigrant communities. Yet the importance of Gaelic games as a meeting place, as well as a sporting and social outlet, was apparent from the manner in which increases in Irish immigration translated into an upsurge in GAA involvement.

Broadly speaking, the 1950s were boom years for the GAA in Britain and the United States. The fresh influx of immigrants helped replenish the numbers in old clubs and led to the creation of new ones. But there was also a steady stream of visits by top county teams, which afforded immigrants an opportunity to maintain a connection with home and see in the flesh some of the finest hurlers and footballers they had left behind.

'The Irish community found each other jobs and digs, far more than through any other source and the GAA was sort of part of that and so, you know, I would say that the GAA probably was the greatest source of community care in those days. It helped Irish men who arrived in the city to find jobs and digs. It was far, far more than just a Gaelic football or hurling thing.' – **Tommy Walsh, GAA Oral History Project Archive, 2008.**

In 1958, for instance, the traditional Easter and Whit Sunday inter-county games in Britain were replaced by a new tournament, the finals of which were played in Wembley stadium. This was a considerable gamble on the part of the London County Board. In choosing such a big venue, the Board hoped not only to provide a better showplace for the games, but to generate enough revenue to reduce a debt on thirteen acres of land they had previously acquired as a permanent home for Gaelic games in New Eltham – the Association's first official ground in the city. Their ambition paid off: over 33,000 people attended the Wembley Tournament, many drawn from GAA units and the wider Irish community across Britain. The success of the venture ensured that the games became a fixture in the GAA calendar until the 1970s.

For the top county teams, playing to emigrant crowds became a matter of almost seasonal routine. It was also a perk, a reward for winning national competitions and an opportunity to travel, to meet estranged family and friends and to broaden their experience of the world. For American-based players, on the other hand, the institution of competitive links with Ireland allowed for traffic in the opposite direction, an opportunity to come home. In 1950, the GAA Annual Congress decided to open the National Leagues to America, by allowing the National League winners to play against an American side on alternate years in Dublin and New York. Although strained relations between the Dublin and New York

'It's like I've two lives over here. I go to work and I talk soccer and rugby all day because that's all that any of them know about. The rest of my life is hurling then. Talking GAA and meeting GAA people. That's what's kept me happy in London.'– **Tommy Harrell from Wexford who emigrated to London in 1960, quoted in Tom Humphries,** *Green Fields: Gaelic Sport in Ireland* **(1996), p. 81.**

Action from a game between Offaly and Kilkenny teams at Gaelic Park in New York in the 1950s. Originally known as Inisfail Park, the ground has been used for Gaelic games in the city since the 1920s. However, the importance of the venue increased with the influx of Irish immigrants after the Second World War, when it became both a focus for GAA and Irish social activity in the city. (*Pickow Collection, NUIG*)

A player quenches his thirst after a St Brendan's Cup hurling game at the Polo Grounds, New York, 1954. In the inaugural competitions, New York faced Cork hurlers and Mayo footballers.
(*Getty Images*)

Christy Ring is congratulated after Cork defeated New York in the inaugural St Brendan's Cup at the Polo Grounds in November 1954. The game was reported in both the Irish and American press, with *Sports Illustrated* magazine describing the Cork star as 'a balding 33-year old Irishman, with broad back, strong legs and hands that could choke a bear'. (*Getty Images*)

Action from a Monaghan Cup game between Kilkenny and Tipperary at Wembley Stadium from the mid-1960s. Gaelic games were played at the spiritual home of English soccer from 1958 until the mid-1970s. (*Getty Images*)

IRISH EMBASSY

London, S.W. 1.

4th November, 1952.

The Secretary,
Department of External Affairs,
Dublin.

In any consideration of the question of
welfare activity in connection with our people here
in Britain, there are certain general, over-riding
factors which it is well to bear in mind.

2.   One is the great number of people of Irish
birth in Great Britain.   There are probably more
Irish-born people in Britain than in the U.S.A. When
the last census was taken in 1931, there were 505,385.
There are about 670,000 today. In 1931, the number of
people resident in this country who were born in the
Twenty-six Counties numbered 367,424. I am reliably
informed that when the results of last year's census
are published, the present number will be found to be
over half-a-million. The vast majority of Irish-born
people in Great Britain come from rural areas and
belong to the wage earning class. Although they are

nothing of the kind in this country. Irish-owned dance
halls, catering specifically for Irish people, are quite
common in London and elsewhere. They help our people to
meet and to get to know one another - a useful enough
service if - as some people say - loneliness is the most
frequent cause of moral lapses among Irish people here.
But, of course, the dance halls are purely commercial
concerns with little or no interest in the general welfare
of their patrons. The G.A.A. is well organised in the
London area and, with the help of an initial grant from
the Central Board, has reached a position in which it not
only does much to strengthen the morale and sense of
dignity of our people, but is financially sound and self-
supporting. In the rest of Great Britain however, there
is a relative dearth of similar provision. The lack of
sports and athletic clubs, and other forms or organised
activity, among the Irish population in this country has
a definite bearing on the problem of their general welfare.

A letter from the Irish
Embassy in London to the
Department of External
Affairs in Dublin addresses
the issue of the welfare of
Irish emigrants in Britain.
This letter underlined the
importance of Irish voluntary
agencies to emigrants and
makes special reference to
the positive influence of the
GAA in the London area.
(D/Taoiseach, S 11582,
National Archives of Ireland)

authorities forced the abandonment of the experiment before it could properly take root, a new international competition – played for the St Brendan's Cup – was introduced in 1954 and ran until 1960.

Within the American GAA, New York remained a singular presence. Through the 1950s, the city removed itself from efforts to establish a nationwide governing body for the Association in America. In 1959, when a North American County Board (NACB) was established, it embraced clubs in twenty-six cities from the east coast to the west, including Canada. New York alone stood apart, its independence rooted primarily in a consciousness of its own size and the strength of its Irish immigrant population. Over the two decades that followed, however, the numbers of Irish immigrants arriving in America fell sharply and no region escaped the effects. In part, the reduction in immigration to America was due to the improvement in Irish economic circumstances, a result of the expansionist policies of Seán Lemass' government from the late 1960s and, from 1973, Ireland's admission into the European Economic Community. But it also had much to do with the passage through the United States Congress of the Immigration Act of 1965, which imposed stricter criteria on entry into the country. As numbers dropped and clubs folded, the big underlying weakness in the American GAA set-up was exposed – it relied almost exclusively for players on Irish-born immigrants rather than their American-born children, who took to other sports as a way of assimilating into American life.

The lesson of this was clear: without proper youth programmes, the GAA abroad was destined to remain wedded to the vicissitudes of the Irish economy. Through the 1970s, there were signs of change as clubs began to recognise the importance of encouraging participation among the younger sections of Irish communities and teams from London and New York started to compete in All-Ireland minor championships, in football at least. The pressure to build from below abated with the economic downturn in Ireland in the 1980s, the decade that began with Joe Connolly's famous Croke Park speech. As unemployment increased, large-scale emigration returned. Some Irish counties were worse affected than others, but the case of Roscommon was illustrative of how deeply the problem cut. In the three years leading up to 1988, the county lost a quarter of its playing population to emigration. One club had an entire team wiped out over the same period. Some within the GAA believed that these difficulties were aggravated by the use of enticements by American units of the Association. In the late 1980s, one leading GAA official in Mayo, another western county ravaged by emigration, complained that clubs in New York, Boston and Chicago were luring players with the promise of 'large sums of money'. This was a recurring concern among Irish clubs and officials, yet it continued through the 1990s and beyond, a reminder of how dependent the American GAA became not merely on long-term emigrants, but equally on transient traffic from Ireland – the student on a summer visa and the big-name county player on a weekend trip. Throughout the 1980s and 1990s, a good county hurler or footballer could jet into New York, Boston or Chicago, play a match and leave again with his wallet fattened by a roll of cash.

For much of the 1990s, American stopovers by county players filled a void left by the suspension of annual All-Stars tours, the players' awards scheme that combined recognition of individual achievement with outreach to Irish emigrant communities. From their inception in the early 1970s through to the early 1990s, the All-Stars had travelled exclusively to cities in North America and Canada, the big centres of Irish settlement. When the tours were revived under new sponsorship in the late 1990s, however, the choice of destination broadened to include such locations as Dubai, Singapore and Hong Kong.

Cumann Lúit Cleas Gaeðeal

SENIOR FOOTBALL CHALLENGE

coronco

v.

muineacán

AT GRATTON PARK, INNISKEEN

· on ·

SUNDAY, 18th SEPT., 1960, at 3.30 p.m.

Referee : M. McArdle.

PRECEDED BY MINOR CHAMPIONSHIP DIVISIONAL FINAL AT 2 P.M.

Castleblayney v. Donaghmoyne

Referee : P. O'Rourke.

ADMISSION 2/-; SIDELINE 1/- extra.

Luaċ - - 3p.

•

N⁰ 75   Please hold your Programme
for Draw at Interval.

•

Printed by R. & S. PRINTERS, MONAGHAN.

The traffic of teams flowed both in and out of Ireland. In the summer of 1911, for instance, a team of Irish expatriate hurlers in America travelled to Ireland to play a series of games. Other teams followed. This is the programme for a challenge match organised between Toronto and Monaghan in 1960. Toronto were reportedly the first ever Canadian football team to tour Ireland and they arrived with a party of 196 people. The Canadians played a number of challenge games against club and county opposition, but attending the All-Ireland football final in Croke Park was the highlight of their visit. (*Monaghan County Museum*)

All-Star footballers play a game against the spectacular Hong Kong skyline in January 2005. Initiated in the 1970s and focused primarily on North America, the destination of All-Star tours has, since the late 1990s, reflected the changing patterns of Irish emigrant settlement. (*Inpho*)

'New York may have done much to kill the goose that lays the golden eggs. Their wholesale importation of players from this country . . . has done much to diminish the popular appeal of county sides from this country in Gaelic Park. Every Sunday of the New York playing season provided its quota of stars from Ireland in Gaelic Park and it in no way surprises me that the novelty of Irish county teams, as a consequence, grew thin.' – **Journalist John D. Hickey, writing in the *Irish Independent*, 23 April 1974.**

These were not exercises in new-found exoticism on the GAA's part. Rather, they were a calculated response to a growing Irish presence in these regions, most visibly expressed in the upsurge of GAA club numbers. In fact, the rise of Gaelic games in regions beyond America and Britain has been a singular feature of the Association's overseas development since the mid-1990s. As air travel became cheaper and Ireland became more and more immersed in the global economy, Irish migration patterns changed. The geography of Gaelic games changed with it. From admittedly small bases, Asia and Europe became major growth areas. The games spread through the increased movement of young, educated professionals – men and women – to work in the areas of education, business and finance. Among them were many who had little involvement with the GAA at home, but found in it abroad a unique way to express their Irish identity and meet with other Irish people. What distinguishes the GAA most of all in these new growth regions, however, is its multinational membership. Throughout Asia and Europe, the GAA has become an umbrella for a kaleidoscope of nationalities who have been seduced by the athletic demands of the sports and the social life around them. In October 2008, when teams gathered in the Malaysian city of Penang for the Asian GAA games, players from more than twenty countries took to the field.

Phenomenal as this expansion has been, it has done nothing to challenge the position of the traditional Irish emigrant centres of the United States and Britain. These remain the GAA's international strongholds. Not only have they more clubs and better facilities than any other region, they have also in recent times moved to break with their dependence on Irish-born immigrants and, as a result, their vulnerability to fluctuations in the Irish economy. After a decade of slowing immigration, both America and Britain have staked their futures on youth programmes and grass-roots development. In 2008 the Irish government weighed in

Hurling on holiday: two Irishmen enjoy a puck around on Bondi Beach, Sydney, January 2000. The 'year out' working holiday in Australia became a rite of passage for thousands of young Irish through the late 1990s and early 2000s. Many maintained a connection with the GAA by joining clubs based around the major Australian cities. (*Inpho*)

with financial support, assisting the GAA in the provision of ten new full-time coaches for Britain and four for the United States. In doing so, the Irish state has recognised that the influence of the GAA among the Irish diaspora reaches well beyond the realm of sport. As well as projecting Irish identity and culture across the globe, the GAA has acted as a welfare resource and a community network for Irish people when they are far from home. When Maurice Davin led his Invasion party across the Atlantic in 1888, he could never have imagined just how far the games would eventually travel. With almost 300 overseas affiliated clubs, the GAA has become a national organisation with a global reach.

'I had no involvement in GAA when I was younger, even in Kerry. And we had an All-Ireland medallist, Billy Casey, as our next-door neighbour. I was tired of the gym, the isolation of it, and I wanted a team sport. It's a great networking and bonding structure. At the same time it provides lots of fun and fitness and opens up the Irish community to you. I know more Irish people as a result of the GAA after six years in China . . . It has also opened me up to the volunteer system. When you're young you take the organisation for granted, but there is a lot of volunteer work that goes on, and nothing would happen without the people here. It means all the best things to me.' – **Angela Keane from Lispole, now resident in Beijing, quoted in** *The Irish Times*, 8 November 2008.

'The number one goal of the club is to bring Gaelic football to kids, and show them what it is and keep it going, that when we're all dead and gone they'll still be playing Gaelic football in America.' – **Niall O'Neill, GAA Oral History Project Archive, 2009.**

The multicultural face of the GAA abroad: members of the Taiwan Celts Gaelic Football Club at the 2007 Asian Gaelic Games tournament in Singapore. Pictured are (l–r): Gabriella Beyer, Canada; Amy Gillian, Canada; Rachel Grimes, Dublin; Courtney McCurdy, USA; Erin Pitkin, Canada; Kathryn Basson, Canada; Chelsea Mason, USA; and Holly Itoga, USA. Founded in 1996 as a social and sporting outlet for Irish expatriates, the Taiwan Celts Gaelic Football Club now attracts an international membership. (*Taiwan Celts Gaelic Football Club*)

This is one of the earliest action shots of Gaelic football. It was taken in the 1890s at Gaelic Field, now known as Fraher Field, in Dungarvan, County Waterford. A striking feature of the early scoring system, depicted here, was the use of side posts and a soccer-style goal scoring area. These remained in place until 1910 when they were replaced with the modern system of uprights and a crossbar. (*Waterford County Images*)

Crossroads

'The idealism has somehow mattered, as much as the speed of the games and the skill of the players.'

Writer Colm Tóibín, speaking on the GAA at the Royal Irish Academy, Dublin, 2 June 2009.

It's meant great friendships with fellas that I have abused and have abused me,
but the amazing thing about it is it makes great lasting friendships, it spans
party politics, you can see anybody from the unemployed or the
unemployable on the team to the doctor, to the politician, to the highflyer . . .
there's no snobbishness in the GAA, or very little anyway, it crosses all
spectrums of life, the local team and the parish.

'The GAA widened the horizon
of the young men, and made them
proud of their country, giving them a new interest in it.
By its strict enforcement of rule on the field, it disciplined the fierce
and tumultuous spirits amongst them.'

Every sport has its own myths. Such myths imagine that rugby was founded by William Webb Ellis who, one afternoon in 1823, is supposed to have caught a ball and run with it across a school field in the midlands of England, thereby inventing rugby, or that Abner Doubleday is said to have stopped a game of marbles outside a barbers' shop in Cooperstown, New York, in 1839 to sketch out a plan which he had just invented for the game of baseball. Neither event happened – their very neatness as defining moments in history is enough to suggest their implausibility. Both rugby and baseball were the product of long processes, not the sporting equivalent of the Big Bang.

The GAA's own invention myth is complex. It sees the story of the foundation of the GAA in political terms and imagines that the GAA was primarily focused on a project of national liberation. This myth was forged by the Association and acquiesced to by historians who have understated the social influence of the GAA, while focusing on its nationalist activities. There is, of course, a certain truth to this myth. The divided politics and contested identities of Ireland in the decades between 1884 and 1921 inevitably coloured the origins and development of the GAA. Nonetheless, the politics of certain of its members and officials – and the radicalism of so many of those who wrote about the games – has tended to over-shadow the reality of the engagement with the GAA as experienced by the vast swathe of its membership. Politics mattered and mattered a lot, but so did much else, and for most people the story of their involvement with the GAA revolves around playing and watching matches (not to mention the delight taken in preview and review, arguments and dreams). The meaning of these stories lies in their importance to the individuals involved. Taken apart, their significance is personal and often local; bound together they are the history of the GAA.

Action from a hurling match at Loughinisland, County Down, *c*. 1915. In this parish, as with other parts of the country at the time, wider social and political events impacted upon the organisation of Gaelic games. In the years before and after this photograph was taken, the playing of hurling and Gaelic football suffered from political unrest. It was not until the mid-1920s that the GAA in Loughinisland enjoyed a resurgence in activity. (*Loughinisland GAC*)

'It is arguable that no organisation had done more for Irish nationalism than the GAA – not the IRB, so influential in its founding but now dissolved, not the Gaelic League, its linguistic counterpart which had failed in its mission to restore the national language, not the Irish Parliamentary Party, which had been unable to adjust to the nationalist revival, not even Sinn Féin which had broken apart under the impact of the Treaty. The Gaelic Athletic Association had fulfilled its mission – to revive the native games of Ireland, and to awaken the national spirit. Throughout all the vicissitudes, harassments, chicaneries, divisions, manipulations and disputes, it had kept the objectives for its existence in view, and had succeeded in achieving them.' – W. F. Mandle, *The Gaelic Athletic Association and Irish Nationalist Politics, 1884–1924* (1987), p. 221.

This accumulation of GAA stories has built traditions and it is commonplace that traditions matter in Gaelic games. Those who are born into a winning tradition can be propelled by that tradition to further success or, alternatively, to be suffocated by its pressures. Others who are battling to escape from under the rubble of decades of failure and to invent their own tradition of success take a particular pleasure in defeating more-storied opponents. How success is attained is also measured against the past, not least by a cadre of 'traditionalists' or 'purists' who analyse the style of winning. This measurement invariably involves notions that a 'golden age' once flourished and that cynicism is a modern illness. It ignores the reality that since the GAA laid down its first rules for hurling and football, styles of play have continuously evolved in pursuit of victory. Clubs and counties that have enjoyed success have not slavishly adhered to any one style. The one constant is that teams have always sought to play in whatever style was considered necessary to win.

The evolution of hurling and Gaelic football as sport and as spectacle is central to understanding the enduring appeal of the GAA. For all that the rule changes and the search for tactical innovation have changed the style of play, the essence of the games as challenges of physique, courage, skill and intelligence remains unaltered. Gaelic games are not merely contests between teams, but also between individuals. The marking system almost always sets up a direct clash between two players and the unfolding of this clash holds much of the attraction in playing and watching games. The most memorable contests are ones not between teams, but between two players, each trying to outdo the other.

'The GAA widened the horizon of the young men, and made them proud of their country, giving them a new interest in it. By its strict enforcement of rule on the field, it disciplined the fierce and tumultuous spirits amongst them . . . The young men learned that skill and self-control were better and nobler than quarelling and fighting, and that deft handling of the Camán was more to be admired than the ability to trounce a brother Irishman with the fist or cudgel.' – **Rev James B. Dollard, in** *The Gaelic Athletic Annual and County Directory, 1907–08*, p. 19.

Across the GAA, memories of contests inevitably invite the drawing of comparisons. Players and teams are judged not just by what they have won, but also against the achievements of the past. It is one of the finer traditions of the GAA to believe that the men of today are not fit to lace the boots of those of yesteryear. This is not a simple matter of ability; it is also about manliness. No generation is ever considered tougher than the one that went before. It is as if the matches played by previous generations were defined by carnage – as if, in every parish across Ireland, Sunday Mass was followed by a re-enactment of the Battle of the Clontarf.

Since its foundation, the GAA has stitched itself into the fabric of local communities. This did not happen overnight. In the early years of the Association, clubs rose and fell in different areas, their very existence dependent on the dedication of a few individuals whose own presence in the community was often at the whim of social and economic forces. Later, as clubs became more established, their place in society evolved. As the twentieth century progressed, teams no longer rented fields or togged out in ditches or the back rooms of public houses. Now, a glorious necklace of GAA fields – often surrounded by stands, a clubhouse which serves as both dressing room and community centre, and lit by brilliant floodlights – provides physical testimony to the centrality of the GAA to communities across Ireland.

Hurling gained a new lease of life. Football was revived. Running, jumping, weight-throwing, wrestling, bowling and handball were practised in districts where they had become only a tradition . . . Thousands of people eagerly gathered to witness hurling and football matches and athletic contests and the dull monotony of Irish rural life was dispelled forever.' – **Summary of the GAA's first year, quoted in T. F. O'Sullivan,** *Story of the GAA* (1916), p. 18.

The people's champion: 37-year-old John Maher is carried from the Thurles sportsfield to Thurles town square after leading Tipperary to victory in the 1945 Munster hurling final. The throng of players and supporters is led by the Moycarkey Pipers. (*Micheál Maher*)

The winning tradition: Norman Ross fills the Sam Maguire at the Royal Hotel on Valentia Island as Kerry's All-Ireland celebrations continue into October 1959. The All-Ireland winning team was captained by islandman Mick O'Connell, later to become an iconic figure in the game. (*Kennelly Archive*)

'Since its foundation the Gaelic Athletic Association has remained consistent and faithful in its active support for everything that is Irish and national – the language movement, the struggle for freedom, Irish industry and manufacture. It taught the young men of Ireland the value of team-work and the meaning of discipline, both on and off the playing field. It played no small part in wiping out *shoneenism* and the false class-distinction imposed, directly or indirectly, by an alien conquerer, with all its consequences; on the Gaelic sports fields master and man stand equal.' – Pádraig Puirséal, *The GAA in its Time* (1982), pp. 280–281.

That the GAA means so much to so many communities is a cause of celebration; that there are many more communities where the GAA has merely a spectral presence is a matter of regret. The reasons for this are complex. Partly, it is a matter of money. Ever since traditional field games were recast in the nineteenth century into modern sports where a network of clubs compete against one another under the control of national and international organisations, participation has been dependent on a certain disposable income. At the founding meeting of the Association in Thurles in 1884, Maurice Davin highlighted the ambition to provide amusement for the poorer sections of Irish society who had been born into what he described as 'an everlasting round of labour'. There are whole areas of Irish cities and towns where the GAA remains an irrelevance, and the inescapable implication is that the Association has not done enough to open its doors to people of limited income.

That the GAA's network of clubs does not extend still further than it already does is also rooted in traditions of play which extend back across centuries. The story of the geography of modern sport is largely that of organisations dominating an area by getting in first and laying formidable foundations. This basic fact is crucial to understanding why rugby league dominates certain of the conurbations of northern England, and why rugby union thrives in south Wales and in Limerick. In many cases, clubs in those areas built on traditions of play which long predate the Victorian sports revolution. On top of that, the peculiar relationship between sport and social class – best observed in the elevated position of certain sports in certain schools – is another relic of the nineteenth century. Across Ireland, the superior presence of soccer in urban working-class communities and of rugby in schools which serve the upper middle classes has built barriers to the spread of Gaelic games.

Closing ranks: a group of Gardaí join spectators at a hurling
match in Clare in the 1950s. For all that Gaelic games drew
communities together, there remained barriers to participation
throughout the twentieth century. Where some had a wider political
and social foundation, some were created by the Association itself.
For much of the twentieth century, the GAA excluded people who
played 'foreign games', attended dances organised by 'foreign
games' clubs or were members of the British armed forces or police.
(*Dorothea Lange Collection, the Oakland Museum of California,*
City of Oakland. Gift of Paul S. Taylor)

'In keeping with a siege mentality established many centuries ago, Protestants in Northern Ireland come to regard individual members of the GAA not merely as potential trouble-makers, but as representatives of an alien tradition which threatens the Protestant and Unionist way of life. The constitutional position of the GAA, concerning the unification of Ireland and the exclusion of the security forces, does nothing to alleviate such suspicions. Neither does the naming of the Provincial stadium after the Republican hero and British traitor, Sir Roger Casement, or the continued practice of using hurley sticks to symbolize Irish nationalism, together with their use by paramilitary punishment squads.' – **John Sugden and Alan Bairner,** *Sport, Sectarianism and Society in a Divided Ireland* (1993), p. 37.

The GAA, for a long time, conspired in the creation of those barriers. Until 1971, the Association had a ban on membership for people who played 'foreign games' (soccer, rugby, cricket and hockey), who attended a dance organised by 'foreign games' clubs, or who were members of the British armed forces or police. Use of GAA grounds was also refused to non-GAA sporting organisations which promoted 'foreign games'. The set of rules was rooted in a commitment to its vision of an 'Irish Ireland' and was the source of enduring opposition from within and without the GAA. They had the impact of alienating from the GAA men and women who were not willing to abandon entirely sports they loved to play. Claiming exclusive loyalty was idealist in nature, but undermined the GAA's ambition to spread its games and to develop its network of clubs.

A striking feature of the GAA's membership is the absence of unionists. History has rendered unionist participation unlikely, if not impossible. The ostentatious presence of the symbols of Catholicism at major GAA events has waned in parallel with a similar decline across Irish public life, but its legacy persists. The GAA has made attempts to develop cross-community programmes in the north of Ireland, but it cannot deny its own history. That the GAA's official guide states that the basic aim of the GAA is to strengthen the national identity through the promotion of Gaelic games emphasises the broader historical mission of the Association. As well as being identified with nationalism, the GAA is embedded in the nationalist community and, in the divided society of the north, this has obvious implications for attracting unionists. Transcending this fact will require decades of persistence and a shift in the aims of the Association. This, in turn, will require change on a scale made all the more difficult by the GAA's own experiences in the Troubles.

The murder of GAA members, the destruction of GAA property, and the requisition of GAA grounds is the raw truth of the decades after 1970 in Northern Ireland. The hostility of loyalist paramilitaries and the British security forces profoundly affected the GAA in the north. The danger of being a member of the GAA was not something that was always understood by Association members in the south and this was the cause of considerable frustration. Even in the north, the GAA itself was divided as to how it might most appropriately respond to the political climate. Some clubs and some counties were more overtly nationalist in their operations than others and this, inevitably, was a source of strain, even bitterness. Just as the GAA was hailed for helping to heal the splits of the Civil War in the south after the 1920s, it is a considerable compliment to the Association that the tension wrought by the Troubles brought no split.

Through its history, being bound into – and, indeed, being a conscious actor in – this issue of forging a national identity has caused problems for the GAA. There can be no doubt that some of the GAA's more significant mistakes have been around this issue of identity. Although it does many things right, the GAA also has the capacity to do wrong. In the process it embarrasses its membership and diminishes itself as an organisation. Sometimes it makes decisions which honour the letter of its rules but entirely subvert the aims of the Association. In history, probably the finest example of this is the decision in 1938 to remove as Patron of the GAA Dr Douglas Hyde on the grounds that he had attended a soccer match in the course of his duties as President of Ireland. By the laws of the Association, the decision was correct; by any measure of commonsense it was

'My beginnings in the GAA are associated very much with a kind of what I would call a fidelity which is comparable to a religious fundamentalism, which I think is the life blood of the GAA and that was expressed for us in the Tipperary hurling teams of the 1950s and the 1960s. I think it's an extraordinary type of respect we had for the men who wore the jersey, the men who supported the local club, the men who were the local champions. We knew nothing about community development at that period, we knew nothing about community. We had the Catholic Church, we had the Garda station and we had the GAA.' – Historical geographer Prof William Nolan speaking at the GAA 125 History Conference, Croke Park, 25 April 2009.

Hawkers go about their business at the Thurles Sportsground, now Semple Stadium, in 1953. As the popularity of Gaelic games has grown, so too has the commercial activity around them. (*Fáilte Ireland*)

ludicrous to deploy such rules against a man who had helped to invent the very ideal of an 'Irish Ireland' which the rules were supposed to help establish.

Over the decades, the GAA's ban rules have steadily been eroded to the point where only the use of its grounds by non-GAA organisations is precluded. Even the opening of Croke Park to rugby and soccer during the redevelopment of Lansdowne Road has weakened this particular ban. The decision to open Croke Park was reached after a long process of debate and dispute. In this – as in much else – the GAA could never stand accused of rushing into things. This is the organisation's greatest weakness, leaving it plagued by an inability to redress obvious grievances. But aversion to change is also its greatest strength. The GAA has never been beholden to those who subvert informed discussion with their own brand of cant and populism. This is just as well given the capacity of the Association to induce the normally sane to turn rabid. First amongst those are individuals for whom the audit of the GAA's value to Irish society has been how much help it provided to its competitors. The characterisation of those – rightly or wrongly – who have stood by certain principles as backwoodsmen is precisely the type of intolerance of which sections of the GAA have been accused routinely.

Ultimately, the GAA is well used to criticism from many quarters and this is to be expected for any organisation of its stature and size. On occasion it can be prickly or resentful in the face of criticism; mostly it is sensible enough to ignore the shouts of the crowd. The criticism that matters in the GAA is the criticism that comes from within. The GAA generally listens to its own, though only when the noise is loud enough. As the Association reached its 125th anniversary, a variety of concerns excited its membership. Prime amongst those were a range of issues with money at their core. Like any progressive organisation the GAA has to raise significant levels of finance if it is to prosper. Indeed, the story of the modern GAA is the story of the practical marriage of voluntarism and commercialism. One without the other would leave the GAA unbalanced and ill-placed to succeed. The amateur status of the GAA's player base has famously allowed it to invest the bulk of its finances in the provision of facilities for its members. This amateurism has come under significant pressure. Managers at club and county level have received payments for their work; players at inter-county level have established an association to lobby for improved conditions and increased rewards. With players from sports in Ireland which draw considerably less support than Gaelic games getting paid for their play, elite GAA players have sought material gain from the increased commercialisation of their games.

'Tá an iomáint ag fáil bháis fós i gceantracha nach raibh sa pheil iontu ach cuach sa nead. Tá sí ag fáil bháis i gcathair Chorcaí agus soir uaithi, a bhuíochas san do bhord an chontae. Tá lucht leanúna anois ag peileadóirí Luimnigh. Aiséirí sa pheil i Loch Garman. Foireann rugbaí na Mumhan chuid d'fhéiniúlacht na dúiche. Más áil leis an gCumann an iomáint a chur chun cinn, caithfear srian a chur leis an bpeil. Tá sé chomh simplí leis sin. Ealaín is ea an iomáint, agus tógann blianta lena foghlaim. Útamáil ar an gcuid is fearr an rud eile. Is fusa breith ar lamhnán muice agus í a lascadh le cóir na gaoithe ná siúl leis na déithe i dtreo na síoraíochta.' – **Alan Titley** highlights the ongoing challenges that face the GAA in promoting the game of hurling, *The Irish Times*, 26 February 2009.

This drift towards professionalism has alarmed those who believe it will undermine the cohesiveness of the GAA and further upset the balance between club and county teams. That is a balance which – in parts of the country – has seen clubs suffer repeated humiliation, their fixture lists the plaything of the managers of county teams who believe too often that their success is dependent on restricting the club activities of the players in their charge. The failure of various county committees to organise a proper programme of games in their counties has frustrated club players who spend the best of the summer engaged in challenge – rather than championship – matches. At its worst, this failure has resulted in the playing of senior county finals in December. For the ordinary club player, the inequity of their treatment remains the single greatest failure of the GAA. Against that, there have been some advances. The All-Ireland club championships have grown in popularity since their establishment in the 1970s, replacing the interprovincial Railways cups as the centrepiece of the Association's St Patrick's Day activity. The inauguration of All-Ireland championships for junior and intermediate clubs means that virtually every player in the country can aspire to reach Croke Park in any given year.

Playing in Croke Park remains the dream of GAA players; walking down Jones' Road on All-Ireland Sunday is precisely what every spectator wishes for at the start of a championship summer. Against the skyline of Dublin, Croke Park stands majestic, surveying the north inner city. It is a miracle of modern Ireland, though it has wrongly been described as a symbol of Celtic Tiger Ireland and of the supposed rebirth of the Irish nation as a people overflowing with confidence, maturity and achievement. It is nothing of the sort. Croke Park is a story of love,

'It's meant great friendships with fellas that I have abused and have abused me, but the amazing thing about it is it makes great lasting friendships. It spans party politics, you can see anybody from the unemployed or the unemployable on the team to the doctor, to the politician, to the highflyer. There's no snobbishness in the GAA, or very little anyway, it covers all spectrums from the rich to the poor.' – **Bobby Goff, GAA Oral History Project Archive, 2009.**

not one of lust – a monument to voluntarism and to people committing to a common cause. It was conceived by the GAA when Ireland was in the depths of the 1980s' recession and rebuilt ahead of schedule as a home for Gaelic games. It is about love of sport, of culture, of locality. It heaves and throbs on big match-days – but not like other stadiums. The noise is different – warm and loud.

GAA people are justly proud of the development of Croke Park, but it is not a stadium without fault. There are times when Croke Park is emblematic of the sense of dislocation that GAA members sometimes feel – a sense that the idea of Croke Park with its corporate boxes and Americanised franchises is too far removed from the reality of their club lives. Rather than being simply an asset at the disposal of the Association, the stadium has gathered a momentum of its own, just by its very presence. This has led to the playing of matches there which would better be played in provincial venues. And this, in turn, has changed the nature of the championship summer. A lot of what is unique about the GAA is the atmosphere in country towns on the days of big matches. When local rivals meet in the provincial championships much of the day is ritual: traffic jams, freestyle parking, men playing banjos, the smell of frying onions, stopping in the same pub or shop. Best of all is the atmosphere in a tight ground, local people standing beside each other on a grassy bank or a terrace, getting burned in the sun and exchanging sneers. Great matches to win; bad matches to lose; terrible matches to miss.

What is true for county matches is even truer of local club rivalries. The story of club championships is one of matches won and lost at the same place to the same people year after year, decade after decade. Local rivalries between neighbouring clubs – or between perennial rivals within counties – are often coloured by battles between successive generations of families. At their worst, these rivalries have mutated into spleen and inherited bitterness. At their best they epitomise everything that is truly great about Gaelic games: hard sporting contests between the white lines and genuine friendship outside those same lines.

The home of Gaelic games sits at the heart of the capital city. The redevelopment of Croke Park is a monument to voluntarism, courage and self-belief. To mark the 125th anniversary of the Association, a fireworks display and light show accompanied the Saturday night National Football League fixture between Dublin and All-Ireland champions Tyrone on 31 January 2009. (*Inpho*)

'Can Kerry ever prosper in hurling while they are landlocked in Munster? Can Kilkenny ever prosper in Gaelic football in the midst of powerful neighbours? These are simple and honest questions. They should be asked loudly and clearly at every annual convention of the association. The GAA is a democratic body, kind of – but it is cursed with men who are terrified of change.' – Con Houlihan, *More Than a Game: Selected Sporting Essays* (2003), pp. 142–143.

The first lesson of sport, of course, is that you will most likely lose far more than you will win. Across the ebb and flow of championship play every club and every county has suffered bitter disappointment, but has also enjoyed memorable successes. Beyond the matter of winning and losing – and not in any way to diminish the extent to which that is important – a vital aspect of Gaelic games is that of representing a place. Largely because of the GAA, the boundaries between counties are sacred lines in Irish life. Each county carries its own stories, a place apart, with its own traditions and its own history. You may be born just a field away from your neighbour, but if a county boundary runs through that field, your neighbour is somehow different. You might learn to love that neighbour, but you would never want to change places with them. And no contest is as intense as that played out between border rivals. People who agree on everything else fall out over football and hurling. From this sporting rivalry flows all manner of other differences. Most often these differences are imagined rather than real – but they are important nonetheless. It is the territorial nature of the rivalries which gives so much spice to the GAA – it gives rivalries a depth and texture not always found in other sports.

There is a notion that changes in modern Irish society will undercut traditional rivalries. The classic city-versus-country rivalry of Dublin and Meath is perceived as a case in point. According to legend, on the morning of matches, big Meath farmers climbed aboard their Massey Fergusons and Range Rovers, and rolled across the countryside like giant Panzer divisions off to conquer Dublin before teatime. Waiting for them, the Dubs stood on the road outside the pubs of Fairview and Drumcondra drinking pints and sneering at the savages up for the day. Not any more. The housing estates of Meath are filled with houses with Dublin flags flying from their windows. GAA summer schools in Navan are full of children wearing Dublin jerseys. Recent demographic changes do not necessarily mean dramatic changes in GAA rivalries, however, as the notion of shifting loyalties

Crowds gather in Clones before an Ulster Championship football final between Armagh and Fermanagh in July 2008. Every summer, local rivalries, played out in provincial venues, bring a unique atmosphere to Irish country towns. (*Sportsfile*)

On the edge of Ireland, at the centre of the community. Set against a spectacular strip of Atlantic coastline, the Na Cealla Beaga (Killybegs) Club in County Donegal plans the next stage of its development. The move from the old pitch at Fintra (on the left), home to club teams since 1967, has paved the way for the club to acquire a ground of its own. The new facilities include a new pitch, photographed here after being re-sown, a new training field and separate men's and women's dressing rooms. In common with similar developments in other clubs, funding has come from a range of sources: lottery funding, grants from Croke Park and the Ulster Council and local fund-raising initiatives, including weekly lottos, fashion shows and a cow-dung drop. (*Fred Reilly*)

is no new phenomenon. For decades, men and women who moved to Dublin often flew the flags of their native counties from the windows of Dublin housing estates and dressed their children in the colours of home. With the passage of time those same children broke the hearts of their parents by standing on the Hill, wearing the blue of Dublin. This Gaelic rite of passage will now occur in reverse and Dublin parents will eventually come to accept their children in the colours of ancient enemies. It might not be easy to stomach, but it is a celebration of the GAA as an agent of social cohesion, as an organisation which helps to bind communities together. Irish people may move from place to place, but the GAA offers a way into most communities.

Maintaining its presence as an organisation that sits at the heart of communities is the greatest challenge facing the GAA. Every decade brings its own obstacles. Often these obstacles are the construct of wider social and economic change. Where once the GAA lost players, teams and clubs to emigration – witness the devastation of the 1950s where almost half a million Irish people were forced to emigrate – the boom of the millennium brought its own pressures. Changes in working patterns, the extraordinary sprawl of the greater Dublin area, the building of new estates around towns and villages all across the country, the rise in the numbers commuting and in the distances being commuted, and the growth in the number of immigrants all redefined social life in Ireland. Through all of this, the GAA prospered, with record numbers of players and record attendances at matches.

As boom returned to bust, the spectre of emigration returned and so too did the certainty that a fall in disposable income will challenge the ambitions of the Association. The network of GAA clubs across the world will most likely profit from home-grown economic woes. In Ireland, the rude health of the GAA is no insulation against the challenges it faces – some age-old, others recent and still more yet to unfold. All told, the challenges facing the GAA require skilful management. The ability, first of all, to identify the key challenges, and then to plot a path forward

'. . . those who control the GAA's affairs must try to differentiate between genuine constructive criticism, from those who wish the Association a long and improved life, and the crepitations of the Humpty McDumptys who, apart from being little squalls in search of teacups, are very often second division mice attempting to be first division rats – and failing.'
– Breandán Ó hEithir, *Over the Bar: A Personal Relationship with the GAA* (1984), p. 214.

will define the future of the Association. This is as true for local clubs as it is for county committees, provincial councils and the central administration of the Association. In the past, the GAA has been well served by the stability and quality of its leadership at local and national level. It will continue to require this. There is nothing inevitable or fated about the GAA's position in Irish society. It is a tribute to untold hours of voluntary commitment. Regardless of the social pressures that emerge, the lure of the Association and its games has always commanded the dedication and loyalty of enough people to guarantee its safe passage.

That is not to suggest that progress will be unrestricted and smooth. Much of the fun in being involved in the GAA is its capacity for controversy. The ability of any one section of the Association to tie itself in knots at any given time is remarkable and persistent. It is a source of no little amusement to those other sections of the Association watching on, relieved that it is not them on this occasion standing in the heat of the fire. In the end, one controversy always passes, quickly to be replaced by another and then another. This is testimony to the place of the GAA in Irish society, to the fact that the affairs of the Association are something of a national conversation.

It is a measure of the change which has framed the story of the GAA that, when the Association was founded in 1884, Ireland was part of the United Kingdom, isolated on the periphery of Europe, with an economy dominated by agriculture and a society dominated by religion. That country is, in many respects, unrecognisable from the one in which the GAA reached its 125th anniversary. The basic ambition laid out by Michael Cusack and Maurice Davin at the founding meeting of the GAA was to change how sport was organised in Ireland. That ambition has been met. The Association they founded is a singular body – part sports organisation, part national movement. In the sweep of its activities and in its presence across Ireland, it is difficult to think of any organisation which more profoundly influences the daily lives of so many people. And that, perhaps, is the finest tribute that might be paid to the Gaelic Athletic Association – its games, its people, its history, its place in Irish life.

The future of the GAA rests on its ability to attract successive generations onto its fields. This is as true for the country as it is for the city. The Association's network of clubs leaves it well placed to meet the demands of the future. However, the degree to which the GAA succeeds in meeting these challenges will inevitably be defined by the commitment of its members. As this photograph from a club in south Dublin makes clear, the pull of the games will still need to be matched by the push of voluntary effort. (*Fred Reilly*)

Notes

Chapter 1: Beginnings

P. 3: 'At 3 p.m. on Saturday 1 November 1884 . . .' There may have been as few as seven – or as many as fourteen – present in the room, depending on which newspaper account is believed. See, for example, *Cork Examiner*, 3 November 1884 and *Tipperary Advocate*, 8 November 1884.

P. 3: 'It was not that there was anything wrong . . .' *Cork Examiner*, 3 November 1884 and *Tipperary Advocate*, 8 November 1884.

P. 4: 'For example, when his one-time friend . . .' *United Ireland*, 19 December 1885.

P. 10: 'He used this knowledge to design and build his own boats . . .' For a full account of the life of Maurice Davin, see Séamus Ó Riain's excellant biography, *Maurice Davin (1842–1927). First President of the GAA* (1994).

P. 16: 'Cusack wrote admiringly of how schools in England . . .' *The Celtic Times*, 14 May 1887.

P. 16: 'Cusack wrote that there was no better game for boys . . .' *The Shamrock*, 8 July 1882.

P. 16: 'Cusack was club secretary and trainer . . .' See Paul Rouse, 'Michael Cusack: sportsman and journalist', in Mike Cronin, William Murphy and Paul Rouse (eds.), *The Gaelic Athletic Association, 1884–2009* (2009), chapter four.

P. 16: 'The first modern athletics meeting to be held . . .' Peter Lovesey, *The Official Centenary History of the Amateur Athletic Association* (1980).

P. 16: 'The annual "College Races" quickly became . . .' *Sport*, 2 June 1883.

P. 16: 'In Cavan, for instance, men would gather weights . . .' Coimisiún Béaloideasa Éireann, vol. 921, pp. 56–7: interview with Peter Clarke, Kilann, County Cavan.

P. 16: 'Several of these old-style practices . . .' Séamus Ó Ceallaigh, *A History of the Limerick GAA* (1987), *passim*.

P. 16: 'In many places, despite the obvious influence . . .' *Sport*, 8 November 1884.

P. 18: 'The reporter also recounted with relish . . .' *Sport*, 29 September 1883.

P. 18: 'It was in that same year that he first met . . .' Tony O'Donoghue, *Irish Championship Athletics* (2005), p. 14.

P. 18: 'Cusack came to regard Davin as the greatest . . .' *Irish Weekly Independent and Nation*, 13 December 1902.

P. 18: 'A notebook which Davin used . . .' Maurice Davin Notebook, GAA Museum and Archives, Croke Park.

P. 18: 'He developed his throwing technique . . .' Maurice Davin Notebook, GAA Museum and Archives, Croke Park; Séamus Ó Riain, *Maurice Davin, (1842–1927). First President of the GAA* (1994), p. 19.

P. 18: 'He was meticulous in his diet . . .' Maurice Davin Notebook, GAA Museum and Archives, Croke Park; Séamus Ó Riain, *Maurice Davin, (1842–1927). First President of the GAA* (1994), p. 19.

P. 18: 'On the strength of two weeks' training . . .' *Irish Weekly Independent and Nation*, 13 December 1902; Pat Davin, *Recollections of a Veteran Irish Athlete* (1938), *passim*. and Séamus Ó Riain, *Maurice Davin, (1842–1927). First President of the GAA* (1994), *passim*.

P. 18: 'The annual athletics championship was on the verge . . .' *Sport*, 6 August 1881.

P. 19: 'On 11 October 1884 the pair went public when Cusack . . .' *United Ireland*, 11 October 1884.

P. 19: 'Cusack railed against the Britishness of everything . . .' *United Ireland*, 11 October 1884.

P. 19: 'In the following edition of the paper, Maurice Davin . . .' *United Ireland*, 18 October 1884.

P. 19: 'Davin told those present that they needed to . . .' See, for example, *Cork Examiner*, 3 November 1884 and *Tipperary Advocate,* 8 November 1884.

Pp. 19–21: 'It was almost as an afterthought that . . .' *United Ireland*, 18 October 1884.

P. 21: 'By the late 1700s, matches were often played . . .' See, for example, the newspaper cuttings carrying reports on hurling matches played around Ireland throughout the eighteenth century in National Library of Ireland, Ms. 8723 (1 to 3).

P. 25: 'Between the end of the Famine and . . .' For a full account of hurling before the GAA, see Art Ó Maolfabhail, *Camán, 2000 Years of Hurling in Ireland* (1973) and Liam P. Ó Caithnia, *Scéal na hIomána: Ó Thosach Ama go 1884* (1980).

P. 25: 'Amongst those who played the game was . . .' T. S. C. Dagg, *Hockey in Ireland* (1944), pp. 30–5.

P. 25: 'The impact of these changes was to make . . .' T. S. C. Dagg, *Hockey in Ireland* (1944), pp. 30–5.

P. 29: 'Four times in early 1883 . . .' *Sport*, 3 February 1883.

P. 29: 'Around twenty players turned up . . .' *Sport*, 17 February 1883.

P. 29: 'Initially, several players had taken part in both . . .' *Sport*, 3 February 1883. Later, after the founding of the GAA, the game of hurley collapsed and just two clubs remained, King's Hospital and High School. They remained faithful to hurley until it became clear in the early 1890s that the game was not about to grow in strength. By then a Hockey Association had been founded in England and a code of rules developed. In the autumn of 1892 both King's Hospital and High School abandoned hurley and turned to hockey. Then, in February 1893, the two clubs drove the formation of the Irish Hockey Union, with the Rev Gibson elected President.

P. 29: 'Michael Cusack was later in no doubt . . .' *The Celtic Times*, 2 April 1887.

P. 29: 'Killimor were believed to be the finest . . .' Padraic Ó Laoi, *Annals of the GAA in Galway,* vol. 1, (1983), *passim*.

P. 32: 'The play of the Galway men, he said . . .' *The Irish Times*, 15 April 1884.

P. 32: 'A letter to the *Western News* made a public . . .' *Western News*, 12, 19 and 26 April 1884.

Chapter 2: Games

P. 37: 'Scores were a rarity, but this was not . . .' *United Ireland*, 11 July 1885.

P. 37: 'It says much for the intense nature of the play . . .' See *United Ireland*, February 1885.

P. 38: 'The "Old Hurler" concluded by defending . . .' *Western News*, 17 October 1885.

P. 38: 'By the spring of 1886 reports suggest . . .' See *United Ireland*, March to May 1886.

P. 40: 'They established the Irish Amateur Athletic Association . . .' W. F. Mandle, *The Gaelic Athletic Association and Irish Nationalist Politics, 1884–1924* (1987), p. 22.

P. 40: 'As Michael Cusack put it, Irish sportsmen . . .' W. F. Mandle, *The Gaelic Athletic Association and Irish Nationalist Politics, 1884–1924* (1987), p. 24.

P. 40: 'Against the backdrop of political and social division . . .' W. F. Mandle, *The Gaelic Athletic Association and Irish Nationalist Politics, 1884–1924* (1987), p. 24.

P. 40: 'By eschewing any prohibition on Sunday play . . .' Neal Garnham, 'Accounting for the early success of the Gaelic Athletic Association', in *Irish Historical Studies*, 33 (133), (2004), pp. 65–79.

P. 40: 'In 1887 the GAA ruled that the dividing lines . . .' *Sport*, 16 April 1887.

P. 42: 'The change did nothing to deflect the progress . . .' Sean Kearns, 'John Kennedy', in James McGuire and James Quinn (eds.) *Dictionary of Irish Biography* (2009).

P. 42: 'By and large, early GAA players were young . . .' Neal Garnham, 'Accounting for the early success of the Gaelic Athletic Association', in *Irish Historical Studies*, 33 (133), (2004), pp. 65–79.

Pp. 42–43: 'In 1908, the journalist P. J. Devlin . . .' *The Gaelic Athletic Annual and County Directory, 1907–08*, p. 17.

P. 46: 'All this underlined the idea of a county identity . . .' Tom Ryall, *Kilkenny – the GAA Story, 1884–1984* (1984), pp. 31–6; Mark Duncan, 'The camera and the Gael: the early photography of the GAA', in Mike Cronin, William Murphy and Paul Rouse (eds.), *The Gaelic Athletic Association, 1884–2009* (2009), chapter seven.

P. 46: 'The book underlined the extent to which . . .' Dick Fitzgerald, *How to Play Gaelic Football* (1914), p. 13.

P. 46: 'As far as Fitzgerald was concerned . . .' Dick Fitzgerald, *How to Play Gaelic Football* (1914), p. 15.

P. 46: 'But the real "genius" of the game, Fitzgerald . . .' Dick Fitzgerald, *How to Play Gaelic Football* (1914), p. 15.

P. 46: 'Training was mostly confined to the weeks . . .' Dick Fitzgerald, *How to Play Gaelic Football* (1914), p. 66.

P. 46: 'The money was raised by subscriptions . . .' Clare County Museum, Clare GAA Circular re: Hurling Championship semi-final for the Championship of Munster, Ennis, July 1914; GAA Museum and Archive, GAA/Laois/2, Circular letter asking people of Leix to contribute to the Training Fund, 29 August 1914.

P. 50: ' ". . . If ye do not", the writer added . . .' GAA Museum and Archives, GAA/Laois/74, anonymous letter to the Leix County Secretary, *c.* October 1914.

P. 50: 'By the end of the 1920s more than 30,000 . . .' See, for example, Marcus de Búrca, *The GAA: A History* (1999), p. 158.

P. 54: 'Despite the rise in quality, a core of GAA . . .' See, for example, reports on GAA Congresses: *Cork Examiner* of March 1940, April 1941, April 1942, 7 April 1947.

P. 54: 'The practice even extended to junior . . .' Dónal McAnallen, ' "The Greatest Amateur Association in the World"?: Amateurism and the GAA', in Mike Cronin, William Murphy and Paul Rouse, *The Gaelic Athletic Association, 1884–2009* (2009), chapter ten.

P. 54: 'Throughout the 1940s, some inter-county . . .' Dónal McAnallen, ' "The Greatest Amateur Association in the World"?: Amateurism and the GAA', in Mike Cronin, William Murphy and Paul Rouse, *The Gaelic Athletic Association, 1884–2009* (2009), chapter ten.

P. 54: 'The reason for this was the widespread . . .' Eamonn O'Sullivan, *The Art and Science of Gaelic Football* (1958), p. 26.

P. 54: 'It was a style of football built on the principle . . .' Eamonn O'Sullivan, *The Art and Science of Gaelic Football* (1958), p. 35.

P. 54: 'In his memorable 1958 book . . .' Eamonn O'Sullivan, *The Art and Science of Gaelic Football* (1958), p. 20.

P. 54: 'By bringing players together, it not . . .' Eamonn O'Sullivan, *The Art and Science of Gaelic Football* (1958), pp. 20 and 28.

P. 56: 'The special subcommittee that recommended . . .' *Cork Examiner*, 19 April 1954.

P. 56: 'As one Congress delegate pointed out . . .' *Cork Examiner*, 19 April 1954.

P. 60: 'For Joe Lennon, coaching was less about . . .' Joe Lennon, *Coaching Gaelic Football for Champions* (1964), p. 3; see, also, Eamonn O'Sullivan, *The Art and Science of Gaelic Football* (1958).

P. 64: 'It was not until 1971, when a special . . .' *Report of the Commission on the GAA* (1971), p. 120.

P. 64: 'In addition to assisting in developing skills . . .' *Report of the Commission on the GAA* (1971), p. 129.

P. 64: 'Competition from Gaelic football at local . . .' As early as 1887, the journalist and hurler, P. P. Sutton, contrasted the difficulty of reviving hurling with the ease of developing football. See *Sport*, 25 June 1887.

P. 64: 'Securing a sufficient supply of ash . . .' *Report of the Commission on the GAA* (1971), pp. 100–1.

P. 65: 'This was originally part of a long-term plan . . .' *Report of the Commission on the GAA* (1971), pp. 100–2. The *Report of the Commission on the GAA* in 1971 recommended that the key objectives of hurling revival include: the 'continuance of the effort to develop Hurling still more in the "strong" counties; 'the intensive promotion of Hurling in areas where it already exists'; and 'special support for smaller pockets of hurling potential in other areas.'

P. 65: 'What was needed was support for the local effort . . .' *Report of the Commission on the GAA* (1971), p. 101. 'The most important factor is the personal enthusiasm of individuals.'

P. 74: 'As one player later recalled . . .' Michael O'Halloran, quoted in Denis Walsh, *Hurling: the Revolution Years* (2005), p. 22.

P. 75: 'In terms of the organisation of games . . .' *Daily Mail*, 6 January 2007. Profile of Pádraig Duffy, GAA's first-ever Player Welfare Officer; *The Irish Times*, 10 October 2007.

P. 75: 'Modern Gaelic football and hurling may be . . .' *The Irish Times*, 23 May 2008.

Chapter 3: Travel

P. 79: 'The carriages of the train were . . .' *Sport*, 6 August 1898.

P. 81: 'Nonetheless, as they took the train home . . .' *Sport*, 6 August 1898.

P. 82: 'Despite the success of the first line . . .' Tom Ferris, *Irish Railways. A New History* (2008), chapter four.

P. 82: 'Later, with the rationalisation of the railways . . .' Tom Ferris, *Irish Railways. A New History* (2008), chapter seven.

P. 82: 'In February 1886, when Cusack organised . . .' Marcus de Búrca, *The GAA: A History* (1999), p. 17.

P. 85: 'In Kerry's absence, Louth were . . .' P. F., *Kerry's Football Story* (1945), pp. 46–9.

P. 85: 'As many as 100 special trains . . .' Colm Creedon, *GAA Excursion Trains: a Centenary Record* (1984), unpaginated.

P. 85: 'A return ticket from Galway cost . . .' *Irish Independent*, 10 June 1922.

P. 87: 'These tired and weary supporters eventually . . .' See interview with Eugene Deane, GAA Oral History Project, 2009.

P. 88: 'Three return trains left for the West . . .' Colm Creedon, *GAA Excursion Trains: a Centenary Record* (1984), unpaginated.

P. 88: 'Inevitably, this touring was tailored . . .' Brian Griffin, *Cycling in Victorian Ireland* (2006), p. 145.

P. 88: 'In his pursuit of the best players for his panel . . .' *Sunday Tribune*, 4 January 2009. See also, Dominic Williams, *The Wexford Hurling and Football bible, 1887–2008* (2008), p. 99.

P. 88: 'He put his knicks in one boot . . .' See interview with Paddy Wickham, GAA Oral History Project, 2008.

P. 92: 'For those who had not been able to cycle . . .' *Nationalist and Leinster Times*, 26 July 1947.

P. 92: 'The secretary of the Laois County Board . . .' *Irish Independent*, 20 January 1943.

P. 96: 'Breandán Ó hEithir later recalled meeting . . .' Breandán Ó hEithir, *Over the Bar: a Personal Relationship with the GAA* (1984), p. 47.

P. 96: 'He was quickly followed by other . . .' Bob Montgomery, *Early Motoring in Ireland* (1999), pp. 3–9.

P. 99: 'The number of private cars reached . . .' *Roads Bulletin, 1993*. Quoted in Anne Buttimer and Taeke Stol, 'Flows of Food and Energy in Germany, Ireland, the Netherlands and Sweden, 1960–1990', in Anne Buttimer (ed.), *Sustainable Landscapes and Lifeways: Scale and Appropriateness* (2001), p. 93.

P. 99: 'Passengers were thrown about . . .' Pat Davin, *Recollections of a Veteran Irish Athlete* (1938), p. 27.

P. 100: 'It was, wrote Pat Davin, a 'very . . .' Pat Davin, *Recollections of a Veteran Irish Athlete* (1938), pp. 23–34.

P. 100: 'Nonetheless, it did still take them . . .' See interview with Mick Higgins, GAA Oral History Project, 2008.

Chapter 4: Places to Play

P. 109: 'Negotiations were set in progress . . .' *Southern Star*, 8 February 1902.

P. 109: 'The writer glumly concluded . . .' *Southern Star*, 8 February 1902.

P. 116: 'Apply to the secretary, St Brendan's club . . .' *Midland Tribune*, 8 March 1888.

P. 116: 'Undeterred, some players uprooted the goalposts . . .' Tim Carey, *Croke Park: a History* (2004), pp. 21–3.

P. 119: 'Such figures were unusual in the Association . . .' Séamus Ó Riain, *Maurice Davin, (1842–1927). First President of the GAA* (1994), p. 206.

P. 119: 'At a meeting of the County Board in 1901 . . .' *Southern Star*, 1 June 1901.

P. 120: 'The GAA did not have a monopoly of use . . .' Tim Carey, *Croke Park: a History* (2004), pp. 19–23.

P. 123: 'The stadium came to symbolise . . .' Tim Carey, *Croke Park: a History* (2004), pp. 42–95.

P. 123: 'In this way, Croke Park . . .' Tim Carey, *Croke Park: a History* (2004), p. 98.

P. 126: 'A fund-raising drive was organised . . .' www.fethardgaa.com

P. 128: 'The expansion of GAA property . . .' Marcus de Búrca, *The GAA: A History* (1999), p. 211.

Chapter 5: Politics

P. 141: 'They did not succeed in their primary objective . . .' See William Nolan (ed.), *The Gaelic Athletic Association in Dublin, 1884–2000*, vol. 1, (2005), p. 131.

P. 142: 'By the beginning of 1887 they had moved . . .' See W. F. Mandle, *The Gaelic Athletic Association and Irish Nationalist Politics, 1884–1924* (1987), W. F. Mandle, 'The IRB and the beginnings of the Gaelic Athletic Association,' in *Irish Historical Studies*, 20 (80), (1977), pp. 418–438, and Paul Rouse, 'Gunfire in Hayes' Hotel: the IRB and the founding of the GAA', in James McConnel and Fearghal McGarry (eds.), *The Black Hand of Republicanism: the Fenians and History* (2009), chapter six.

P. 142: 'The GAA was thriving beyond all expectation . . .' *Sport*, 27 March 1886.

P. 144: 'In 1887, aware of the influence of the IRB . . .' Paul Rouse, 'Gunfire in Hayes' Hotel: the IRB and the founding of the GAA', in James McConnel and Fearghal McGarry (eds.), *The Black Hand of Republicanism: the Fenians and History* (2009), chapter six.

P. 144: 'In the same year Dublin Castle commissioned . . .' Quoted in Marcus de Búrca, *The GAA: A History* (1999), p. 40.

P. 145: 'Another observer, Maurice O'Halloran . . .' National Archives of Ireland, CBS 126/S, Maurice O'Halloran letter, 9 November 1887.

P. 147: 'Club numbers increased again . . .' See W. F. Mandle, *The Gaelic Athletic Association and Irish Nationalist Politics, 1884–1924* (1987).

P. 147: 'The club also had a song . . .' For the GAA and the Boer War, see Deirdre McMahon, 'Ireland, the Empire and the Commonwealth' in Kevin Kenny (ed.), *Ireland and the British Empire* (2004), pp. 182–219; Alan Bairner, 'Ireland, Sport and Empire', in Keith Jeffery (ed.), *An Irish Empire? Aspects of Ireland and the British Empire* (1996), pp. 57–76; and Mike Cronin, 'Enshrined in blood. The naming of Gaelic Athletic Association grounds and clubs', *The Sports Historian*, 18 (1), (1998), pp. 90–104.

P. 148: 'Later, this suite of rules was extended . . .' Paul Rouse, 'The politics of culture and sport in Ireland: a history of the GAA ban on foreign games, 1884–1971. Part One: 1884–1921', in *International Journal of the History of Sport*, 10 (3), (1993), pp. 333–360.

P. 148: 'Evidence of the close ties was readily apparent . . .' Paul Rouse, 'The politics of culture and sport in Ireland: a history of the GAA ban on foreign games, 1884–1971. Part One: 1884–1921', in *International Journal of the History of Sport*, 10 (3), (1993), pp. 333–360.

P. 148: 'Killaloe GAA Club in Clare . . .' William Murphy, 'The GAA during the Irish revolution, 1913–23', in Mike Cronin, William Murphy and Paul Rouse (eds.), *The Gaelic Athletic Association, 1884–2009* (2009), chapter five.

P. 151: 'Estimates of the numbers of GAA members . . .' William Murphy, 'The GAA during the Irish revolution, 1913–23', in Mike Cronin, William Murphy and Paul Rouse (eds.), *The Gaelic Athletic Association, 1884–2009* (2009), chapter five and William Nolan (ed.), *The Gaelic Athletic Association in Dublin, 1884–2000*, vol. 1, (2005), pp. 125–37.

P. 151: 'Immediately, the GAA issued a statement . . .' Paul Rouse, 'The politics of culture and sport in Ireland: a history of the GAA ban on foreign games, 1884–1971. Part One: 1884–1921', in *International Journal of the History of Sport*, 10 (3), (1993), pp. 333–360.

P. 151: 'While the prisoners also wanted to play hurling . . .' W. J. Brennan-Whitmore, *With the Irish in Frongoch* (1917), p. 38; Sean O'Mahony, *Frongoch: University of Revolution* (1987), pp. 99–101; Lyn Ebeneezer, *Frongoch and the Birth of the IRA* (2006), pp. 48–49.

P. 151: 'Tournaments were staged to raise money . . .' William Murphy, 'The GAA during the Irish revolution, 1913–23', in Mike Cronin, William Murphy and Paul Rouse (eds.), *The Gaelic Athletic Association, 1884–2009* (2009), p. 67.

P. 152: 'The success of their protest . . .' Marcus de Búrca, *The GAA: A History* (1999), p. 112.

P. 152: 'The GAA was involved in the emergence . . .' William Murphy, 'The GAA during the Irish revolution, 1913–23', in Mike Cronin, William Murphy and Paul Rouse (eds.), *The Gaelic Athletic Association, 1884–2009* (2009), p. 69; Fearghal McGarry, *Eoin O'Duffy: a Self-made Hero* (2005).

P. 154: 'This was now more than merely a playing field . . .' See Anne Dolan, 'Killing and Bloody Sunday, November 1920', in *Historical Journal*, 49 (3), (2006), pp. 789–810 and David Leeson, 'Death in the afternoon: the Croke Park Massacre, 21 November 1920', in *Canadian Journal of History*, 38 (1), (2003), pp. 43–67.

P. 154: 'Cork, too, refused to play Offaly . . .' Marcus de Búrca, *The GAA: A History* (1999), pp. 129–131.

P. 162: 'When the matter was raised by a Connacht . . .' Marcus de Búrca, *The GAA: A History* (1999), p. 167.

P. 162: 'GAA stalwart and political activist . . .' Brendan MacLua, *The Steadfast Rule* (1967), p. 57.

P. 163: 'In 1953, the then President of the GAA . . .' *Irish Independent*, 6 April 1953.

P. 163: 'Equally, it was decided that the ban . . .' Paul Rouse, 'Sport and the Politics of Culture: a History of the GAA Ban on Foreign Games, 1884–1971' (MA thesis, UCD, 1992).

P. 166: 'The Ulster Freedom Fighters placed the GAA . . .' *Irish Independent,* 9 October 1991.

P. 166: 'Amidst the repeated intimidation of members . . .' Desmond Fahy, *How the GAA Survived the Troubles* (2001), *passim*.

P. 170: 'In February 1988 McAnespie . . .' Desmond Fahy, *How the GAA Survived the Troubles* (2001), *passim*.

P. 170: 'He was also a member of . . .' See Public Records Office of Northern Ireland, *Troubled Images* CD.

P. 174: 'Ultimately, the rule was deleted . . .' David Hassan, 'The Gaelic Athletic Association, Rule 21 and police reform in Northern Ireland', in *Journal of Sport and Social Issues*, 29 (1), (2005), pp. 60–78.

Chapter 6: Media

P. 179: 'Indeed, the very notion of the live broadcast . . .' P. D. Mehigan ('Carbery'), [ed. Seán Kilfeather], *Vintage Carbery* (1984), pp. 31–3; Dick Booth, *Talking of Sport: the Story of Radio Commentary* (2008), pp. 134–7.

P. 180: 'Eventually, his equipment was swept . . .' P. D. Mehigan ('Carbery'), [ed. Seán Kilfeather], *Vintage Carbery* (1984), pp. 31–3; Dick Booth, *Talking of Sport: the Story of Radio Commentary* (2008), pp. 134–7.

P. 180: 'When the protestors left the box . . .' P. D. Mehigan ('Carbery'), [ed. Seán Kilfeather], *Vintage Carbery* (1984), pp. 31–3; Dick Booth, *Talking of Sport: the Story of Radio Commentary* (2008), pp. 134–7.

P. 183: 'In Cavan, the end of the broadcast . . .' Mick Dunne, *The Star Spangled Final: the Story of the 1947 All-Ireland Football Final in New York* (1997), p. 42.

P. 183: 'It drove newspapers to increase their coverage . . .' P. D. Mehigan ('Carbery'), [ed. Seán Kilfeather], *Vintage Carbery* (1984), pp. 31–3.

P. 183: 'One GAA stalwart had even predicted . . .' P. D. Mehigan ('Carbery'), [ed. Seán Kilfeather], *Vintage Carbery* (1984), pp. 31–3.

P. 184: 'Getting that column, wrote Cusack . . .' *The Celtic Times*, 19 November 1887.

P. 184: 'Column after column stressed . . .' *United Ireland*, 8 November 1884.

P. 184: 'It immediately stressed its nationalist credentials . . .' W. F. Mandle, *The Gaelic Athletic Association and Irish Nationalist Politics, 1884–1924* (1987), p. 24.

P. 189: 'A journalist in the weekly newspaper . . .' *Sport*, 19 December 1885.

P. 189: 'Michael Cusack accused the mainstream press . . .' *United Ireland*, 8 November 1884.

P. 189: '*The Irish Sportsman*, another weekly . . .' Quoted in T. S. C. Dagg, *Hockey in Ireland* (1944), p. 39.

P. 189: 'The minimum of space is doled out to us . . .' *The Gaelic Athletic Annual and County Directory, 1910–11*.

P. 195: 'Writing in *The Irish Times*, Flann O'Brien . . .' This section relies heavily on the work of Seán Crosson who has written extensively on the relationship between the GAA and film. See, for example, Seán Crosson, 'Gaelic games and the movies', in Mike Cronin, William Murphy and Paul Rouse (eds.), *The Gaelic Athletic Association, 1884–2009* (2009), chapter eight.

P. 201: 'In 2006, for instance . . .' See Paul Rouse, *The Impact of Pay-TV on Sport* (2007).

P. 201: 'The former President of the GAA . . .' *The Irish Times*, 14 April 1997.

Chapter 7: Community

P. 211: 'The meeting then resumed . . .' Breandán Ó hEithir, *Over the Bar: A Personal Relationship with the GAA* (1984), p. 7.

P. 211: 'It aimed to do this by building . . .' It was decided that a club, if possible, should be established in every parish throughout the country. GAA Oral History Project, Jim Cronin Papers, Newspaper report on GAA Convention, 17 January 1885.

P. 212: 'The players were the butt of sneers . . .' *The Celtic Times*, 9 July 1887.

P. 215: 'The large numbers of women attending matches . . .' *The Celtic Times*, 23 July 1887.

P. 215: 'Away from the playing fields . . .' For details on the social life of GAA clubs in Westmeath, see Tom Hunt, *Sport and Society in Victorian Ireland: the Case of Westmeath* (2007), pp. 158–161.

P. 215: 'Cusack believed the affect on the social tastes . . .' *The Celtic Times*, 26 November 1887.

P. 215: 'This was as true for those who joined . . .' Tom Hunt, 'The GAA: social structure and associated clubs', in Mike Cronin, William Murphy and Paul Rouse (eds.), *The Gaelic Athletic Association 1884–2009* (2009), chapter eleven.

P. 215: 'Such, indeed, was the lack of identification . . .' David Gorry, 'The Gaelic Athletic Association in Dublin, 1884–2000: a Geographic Analysis' (M.Litt thesis, UCD, 2001), pp. 92–93.

P. 215: 'At the founding meeting of the Association . . .' W. F. Mandle, *The Gaelic Athletic Association and Irish Nationalist Politics, 1884–1924* (1987), p. 7.; Séamus Ó Riain, *Maurice Davin (1842–1927). First President of the GAA* (1994), p. 57.

P. 215: 'The Association organised itself . . .' Neal Garnham, 'Accounting for the early success of the Gaelic Athletic Association', in *Irish Historical Studies*, 33 (133), (2004), pp. 65–79.

P. 216: 'This revenue was ploughed back into games . . .' See summary of Provincial Council Balance Sheets presented to Annual Convention, 24 February 1907, in *The Gaelic Athletic Annual and County Directory, 1907–08*, p. 55.

P. 216: 'As inter-county competition increased . . .' Dónal McAnallen, ' "The Greatest Amateur Association in the World"?: Amateurism and the GAA', in Mike Cronin, William Murphy and Paul Rouse (eds.), *The Gaelic Athletic Association, 1884–2009* (2009), chapter ten.

P. 216: 'With only twenty members, Monadrehid . . .' GAA Musuem and Archive, GAA/Laois/38, Letter from Joe Byrne to John J. Higgins, 16 October 1914.

P. 216: 'The games should be played . . .' Dick Fitzgerald, *How to Play Gaelic Football* (1914), p. 67.

P. 216: 'Soccer was a case in point . . .' Neal Garnham, *Association Football and Society in Pre-partition Ireland* (2004), p. 69.

P. 220: 'In 1913, for instance, *The Gaelic Athlete* . . .' See Dónal McAnallen, ' "The Greatest Amateur Association in the World"?: Amateurism and the GAA', in Mike Cronin, William Murphy and Paul Rouse (eds.), *The Gaelic Athletic Association, 1884–2009* (2009), chapter ten; *The Gaelic Athlete*, 31 May 1913. See, also, Neal Garnham, *Association Football and Society in Pre-partition Ireland* (2004), p. 81.

P. 220: 'Between 1924 and 1945, for example . . .' Marcus de Búrca, *The GAA: A History* (1999), pp. 150, 161.

P. 223: 'Fr Cogavin, principal of St Joseph's College . . .' *Irish Independent*, 27 December 1930.

P. 223: 'The following year the Dublin County Board . . .' *Irish Independent*, 5 October 1931.

P. 228: 'While many members joined . . .' GAA Oral History Project, Jim Cronin Papers, Annual Congress Newspaper report, 19 April 1941.

P. 228: 'Across all counties and at all levels . . .' *Irish Independent*, 12 September 1946.

P. 228: 'A member of the local development association . . .' See interview with Donal Kearney, GAA Oral History Project, 2009.

P. 229: 'The GAA shared with groups like Muintir na Tíre . . .' For examples of the overlapping interests of the GAA and Muintir na Tíre, see *Irish Independent*, 22 August 1955 and 2 April 1958.

P. 231: 'For the GAA, this would entail the provision . . .' Pádraig Ó Caoimh spoke on a number of occasion of the need for GAA clubs to assume a bigger role in the life of their communities. See, for example, *Irish Independent*, 6 April 1954 and 10 April 1957; See also GAA President S. MacFerran speaking on the theme 'The Parish and the Nation' at Munitir na Tíre week, *Irish Independent*, 22 August 1955.

P. 231: 'As one newspaper reported . . .' *Sunday Press*, 5 June 1955, quoted in Dónal McAnallen, ' "The Greatest Amateur Association in the World"?: Amateurism and the GAA', in Mike Cronin, William Murphy and Paul Rouse (eds.), *The Gaelic Athletic Association, 1884–2009* (2009), chapter ten.

P. 231: 'By the 1960s, Ireland was becoming . . .' By 1971, 52.2 per cent of the Irish population were living in urban settings. William Nolan (ed.), *The Gaelic Athletic Association in Dublin, 1884–2000*, vol. 2, (2005), p. 515.

P. 231: 'Social centres were particularly important . . .' David Gorry, 'The Gaelic Athletic Association in Dublin, 1884–2000: a Geographic Analysis' (M.Litt thesis, UCD, 2001), pp. 179–180.

P. 232: 'Alongside playing fields, facilities were provided . . .' William Nolan (ed.), *The Gaelic Athletic Association in Dublin, 1884–2000*, vol.2, (2005), pp. 532–537.

P. 232: 'In 1971, the report of a special commission . . .' *Report of the Commission on the GAA* (1971), p. 15; *Irish Independent*, 8 December 1971.

P. 232: 'A system of grants had by then been put in place . . .' GAA, *Dressingrooms and Social Centres for GAA Clubs* (1975), p. 16. In the case of Ballyboden St Enda's, club member and builder Pat Corrigan provided development plans for free, see William Nolan (ed.), *The Gaelic Athletic Association in Dublin, 1884–2000*, vol. 2, (2005), p. 536.

P. 232: 'The success of the bingo, which was still running . . .' *Southern Star*, 12 November 2005.

P. 237: 'The Association's appeal transcended social class . . .' Liam Delaney and Tony Fahey, *Social and Economic Value of Sport in Ireland* (2005), pp. 27, 35 and 38.

P. 239: 'A line remains drawn at pay-for-play . . .' See, for example, GAA, *Summary of Strategic Review: Enhancing Community Identity* (2002), pp. 6–7; *The GAA Strategic Vision and Action Plan, 2009–2015* (2008), p. 15.

Chapter 8: Religion

P. 243: 'Having thrown the ball between the opposing players . . .' *The Irish Times*, 29 September 1958.

P. 246: 'The Pope's subsequent expression of gratitude . . .' From an analysis of the GAA in the 1930s, see Tadhg Ó hAnnracháin, 'The heroic importance of sport: the GAA in the 1930s', in *International Journal of the History of Sport*, 25 (10), (2008), pp. 1326–1337.

P. 248: 'In reaction against this . . .' Emmet Larkin, 'The devotional revolution in Ireland 1850–1875', in *The American Historical Review*, 77, (1972), pp. 625–52.

P. 248: 'Once you went into the Ecclesiastics . . .' See interview with Martin White, GAA Oral History Project, 2008.

P. 251: 'The *Irish Independent* reported . . .' *Irish Independent*, 10 and 13 August 1960; *Fermanagh Herald*, 26 August 2008.

P. 253: 'With this in mind, he called . . .' Reprinted in Séamus Ó Riain, *Maurice Davin (1842–1927). First President of the GAA* (1994), appendix one.

P. 253: 'Sticks were brandished, punches thrown . . .' *Sport*, 12 November 1887.

P. 259: 'It was reopened later in 1916 by a former pupil . . .' Elaine Sisson, *Pearse's Patriots: St Enda's and the Cult of Boyhood* (2004), pp. 5, 127–8 and 157.

P. 259: 'He promoted hurling in the school . . .' *Waterford News and Star*, 29 June 2007; www.seanoheslinsgaa.com and www.kilkennycats.com.

P. 260: 'John Stephen O'Sullivan, a retired teacher himself . . .' See interview with John Stephen O'Sullivan, GAA Oral History Project, 2008.

Chapter 9: Music, Parades and Culture

P. 267: 'The whole day was to conclude with a tug-o'-war event . . .' *Anglo-Celt,* 6 June 1964.

P. 269: 'Observers (somewhat wishfully) believed . . .' *The Celtic Times,* 26 February 1887.

P. 269: 'Later, it changed its rules to allow girls to join . . .' GAA, A *century of service* (1984).

P. 269: 'For example, when the Kanturk Brass Band . . .' *The Celtic Times,* 2 April 1887.

P. 274: 'Throughout much of Irish history . . .' Maura Cronin, 'Claiming the landscape: popular balladry in pre-famine Ireland', in Úna Ní Bhroiméil and Glenn Hooper (eds.), *Land and Landscape in Nineteenth-Ccentury Ireland* (2008), pp. 36–9.

P. 277: 'During the Irish Language Week parade . . .' *Freeman's Journal,* 19 September 1910.

P. 277: 'He agreed with Douglas Hyde . . .' Douglas Hyde, 'The necessity for de-Anglicising Ireland', in Arthur Mitchell and Pádraig Ó Snodaigh (eds.), *Political Documents, 1869–1916* (1989), p. 85 and Breandán Ó Conaire (ed.), *Language, Lore and Lyrics: Essays and Lectures/Douglas Hyde* (1986), p. 169.

P. 278: 'Cusack, for his part . . .' See Brian Ó Conchubhair, 'The GAA and the Irish language' in Mike Cronin, William Murphy and Paul Rouse (eds.), *The Gaelic Athletic Association, 1884–2009* (2009), chapter ten.

P. 281: 'As early as 1887 suggestions were put forward . . .' *The Celtic Times,* 26 February 1887.

P. 281: 'The birth of Scór offered a practical platform . . .' Background to Scór on GAA website, www.gaa.ie/page/scor.html.

P. 283: 'Their moment of glory had come at last . . .' *Tuam Herald,* 29 April 1995.

P. 289: 'Bands such as The Saw Doctors . . .' See Mike Cronin, 'Beyond sectarianism: sport and Irish culture' in Liam Harte and Yvonne Whelan (eds.), *Ireland Beyond Boundaries: Mapping Irish Studies in the Twenty-First Century* (2007), pp. 215–38.

Chapter 10: Hats, Flags and Rosettes

P. 295: 'In their first county final . . .' Seán Seosamh Ó Conchubhair, *Kilmoyley to the Rescue* (2005), pp. 91–92.

P. 298: 'They recalled that their time was filled . . .' *The Avondhu,* 4 September 2008.

P. 298: 'Shorts, or what were then referred to . . .' *Freeman's Journal,* 3 December 1923.

P. 298: 'The archaeology of Ireland includes . . .' See the collections of the National Museum of Ireland.

P. 298: 'By contrast, in Dublin, the journalist and hurler . . .' *Sport,* 17 January 1889.

P. 301: 'He also claimed to have heard of . . .' Sceilg, 'An Camán', in Seamus Ó Ceallaigh, *Gaelic Days* (1944), p. 11.

P. 301: 'In December 1887, a match in Carrick-on-Suir . . .' *The Celtic Times,* 24 December 1887.

P. 301: 'During the American Invasion of 1888 . . .' Pat Davin, *Recollections of a Veteran Irish Athlete* (1938), p. 24.

P. 301: 'The clash of the hickory did not . . .' Pat Davin, *Recollections of a Veteran Irish Athlete* (1938), p. 24.

P. 301: 'They favoured a ball . . .' *Sport*, 20 February 1886; *United Ireland*, 20 February 1886; *The Celtic Times*, 29 October 1887.

P. 305: 'As one delegate told the GAA's Annual Congress . . .' *Irish Independent*, 25 March 1940.

P. 307: 'In a resolution passed at the Ulster . . .' Cardinal Ó Fiaich Library and Archive, Ulster Council Minutes, 17 March 1917.

P. 310: 'The joy proved short-lived . . .' See interview with Sean Scollon, GAA Oral History Project, 2009.

P. 310: 'At the same auction another item . . .' Mealys Auction House, Collector's Sale: Sport, May 2008, www.mealys.com/res0508.php.

P. 310: 'The medal of one of the Limerick Commercial's . . .' www.anfearrua.com, 13 March 2009.

Chapter 11: Women and the GAA

P. 317: 'In the end, however, those same diehards . . .' *Evening Press*, 30 July 1973.

P. 319: '*Sport*, a weekly sports paper, noted . . .' Paul Rouse, 'Sport and Ireland in 1881', in Alan Bairner (ed.), *Sport and the Irish: Histories, Identities, Issues* (2003).

P. 319: 'According to Cusack, Tipperary women . . .' *The Celtic Times*, 12 March 1887.

P. 320: 'Indeed so much taken was one of them . . .' See Paul Rouse, 'Michael Cusack: sportsman and journalist', in Mike Cronin, William Murphy and Paul Rouse (eds.), *The Gaelic Athletic Association, 1884–2009* (2009), chapter four.

P. 320: 'For example, in 1887, the Chairman . . .' Jennifer Hargreaves, *Sporting Females: Critical Issues in the History and Sociology of Women's Sports* (1997), p. 45.

P. 320: 'The founder of the modern Olympic Games . . .' Joseph Levy, 'Fanny "Bobbie" Rosenfeld: Canada's woman athlete of the half century', in *Journal of Sport History*, 26 (2), (1997), pp. 392–6.

P. 320: 'The general tendency of the Victorian sporting world . . .' *Sport*, 21 May 1881.

P. 321: 'The game was played at the Hill of Tara . . .' Margaret Ó hÓgartaigh, 'Shedding their "reserve": camogie and the origins of women's sport in Ireland', in *High Ball* (July, 2003); Tomás Ó Domhnalláin, 'Donlon Family History, 1988', in *Ríocht na Midhe*, 14, (2003), pp. 136–143.

P. 323: 'The final score saw Keatings claim victory . . .' Anon., *Scéal na Camógaíochta* (*c.* 1984), p. 8.

P. 323: 'That the game was played in areas where hurling . . .' Anon., *Scéal na Camógaíochta* (*c.* 1984), p. 9.

P. 323: 'I will gladly be president of the Association . . .' Máire de Buitléir's article, 'Camoguidheacht Association', published on 21 April 1911 in a newspaper (probably the *Evening Telegraph*). The report survives in a scrapbook which forms part of the Sean O'Duffy collection, held by the Camogie Association.

P. 326: 'Only a little organisation should be needed . . .' Camogie Association, Sean O'Duffy Collection, Newspaper clipping (probably the *Evening Telegraph*), 1911.

P. 326: 'Then, in the 1915–16 season . . .' Anon., *Scéal na Camógaíochta* (*c.* 1984), p. 8.

P. 326: 'When we have secured national freedom . . .' Camogie Association, Sean O'Duffy Collection, Newspaper clipping (probably the *Evening Telegraph*), 1911.

P. 328: 'By 1935, camogie was being played . . .' Anon., *Scéal na Camógaíochta* (*c.* 1984), p. 14.

P. 329: 'She had first played for the county in 1941 . . .' Anon., *Scéal na Camógaíochta* (*c.* 1984), p. 16.

P. 332: 'By the end of 2008 there were 132,000 . . .' Information received from Ladies' Gaelic Football Association.

Chapter 12: Exile

P. 345: 'On board was some of the best Irish sporting talent . . .' Séamus Ó Riain, *Maurice Davin, (1842–1927). First President of the GAA* (1994), p. 171.

P. 346: 'The country had been a focus of Irish emigration . . .' Mike Cronin, David Doyle and Liam O'Callaghan, 'Foreign fields and foreigners on the field: Irish sport, inclusion and assimilation', in *International Journal of the History of Sport*, 25 (8), (2008), pp. 1010–1030.

P. 346: 'America, too, had a long attachment to Gaelic sports . . .' Paul Darby, 'Gaelic Games and the Irish Diaspora in the United States', in Mike Cronin, William Murphy and Paul Rouse (eds.), *The Gaelic Athletic Association, 1884–2009* (2009), chapter twelve.

P. 346: 'The Invasion tour, led by Maurice Davin . . .' Séamus Ó Riain, *Maurice Davin, (1842–1927). First President of the GAA* (1994), p. 162.

P. 346: 'Wherever the touring party went . . .' Mike Cronin, 'The Gaelic Athletic Association's invasion of America, 1888: travel narratives, microhistory and the Irish American "Other" ', in *Sport in History*, 27 (2), (2007), pp. 190–216.

P. 346: 'This loss of international competition inevitably . . .' Mike Cronin, 'The Gaelic Athletic Association's invasion of America, 1888: travel narratives, microhistory and the Irish American "Other" ', in *Sport in History*, 27 (2), (2007), pp. 190–216; Séamus Ó Riain, *Maurice Davin, (1842–1927). First President of the GAA* (1994), p. 177.

P. 348: 'County loyalties frequently re-formed . . .' Paul Darby, 'Gaelic Games, ethnic identity and Irish nationalism in New York City *c.* 1880–1917 [1]', in *Sport in History*, 10 (3), (2007), pp. 347–367.

P. 348: 'This practice was particularly common . . .' Paul Darby, 'Gaelic Games, ethnic identity and Irish nationalism in New York City *c.* 1880–1917 [1]', in *Sport in History*, 10 (3), (2007), pp. 347–367; GAA, *A Century of Service, 1884–1984* (1984), p. 78.

P. 349: 'This again was standard practice in Ireland . . .' Mike Cronin, 'Enshrined in blood: the naming of Gaelic Athletic Association grounds and clubs', in *The Sports Historian*, 18 (1), (1998), p. 96.

P. 349: 'For that very reason, the Association enjoyed the support . . .' Paul Darby, 'Gaelic

Games and the Irish Diaspora in the United States', in Mike Cronin, William Murphy and Paul Rouse (eds.), *The Gaelic Athletic Association, 1884–2009* (2009), chapter twelve.

P. 349: 'Many years later, the New York GAA Board reflected . . .' Quoted in Paul Darby, 'Gaelic Games, ethnic identity and Irish nationalism in New York City *c.* 1880–1917 [1]', in *Sport in History*, 10 (3), (2007), pp. 347–367.

P. 349: 'This would prove an ongoing problem . . .' Seamus King and Paul Darby, 'Becoming *Irlandés*: Hurling and Irish identity in Argentina [1]', in *Sport in Society*, 10 (3), (2007), pp. 425–438.

P. 352: 'Later that year, the London County Board . . .' Seamus King, *The Clash of the Ash in Foreign Fields: Hurling Abroad* (1998), p. 42.

P. 355: 'One of those was Michael Collins . . .' Peter Hart, *Mick: the Real Michael Collins* (2005), pp. 37–51; Mike Cronin, 'Sam Maguire: 'forgotten hero and national icon', in *Sport in History*, 25 (2), (2005), pp. 189–205.

P. 356: 'Comparisons with the Invasion tour of 1888 . . .' Thomas J. Kenny, *Tour of the Tipperary Hurling Team in America, 1926* (1928), p. 3.

P. 356: 'Legitimate concerns over costs and logistics . . .' Mick Dunne, *The Star Spangled Final: the Story of the 1947 All-Ireland Football Final in New York* (1997), pp. 11, 17.

P. 356: 'Not only did it succeed in raising the profile of Gaelic games . . .' Pádraig Puirséal, *The GAA in its Time* (1982), p. 254.

P. 356: 'The extent of the exodus was borne out by the figures . . .' Gearóid Ó Tuaithaigh, 'The GAA as a force in Irish Society: an overview', in Mike Cronin, William Murphy and Paul Rouse (eds.), *The Gaelic Athletic Association, 1884–2009* (2009), chapter fourteen.

P. 359: 'According to Ó Caoimh, many of the country's clubs . . .' *Irish Independent*, 6 April 1954 and 2 April 1958.

P. 359: 'Young men and women continued to leave . . .' Mary Daly, *The Slow Failure: Population Decline and Independent Ireland, 1920–1973* (2006), p. 191.

P. 359: 'GAA clubs and events held an obvious attraction . . .' National Archives of Ireland, Department of An Taoiseach S/1953, Memorandum from the Department of External Affairs to Government regarding the appointment of a welfare officer at the Irish embassy in London, June 1953. The Department stressed the importance of the link between voluntary organisations and emigrant welfare. Although the GAA was acknowledged to be well organised in the London area , 'the lack of sports and athletic clubs, and other forms of organised activity, among the Irish population in this country has a definite bearing on the problem of their general welfare.'

P. 359: 'The fresh influx of immigrants helped replenish . . .' See Seamus King, *The Clash of the Ash in Foreign Fields: Hurling Abroad* (1998), p. 50; and Paul Darby, 'Gaelic Games and the Irish Diaspora in the United States', in Mike Cronin, Mark Duncan and Paul Rouse (eds.), *The Gaelic Athletic Association, 1884–2009* (2009), chapter twelve.

P. 360: 'In 1958, for instance, the traditional Easter . . .' *Irish Independent*, 31 October 1957.

P. 360: 'In choosing such a big venue, the Board hoped . . .' *Irish Independent*, 24 May 1958; Seamus King, *The Clash of the Ash in Foreign Fields: Hurling Abroad* (1998), p. 53.

P. **360**: 'Their ambition paid off . . .' *Irish Independent*, 26 May 1958.

P. **367**: 'As numbers dropped and clubs folded . . .' GAA, *A Century of Service, 1884–1984* (1984), p. 79.

P. **367**: 'Through the 1970s, there were signs of change . . .' See, for example, *Irish Independent*, 5 August 1974, 31 March 1975, 15 December 1976 and 31 March 1982.

P. **367**: 'One club had an entire team wiped out . . .' *Irish Independent*, 18 August 1988.

P. **367**: 'In the late 1980s, one leading GAA official . . .' *Irish Independent*, 22 January 1988.

P. **372**: 'In October 2008, when teams gathered . . .' *The Irish Times*, 8 November 2008.

P. **372**: 'In 2008 the Irish government weighed in . . .' PA Newswire: Ireland, 24 June 2008.

Index